GLOBALIZATION AND HUMAN SECURITY

GLOBALIZATION

Series Editors
Manfred B. Steger
Royal Melbourne Institute of Technology and University of Hawai'i–Mānoa
and
Terrell Carver
University of Bristol

"Globalization" has become *the* buzzword of our time. But what does it mean? Rather than forcing a complicated social phenomenon into a single analytical framework, this series seeks to present globalization as a multidimensional process constituted by complex, often contradictory interactions of global, regional, and local aspects of social life. Since conventional disciplinary borders and lines of demarcation are losing their old rationales in a globalizing world, authors in this series apply an interdisciplinary framework to the study of globalization. In short, the main purpose and objective of this series is to support subject-specific inquiries into the dynamics and effects of contemporary globalization and its varying impacts across, between, and within societies.

Globalization and Sovereignty
John Agnew

Globalization and War
Tarak Barkawi

Globalization and Human Security
Paul Battersby and Joseph M. Siracusa

Globalization and American Popular Culture
Lane Crothers

Globalization and Militarism
Cynthia Enloe

Globalization and Law
Adam Gearey

Globalization and Feminist Activism
Mary E. Hawkesworth

Globalization and Postcolonialism
Sankaran Krishna

Globalization and Social Movements
Valentine Moghadam

Globalization and Terrorism
Jamal R. Nassar

Globalization and Culture, Second Edition
Jan Nederveen Pieterse

Globalization and International Political Economy
Mark Rupert and M. Scott Solomon

Globalisms, Third Edition
Manfred B. Steger

Rethinking Globalism
Edited by Manfred B. Steger

Globalization and Labor
Dimitris Stevis and Terry Boswell

Globaloney
Michael Veseth

 Supported by the Globalization Research Center at the University of Hawai'i, Mānoa

GLOBALIZATION AND HUMAN SECURITY

PAUL BATTERSBY
AND
JOSEPH M. SIRACUSA

ROWMAN & LITTLEFIELD PUBLISHERS, INC.
Lanham • Boulder • New York • Toronto • Plymouth, UK

ROWMAN & LITTLEFIELD PUBLISHERS, INC.

Published in the United States of America
by Rowman & Littlefield Publishers, Inc.
A wholly owned subsidiary of The Rowman & Littlefield Publishing Group, Inc.
4501 Forbes Boulevard, Suite 200, Lanham, Maryland 20706
www.rowmanlittlefield.com

Estover Road, Plymouth PL6 7PY, United Kingdom

British Library Cataloguing in Publication Information Available

Library of Congress Cataloging-in-Publication Data

Battersby, Paul, 1961–
Globalization and human security / Paul Battersby and Joseph M. Siracusa.
    p.   cm.
Includes bibliographical references and index.
ISBN-13: 978-0-7425-5652-2 (cloth : alk. paper)
ISBN-10: 0-7425-5652-2 (cloth : alk. paper)
ISBN-13: 978-0-7425-5653-9 (pbk. : alk. paper)
ISBN-10: 0-7425-5653-0 (pbk. : alk. paper)
[etc.]
    1. Globalization.   2. National security.   3. Security, International.   4. Human
rights.   5. World politics—21st century.   I. Siracusa, Joseph M.   II. Title.
JZ1318B38   2009
355'.033—dc22   2008042060

Printed in the United States of America

It is wiser to be pessimistic; it is a way of avoiding disappointment and ridicule, and so wise people condemn optimism. The essence of optimism is not its view of the present, but the fact that it is the inspiration of life and hope when others give in; it enables a man to hold his head high when everything seems to be going wrong; it gives him strength to sustain reverses and yet to claim the future for himself instead of abandoning it to his opponent.

—Dietrich Bonhoeffer

CONTENTS

TABLES AND BOXES

TABLES

BOXES

ACKNOWLEDGMENTS

The ideas and arguments presented in this book have evolved over many years of teaching and research in the fields of international security, history, political economy and international relations, global risk and global governance. A work of synthesis, *Globalization and Human Security* necessarily stands on the shoulders of giants without whose extensive research and scholarly insight a book of this nature could not be written. I owe a debt of gratitude to the School of Global Studies, Social Science and Planning, which granted me leave to think and to conceptualize this project in the second half of 2007. Thanks are also due to the series editors, Manfred Steger and Terrell Carver, for believing in this work and for supporting the project from its inception. Valuable research assistance was provided by one of my doctoral students, Sasho Ripiloski, who tracked down important public documents, key speeches and newspaper reports. Finally, I would like to thank my coauthor, Joe Siracusa, for his supportive and constructive approach to our collaboration.

—Paul Battersby

To begin at the beginning, my first vote of gratitude goes to the editors of this highly innovative series for their kind invitation to embark on this odyssey into the realm of globalization; my second vote goes to my friend and colleague Paul Battersby, whose keen sense of direction got us where we wanted to go. I should also be remiss if I did not acknowledge the support and unfailing courtesy of Susan McEachern, Rowman & Littlefield's editorial director. My intellectual debts are at once overwhelming and obvious and are recognized in the text and bibliography that follows. Last but not least I should like to thank Richard Dean Burns and Lester H. Brune for their generosity in sharing their vast knowledge of America's ill-fated intervention in Somalia.

—Joseph M. Siracusa

INTRODUCTION

We entered this war because violations of right had occurred which touched us to the quick and made the life of our own people impossible unless they were corrected and the world secure once for all against their recurrence. What we demand in this war, therefore, is nothing peculiar to ourselves. It is that the world be made fit and safe to live in; and particularly that it be made safe for every peace-loving nation which, like our own, wishes to live its own life, determine its own institutions, be assured of justice and fair dealing by the other peoples of the world as against force and selfish aggression. All the peoples of the world are in effect partners in this interest, and for our own part we see very clearly that unless justice be done to others it will not be done to us.

—President Woodrow Wilson

The dismantling of the Berlin Wall on that fateful evening of November 8–9, 1989, is one of the more enduring images of the twentieth century—that is, for the generation that lived daily with the frightening prospect of nuclear Armageddon. It marked the end of the tense military and ideological rivalry between the United States and the former Soviet Union known as the Cold War and, so it was optimistically assumed at the time, heralded a new era of cooperation in international affairs. As the Soviet Union was dismantled, the unexpected flowering of popular democracy across Eastern Europe signaled the possibility that all the old antagonisms could be buried and the disquieting competition between East and West, between Soviet-oriented Communism and liberal capitalism, would dissolve. In the West, the sudden unraveling of the Soviet empire—an unintended side effect of Mikhail Gorbachev's reforms—became synonymous with no less than the triumph of individualism, a victory for the right of individuals to pursue their own aspirations free from the dead hand of Communist central planning.

But then, on September 11, 2001, two passenger aircraft flying out of Logan Airport, Boston, were hijacked by educated and urbane-looking Islamist militants seeking to martyr themselves and strike at the United States in a suicidal assault on the symbols of American financial and military power. The two planes each plunged into one of the World Trade Center's twin towers. Two more flights, out of Washington and Newark, respectively, were also hijacked by militants, one crashing into the Pentagon while the other was downed in a struggle between passengers and hijackers en route to an unknown target.[1] For a Western world that had hardly put to rest the menace of the Cold War, these images of destruction marked the dawn of a new era in global affairs, one characterized by fear of the unknown and the unseen.

The United States embarked on a "global war on terror" that both altered the tenor of global affairs and offered the nation-state a new lease on life as the principal guarantor of security in an uncertain post–Cold War world. Military security, which slipped down the scale of global priorities after the Soviet bloc's demise, returned to the top of the global agenda as the United States and its coalition partners intervened first in Afghanistan, the seat of Islamist terror mobilization in the Middle East and South Asia, and then, tragically, in Iraq. The significance of this new post-9/11 terror dynamic in international affairs should not, however, be exaggerated. Much that was familiar for the global majority remained the same. Economic globalization proceeded unchecked, and with it the ever present risks of regional and global financial catastrophe. In Africa, millions continued to die of preventable diseases for want of access to proper medication; child soldiers participated in genocides and massacres from Sierra Leone to Sudan and Somalia. Old challenges, however, acquired a new global importance, adding greater urgency to the search for new operating principles to govern a volatile global system.

This search for a new world order began with the collapse of Moscow-dominated Communism, but, unlike previous watershed moments in twentieth-century history, no state was willing to take the lead. Instead, leadership was split, and thus diluted, between a reluctant United States and the United Nations. While U.S. presidents hinted at a new world order, it was the UN that gave shape and substance to the debate. The United Nations Development Programme (UNDP), in its landmark 1994 *World Development Report*, reminded the developed world that all was not well— that life was still precarious for the greater proportion of the world's rapidly growing population. The World Bank made poverty alleviation its number one priority in recognition of the multiple links between poverty, illiteracy, malnutrition, disease and political chaos. Still, overseas development assistance (ODA), the perennial measure of developed world concern with the daily struggle for survival in developing countries, declined. Resentment for Western affluence ran deep in the developing world, where, in Afghanistan or Sudan, for example, hope for a better future remained crushed by endemic civil conflict. "The market," a globally connected amalgam of financiers, investors, producers, traders and consumers, continued to generate enormous wealth but offered few if any durable solutions to the political challenges created by the punishing extremes of inequality.

The neologism "human security" entered public discourse through the 1994 UNDP report. The principal agency for UN development efforts since the institution's inception in 1945, the UNDP argued that a new and comprehensive approach to security was necessary to address critical humanitarian challenges in a post–Cold War world.[2] An integrated approach to human well-being was called for, one that emphasized the interrelationships between poverty, human rights, public health, education and political participation. This human security idea quickly merged with the "new security" agenda proposed by former Secretary-General Boutros Boutros-Ghali (1992–1996) in his *Agenda for Peace* (1992). While the UNDP approach emphasized development intervention, Boutros-Ghali argued a case for overriding the sovereign rights of states "when all peaceful means have failed," to put an end to intrastate conflicts.[3] Advocating a principle of humanitarian intervention, Boutros-Ghali stated that the international community had a "responsibility to protect" (R2P) the populations of states, especially against aggression from their own governments. Synthesizing these two strands of security thinking, the UN Commission on Human Security declared in its 2003 report, *Human Security Now*, "The international community urgently needs a new paradigm of security," not least because the state, for so long the "fundamental purveyor of security," cannot be relied upon to guarantee the welfare of its people.[4] To the UN human security agenda was thus added a crucial third strand: namely, systemic transformation in which the relationship between sovereign nation-states and international institutions had to fundamentally change.

This paradigm shift advocated at the highest levels at the UN mirrored intellectual currents among scholars of international relations and international development. The development strand of human security was influenced substantially by the work of Amartya Sen, an adviser to the World Bank and UN, and a consultant for the 1994 report, who in the 1990s designed a set of indicators that shifted the measurement of poverty away from household income to include a range of factors: health, literacy, gender equity and respect for fundamental human rights.[5] Feminist writers drew attention to the interrelationship between global politics and the "local" domain of family and community and the plight of women and children "locked down" or sexually exploited in patriarchal society. Gender equity was consequently enshrined as one of the pillars of the UN's Millennium Development Goals (MDGs) unveiled at the Millennium Summit in the year 2000. Frustrated with statecentric readings of security, scholars such as Barry Buzan and the Copenhagen School critiqued the utility of national security in a world where national securities were becoming increasingly internationalized and where states could only logically achieve security through participation in their neighborhood "security community."[6] The international scholarly consensus was that the world was changing rapidly and hence national and global institutions had to change accordingly.

At the national level, human security became incorporated into the security discourse of Canada, Japan, Finland and Norway, which in the late 1990s formed a human security network of states extending to Chile in Latin America, but the concept failed to capture the imagination of policymakers in Washington, London or Paris. Not that there was anything radical or new in arguing that international peace could be achieved through the pursuit of social justice on an international scale. U.S. President Woodrow Wilson proposed no less at the Versailles peace talks in 1919 with his Fourteen Points, in which he set out some ground rules for a new world order that would prevent a repeat of the carnage of World War One (1914–1918). Wilsonian idealism pervaded the rhetoric of U.S. foreign policy in the twentieth century and informed U.S. global institution building at the end of a second world war in 1945. UN secretaries-general are apt to remind U.S. policymakers of the connection between the UN's formation and the idealism of presidents Wilson, Franklin D. Roosevelt and Harry S. Truman. U.S. policymakers are in return apt to remind UN secretaries-general of the uncomfortable realities of international power politics and the limits to intervention, learned from repeated bitter experience, as a means of resolving conflict within states. Human security cannot be separated from questions about the structure and nature of international order. Debate oscillates between the optimistic view that a just and durable global order is possible and the pessimistic view that well-being cannot be enjoyed in equal measure by the world's 6.25 billion people. To borrow a phrase from Karl Marx (who, in turn, borrowed it from Martin Luther), the world remains "the devil's beer house," where aspirations for a better life must be tempered by experience.

Conceived as a set of dynamic and interrelated processes of social, economic, technological and cultural change, globalization is most commonly associated with instantaneous communication, shrinking travel times to distant destinations, rising trade interconnectedness, footloose capital and global consumer markets. Globalization both accentuates the connections between security in the developed and the developing world and accelerates the global impacts of local security crises. The relative ease with which visible and invisible human security risks can spread across the globe, from narcotics to lethal pathogens or a radioactive cloud, is but further proof of the double-edged nature of globalization. These are global risks that affect state and individual security alike and that map out new patterns of reciprocal exchange within an evolving global system.

Globalization and Human Security is thus concerned with the tension between globalizing security relations and the prevailing state-centered conceptual apparatus with which these relations are interpreted and addressed at the nation-state level. An empirical study of the concept of human security, the book explores this tension through the prism of international and global history. Historical memory is an essential foundation upon which to construct a view of the present that is neither jaundiced nor

naive. History is unfashionable, yet sociologists, political scientists, economists and "critical theorists" are all too often prone to deploy historical
generalizations in defense of their point of view. Likewise, for historical
reasons it is unlikely that swords will be beaten into plowshares in the near
or even distant future. Rather than agonize about the elusiveness or subjectivity of history, we argue that an appreciation of the cumulative nature of
contemporary human security crises and risks is a prerequisite to meaningful analysis of contemporary issues. World history also offers potent re-
minders of the capacity for inhumanity in advanced industrialized
countries—a reality often obscured by media images of famine, death and
conflict in Africa and the Middle East.

While it is possible to plot a very long historical trajectory for any contemporary human security crisis, we limit our terms of reference here to
the past century. Chapter 1 interrogates the concept of national security.
State sovereignty was considered the guarantor of security for small and
midsized states when the United Nations was founded at the 1945 San
Francisco Conference, but in a world where threats to humanity are demonstrably beyond the capacity of any one nation to address through unilateral action, the principle of sovereignty has to be re-envisioned.
Prescriptions for a safer and more prosperous world differ according to
one's perspective on the nature of international or global relations. Chapter
2 therefore examines approaches to human security from key theoretical
perspectives on international relations: political realism, liberalism, neo-
Marxism, postcolonialism and feminism. There are tensions between realist views about how the world is, or appears to be, and idealist aspirations
for global peace, but this is not a struggle between polar opposites. Human
security advocates must grapple with the limited capacity of the international system as it is currently constructed to respond to new security challenges.

Without a standing international army under UN direction, responsibility and hence costs of humanitarian intervention inevitably devolves to
the most powerful states, which bear the brunt of ensuing human, political
and financial costs. Chapter 3 explores what happens when humanitarian
interventions go horribly wrong. The U.S.-led intervention in Somalia in
1993 is a cautionary tale in the application of just force to neutralize a
complex humanitarian crisis. For any intervention to be effective, in both
the short and medium terms, planning has to take account of the political
and social complexities of such crises. Human security risks are cumulative
and multidimensional or polymorphous; and failure to conceive these risk

dynamics can leave the agents of intervention dangerously exposed. Chapter 4 examines the labyrinthine interconnections between conflict, refugee flows, public health crises and official corruption, drawing upon case studies from Africa, the Middle East and Asia.

Human security is inextricably linked to questions of political legitimacy and to social and economic justice. Chapter 5, while recognizing the myriad obstacles to an effective global human rights regime, maps out a pragmatic defense of human rights as the foundation of human and global security. International regimes are, of course, subject to the self-interested pursuit of political and strategic advantage. Chapter 6 traces the evolution of an international nuclear nonproliferation regime and looks at how and why states have repeatedly failed to comply with international rules and norms governing the development of nuclear weapons. In Chapter 7 we examine the idea of human security, not as a new paradigm of international relations, but as a framework through which to negotiate new approaches to the governance of global risks.

If security in its broadest sense means the maintenance or restoration of social, economic and cultural conditions that restrain the resort to political violence, then there is an urgent need for governments to adequately address the human dimension of global security. Indeed, in such complex and volatile times, there are serious questions as to whether traditional approaches to security, guided by the dominant state-centric or statist logic of political realism, are sufficient to secure the survival of humankind. For human security to be realized, security analysis and planning must incorporate three related strands: human development, the responsibility to protect and the urgent need for a more responsive and supportive system of global governance. Students of human security must, however, recognize that we live in a less-than-perfect world where idealism needs to be moderated by recognition of the practicalities of international politics.

CHAPTER 1

GLOBALIZING NATIONAL SECURITY: ENVISIONING SECURITY BEYOND THE NATION-STATE

We live in a world captured, uprooted and transformed by the titanic economic and techno-scientific processes of the development of capitalism, which has dominated for the past two or three centuries. We know or at least it is reasonable to suppose, that it cannot go on *ad infinitum*. The future cannot be a continuation of the past.

—Eric Hobsbawm

The threats to human well-being are undoubtedly greater in number and scope today than when the United Nations system came into being in 1945. The scale of security challenges has "blown out" as a consequence of rapid population growth and the increased sophistication of communications and weapons technologies, which in turn has quickened the pace at which security threats can be transmitted within and across national boundaries.

Risk is conceived in terms of potential scale or scope measured in human terms by numbers of people potentially affected by an untoward event—a nuclear explosion, disease pandemic or sudden political transition. Simplistically, preventable diseases kill more people in the world today because there are billions more people at risk of contracting and dying from them—especially in the developing world, where population growth is greatest.

War claimed tens of millions of lives in the twentieth century, but so too did totalitarianism, in Germany, Russia, China and many smaller states in Asia, Latin America and Africa. Radical political transitions in Eastern Europe and throughout the decolonized world brought political oppression, conflict, famine and disease. In 1945 there was only one nuclear power, the United States, but by the end of the millennium there were at least eight nuclear-armed states with dozens more acquiring or seeking to acquire the means to develop nuclear weapons. The irony of international or global security in the twenty-first century is that states have reinvested in their national security to combat the subterranean threat of terrorism, yet technology ensures that security, whether we make people or nation-states our primary referent, is being globalized to the point where no one state acting in isolation can guarantee the welfare of its people.

THE LANDSCAPE OF HUMAN (IN)SECURITY

Momentous shifts in world history invite grand declarations of intent. At the end of World War One, the "Great War" mistakenly cast as "the war to end all wars," Woodrow Wilson's Fourteen Points set out a formula for durable peace. As the Second World War (1939–1945) neared conclusion, Franklin D. Roosevelt sought an end to war through new international institutions to promote economic stability, development and justice. Both Wilson and Roosevelt proposed ground rules for their respective eras because they could. By the end of 1945 if not the end of 1918, the United States was undoubtedly the world's foremost economic and military power, a hegemon, poised to claim the mantle of global leadership from imperial Britain.

THE "DEVIL'S BIERHAUS"

Both presidents looked out on a world shocked by the human cost of war. The Great War reaped a staggering 9,720,453 military deaths and

8,865,649 civilian deaths with another 21,228,813 military wounded. World War One was confined largely to Europe. Wars between France and its neighbors over a twenty-three-year period from 1792 to 1815 claimed the lives of over three million combatants and at least one million civilians—a "mere" fraction of casualties inflicted a century later in shorter but more intense conflicts. World War Two was by contrast fought across the Pacific, Asia and North Africa. Advances in the technology of killing meant that this Second World War ushered in an era of total war, in which civilians became the targets of systematic bombing campaigns designed to sap enemy morale. The greater scope of operational "theaters," larger armies and more numerous conflict parties contributed to higher death counts. There were twenty-five million military combat-related deaths in total with at least another forty to forty-five million civilian deaths arising from combat operations, famine and disease. Counting from the invasion of Manchuria in 1931 to its surrender in 1945, the Japanese imperial army directly and indirectly caused the deaths of anywhere from fifteen to thirty million civilians across Asia and the Pacific.

The international community had worked hard to avoid these tragedies. Woodrow Wilson's prescription for the world as of 1919 was an international system founded upon trust, fairness and justice. The League of Nations was created to implement Wilson's ideas, although without U.S. involvement, the League was ineffectual. The principle of self-determination challenged the interests of the colonial powers—Britain and France—which had no intention of giving up their imperial possessions to immediate independence. The League had no effective power to punish member states that stepped outside the bounds of decent behavior. Though anxious to be admitted to the international club of nations at Versailles in 1919, Japan invaded Manchuria and promptly withdrew from the League. Herein lay the weakness of the League and of post-1945 international institutions such as the UN where, despite an array of agreements, charters and conventions, compliance is also voluntary. Without adequate means for enforcement, international rules and laws carry no legal force and moral suasion carries little weight when presumed national interests are at stake.

The focus of human security at the end of the twentieth century was squarely on the developing world—once termed the third world but now more popularly referred to as the Global South. Yet Western civilization delivered to the world the two most murderous dictators of the twentieth century. German chancellor Adolf Hitler (1933–1945) and general secretary of the Central Committee of the Communist Party of the Soviet Union

Joseph Stalin (1922–1953) cast long and menacing shadows over world affairs, in Hitler's case for many decades after his suicide on the eve of Germany's defeat in 1945. Both leaders became synonymous with the century's political extremes and the epitome of totalitarianism. Nineteenth-century European ideas about race and human evolution received their ultimate expression in Hitler's National Socialist state in which Aryan racial purity was equated with individual virtue and national strength. As chancellor, Hitler plotted the dawn of a global Aryan epoch, the Third Reich, and presided over a Nazi regime that assassinated political opponents and exterminated an estimated six million Jews. It was Hitler's personal ambition to dominate Europe that propelled the world toward war in 1939.

Driven by an extreme reading of the works of German political economist and philosopher Karl Marx and intoxicated by absolute power, Stalin came to epitomize the worst features of Soviet-style Communist ideology. Stalin presided over the expansion of Soviet power in Eastern Europe and Central Asia and brutal purges of "dissident" voices, both inside and outside the Communist Party of Russia. Unlike Hitler, Stalin's record for political murder passed relatively unnoticed—in part because after 1940 the Soviet Union, the United States and Britain were allied against Germany and Japan. Stalin's purges of "counterrevolutionaries" during 1937 and 1938 accounted for 681,692 deaths by execution. This was but the tip of the iceberg. Forced collectivization of agriculture led to famines that, in 1932–1933 alone, cost the lives of an estimated six million peasants. Systematic imprisonment of opponents in prison labor camps or "gulags," arbitrary and summary executions and violent reprisal were essential features of a Soviet system created to liberate the oppressed masses from the yoke of capitalism.[1]

Three years of civil war in China ended in 1949 with victory to the Communists led by Mao Zedong—Chairman Mao. Driven by a version of Marxism modified to suit peasant as opposed to industrial society, Mao also sought the root and branch transformation of Chinese society. As in Soviet Russia, the human costs of this radical transformation were high. Purges of "bourgeois" elements, including intellectuals, small business owners and Christian clergy, in the first ten years of Communist rule claimed the lives of as many as two million people. Mao's Great Leap Forward also included the forced collectivization of agriculture and, as in the Soviet Union, millions of Chinese peasants died as a result of famine generated by radical changes to farming practices and livelihoods. But in China the human toll of famine reached as high as forty-three million people.[2]

Political purges continued through the Cultural Revolution of the 1960s and early 1970s until Mao's death.

SYSTEMIC BALANCES

After the carnage of World War One and World War Two, the developed world enjoyed an era of prolonged peace while perversely, the two superpowers, the United States and the USSR, developed their capacity to destroy life through the expansion of increasingly sophisticated nuclear arsenals. The nuclear devices dropped on Hiroshima and Nagasaki in 1945 killed an estimated 130,000 people and left a legacy of hereditary abnormalities for generations and elevated incidences of cancer in and around ground zero in each city. The bomb dropped on Hiroshima had the equivalent explosive force of 20,000 tons of TNT. By 1952 the United States had developed a thermonuclear bomb with an equivalent explosive power of seven million tons of TNT—a seven megaton bomb. Driven by the impulse to achieve absolute security, both superpowers manufactured the means to devastate entire countries with a single explosive device.

Over the next four decades, a tense nuclear balance of terror between the superpowers maintained relative peace and stability in the geographical heartlands of the West and the former Soviet bloc. Dubbed the "Cold War era" because U.S. and Soviet troops never confronted each other in open battle but rather faced off in numerous proxy wars fought across the developing world, international order was shaped by two competing ideological systems and the interests and tactics of Washington and Moscow.

Within the Western and liberal capitalist sphere, new systems for regulating transnational production and trade emerged, founded upon global institutions such as the United Nations, World Bank, International Monetary Fund (IMF) and the General Agreement on Tariffs and Trade (GATT), superseded by the World Trade Organization. Though defeated militarily in the Pacific, Japan became the center of an Asian economic boom, dubbed the "Asian miracle" by economists at the World Bank. Globalization, it was asserted, was changing the nature of interstate relations to the point where economic prosperity mattered more than the accumulation of military power.

Monetary flows were changing with the emergence of a new global economy. Oil has played a central part in this shift in a number of ways. First, Arab oil-producing states, dissatisfied with the disregard for governments and the profits reaped by Western oil majors, formed the Organiza-

---

TWENTIETH CENTURY: PIVOTAL EVENTS, 1900–1950

The Great War	August 1914–November 1918
Versailles Peace Conference	1919
Bolshevik Revolution	October 1917
Japan's invasion of Manchuria	1931
World War Two:	
European Theater	September 1939–May 1945
Pacific Theater	December 1941–August 1945
Nuclear bombings of Hiroshima	
and Nagasaki	August 1945
Chinese Civil War	1946–1949
International Institutions:	
United Nations	1945
Bretton Woods	1948

---

tion of Petroleum Exporting Countries (OPEC) comprising Saudi Arabia, Kuwait, Iraq, Iran and Venezuela. The OPEC cartel sought to limit production to ensure a favorable oil price and raise oil revenues. However, through the 1960s, even amid rising Western oil dependency, the oil majors were able to apply political pressure on OPEC through the U.S. and British governments. OPEC realized its producer power in 1974 when, to pressure the U.S. government over Israel's continued occupation of Syrian and Egyptian territory following the 1973 Arab-Israeli War, OPEC oil production was severely curtailed.

The sharp rise in oil prices delivered windfall royalties to OPEC governments. "Petrodollars" entered the world banking system, creating vast pools of investment capital that found its way into Latin America and other parts of the developing world. This rise in global liquidity caused severe problems for countries that borrowed heavily but were unable to sustain debt burdens in times of economic hardship. In the 1980s, Brazil and Argentina were so indebted that they could not meet interest payments on their loans from North American and European creditors. The "Washington Consensus" began as a plan formulated by the U.S. Federal Reserve to address the root causes of the Latin American debt crisis by imposing strict economic restructuring conditions to IMF and World Bank loans. In return for assistance, countries henceforth were required to adopt strict fiscal discipline. Structural adjustment became the principal policy prescription for global financial institutions in the 1990s. IMF and World Bank funding assistance to Latin American countries, to Thailand in 1997 and to Russia in 1998 came with strings attached—all designed to guarantee equilibrium in a globalized system of payments.

THE LIBERAL TRIUMPH

One event, seen as insignificant in January 1989, actually started the process that would cause the collapse of the Soviet Empire. From January 15 to January 21, army units in Prague suppressed crowds demonstrating against Communism and arrested over 400 protesters. The repression was temporary, however, as protests grew in size until Czech leaders agreed to hold multiparty elections, which, on December 29, 1989, resulted in the election of Václav Havel as president—a dissident who had been imprisoned in January.

Throughout 1989, the Czech experience was duplicated in different ways in other Warsaw Pact nations. East German protests led to the fall of the Berlin Wall in November 1989 and the reunification of the two Germanys in 1991. Polish protests succeeded when the Communists yielded power to the anticommunist Solidarity Party on August 24. Hungary's Communists permitted multiparty elections, leading to noncommunist victories; Romanian protests led to the overthrow and execution of their Communist leader; the Bulgarians forced their president to resign after approving multiparty elections, but he renamed his party and kept control of parliament.

In Moscow, Gorbachev discovered that his reforms—involving economic changes and a public openness (glasnost)—and dissent in Eastern Europe's Communist states prompted the individual Soviet republics to seek their independence. Gorbachev's successor, Boris Yeltsin, survived a coup by hard-line Communists in August 1991 but could only watch as various Soviet republics seceded from the Soviet Union. The Russian Republic joined the Ukraine, Byelorussia and eight other Soviet republics to form the Commonwealth of Independent States (CIS) in December 1991, and on December 25, 1991, Gorbachev resigned as Soviet president. The red hammer and sickle flag was lowered for the last time from the Kremlin wall.

As the Berlin Wall came down, U.S. president George H. W. Bush envisaged a new world order of liberal capitalist expansion under U.S. auspices. Liberal triumphalism was encapsulated in the title of Francis Fukuyama's controversial book *The End of History and the Last Man* (1992) in which Fukuyama, a State Department adviser in the Bush and Clinton administrations, asserted that

> The most remarkable development of the last quarter of the twentieth century has been the revelation of enormous weaknesses at the core of the world's seemingly strong dictatorships, whether they be of the military-authoritarian Right, or the communist-totalitarian Left. . . . And while they have not given way in all cases to stable liberal democracies, liberal democracy remains the only coherent political aspiration that spans different regions and cultures around the globe.[3]

Fukuyama had a point. In the 1980s Latin America witnessed a series of "democratic transitions" from military to democratic rule, bookmarked by the rapid demise of successive military governments in Argentina between 1981 and 1983 and culminating in a return to civilian rule and the handover of power by Chile's infamous general Augusto Pinochet in 1989. Military regimes too fell out of favor in Asia, adding to the tectonic shift in world politics generated by the Soviet collapse. China and Indochina retained Communist one-party systems but were forced to open up to Western capital, raising questions about the long-term future of Communist rule. Fukuyama expressed the liberal view that, with all alternatives discredited, capitalism was sweeping all before it. The logic of history did not favor a world socialist state but instead pointed toward a complementary balancing of liberal democracy and free markets.

Latin America's transitions occurred because people refused to tolerate the economic failures of their authoritarian governments.[4] Ballooning debt crises also threatened the foundations of the world economy, highlighting the precariousness of a new world economic system underpinned by massive financial movements across state borders. Still, according to liberal optimists, the forces of modernization were working conveniently under their own momentum to refashion world order that would one day be entirely constituted by liberal democracies. Logically, Fukuyama argued, because within democratic states state power is balanced by the popular will expressed through the ballot box, the world would enter an era of unprecedented peace.

China deflected the political winds of globalization but not globalizing economic forces. Demonstrators in Tiananmen Square in June 1989 called

TWENTIETH CENTURY: PIVOTAL EVENTS, POST-1950

U.S. intervention in Vietnam	1962–1975
First and second oil shocks	1973 and 1979
Iranian Revolution	1979
Collapse of Communism	1989–1991
First American Gulf War	1991
9/11	2001
"War on Terror" Interventions:	
Afghanistan	2001
Iraq	2003

for China's democratization but were quickly dispersed by soldiers and tanks. China's leaders, among them Deng Xiaoping, the author of the country's policy of economic modernization, determined that one-party rule would remain and that China would not go the way of the USSR. China adopted market-oriented economic reforms—privatization of state-owned enterprises, openness to foreign investment, encouragement of individual entrepreneurship and capital accumulation—but politics remained firmly under state control. Joining the WTO, the country cast off the political ideology of Mao to become a Communist state in name only.[5]

The demise of Soviet Communism stripped the United States of its principal rationale for maintaining its global security role. From 1989 to 1991, President George H. W. Bush's national security team watched approvingly but passively as bloodless revolutionary events demolished the Soviet Empire and new, independent states emerged in the former Soviet Union. Overall, of course, Bush faced the daunting task of defining post–Cold War policy for the United States. The United States was unchallenged and unchallengeable as the world's only military superpower, but the foundations upon which a new liberal international order were to be built appeared decidedly shaky. As the Soviet system unraveled, civil wars in Eastern Europe, the Caucasus and Central Asia added to the human costs of twentieth-century revolutionary change. In 1998 the world economy came close to collapse as Russia teetered on the brink of economic implosion after devaluing the ruble and defaulting on loan repayments to Western banks. IMF assistance valued at US$11.2 billion was expeditiously put together before a major debt crisis triggered a general worldwide recession—such was the level of financial risk sensitivity in a globally networked world.

SYSTEMIC IMBALANCES

UN Secretary General Boutros Boutros-Ghali and his successor, Kofi Annan (1996–2006), feared that the United States might abdicate its self-appointed mission to promote peace, democracy and development when so much was left to be done to address the legacies of colonialism and the human toll of uneven development. Two world wars in quick succession caused the fatal hemorrhaging of the old European-centered imperial order that for the best part of three centuries had divided the world into competing imperial blocs. The spread of a European-centered imperial order across first the Americas, then Asia, Oceania and Africa, disrupted long-established political traditions and economic patterns with catastrophic consequences for indigenous populations.

Globalization as imperialism laid out the infrastructure of a new international economy powered first by coal and steam and then by oil and electricity. New social stresses were introduced into colonized worlds between colonizer and colonized, between immigrant and "indigenous" and between ethnolinguistic communities thrown together by unwelcome colonial state formations. Colonial regimes created incongruous colonial states designed to service the economic needs of the colonizers and not the communal or political interests of the colonized. As the Commission for Africa summarized, "the division of Africa into its present countries was the product of Western interests, not African minds."[6]

The consequences of this colonial era were still to be addressed at the global and regional levels while, all the time, demographic change amplified the human costs of conflict and disease. At the dawn of the Industrial Revolution in the late 1700s, an estimated seven hundred million people inhabited the globe, rising to nine hundred million by 1800. Over the next two hundred years, world population rose by more than five times to six billion people, with the most rapid increase occurring after 1950 and mainly outside the industrialized or developed world. By the middle of this century world population could peak at around nine billion people with the majority living in Africa, South Asia and East Asia. Not only does this population trajectory amplify the impact of human activity upon the natural environment through rising material consumption, it raises the actual

NEW SECURITY CHALLENGES

We have entered a time of global transition marked by uniquely contradictory trends. Regional and continental associations of States are evolving ways to deepen cooperation and ease some of the contentious characteristics of sovereign and nationalistic rivalries. National boundaries are blurred by advanced communications and global commerce, and by the decisions of States to yield some sovereign prerogatives to larger, common political associations. At the same time, however, fierce new assertions of nationalism and sovereignty spring up, and the cohesion of States is threatened by brutal ethnic, religious, social, cultural or linguistic strife. Social peace is challenged on the one hand by new assertions of discrimination and exclusion and, on the other, by acts of terrorism seeking to undermine evolution and change through democratic means.

Source: Boutros Boutros-Ghali, *An Agenda for Peace: Preventive Diplomacy, Peacemaking, and Peace-Keeping*, 1992.

and potential costs in terms of human life of armed conflicts, be they conventional or nuclear, environmental disasters, pandemics or famine.[7]

Decolonization in the 1950s and 1960s exposed the depth of these fissures and the failure of colonial powers to lay firm foundations for democratic political development. In Africa independence was accompanied by high expectations borne of promising economic conditions. However, within the space of a decade, democratic independence governments were eliminated through coups and civil wars, replaced by military dictatorships or authoritarian one-party states governed by political strongmen and dominated by large tribal groups. Underdevelopment, the condition of stagnant or falling incomes relative to the rest of the world, combined with declining life expectancy rates, high infant and maternal mortality, extensive and increasing illiteracy. States were created in the absence of popular consensus, where, to borrow from Buzan, "the idea of the state" remained in dispute, in terms of both political boundaries and also politico-religious character.

Living standards in the developed and parts of the developing world grew at an unprecedented pace, while in Africa especially, the inhabitants of many newly independent states became locked into vicious cycles of violence, impoverishment and often starvation. Expanding transport and communications matrices shrank space and time, giving impetus to the race to conquer outer space, but billions of new human beings entered a world that provided them with barely enough to eat. It is hardly surprising that the most pressing human security challenges are found in the developing world.

Historical wealth distribution data from Angus Maddison for the period 1500–2001 highlight the shuddering impact of globalization upon Asian productivity relative to Western Europe and North America. Accounting for nearly two-thirds of global gross domestic product at the beginning of the eighteenth century, Asia's share fell below one-quarter by 1913. Productivity climbed back above one-third in the late twentieth century, led by Japan, but in Africa the share of global GDP remained virtually stagnant throughout with, as of 2001, a paltry 3.3 percent for a continent of 1.2 billion people and rising.[8]

For more than four-fifths of humanity, the nuances of ideological debate are less important than the daily struggle with economic hardship, hunger, political chaos and recurring civil unrest or the threat of debilitating illness and disease. New countries were torn by conflict between rival ethnic and tribal groups over the legitimacy of their colonial inheritance or between the state and its people. Since 1945 an estimated forty-one million people, civilians and combatants, have died as a result of interstate conflict and bitter civil wars fought across the Middle East, Asia, Latin America and Africa in the name of nationalism, anticolonialism and socialism or purely for private gain.[9]

Economic mismanagement effected in the name of socialism, but in practice intended to strengthen elite control, sent the economies of prosperous countries such as Ghana, Tanzania, Mali and Zambia into a tailspin.[10] The most striking feature of new states was their fragmented nature and hence vulnerability to disintegration through conflicts over the idea of the state and the character of government. Political rivalries coalesced around questions as to the proper role of religion and religious law, political representation and the allocation of economic dividends. So fragmented were newly independent states that the actual political reach of governments did not correspond to territorial jurisdictions conferred by international law. In practice, territorial borders were mere frontiers where central power was weak and contested and where refugees fleeing brutal regimes begged for sanctuary in neighboring countries.

While great strides were made globally in absolute poverty reduction over the past quarter century, inequality was increasing. Gaping wealth disparities between urban and rural populations mirror wealth disparities between developed and developing countries but are masked by aggregate per-capita purchasing power parity (PPP) or productivity ratios. A global poverty line of US$1.07 per day is cold comfort for those at or just above this level whose economic prospects and those of their family are limited.

A New World Disordered

Although the end of the Cold War surprised President George H. W. Bush and America's foreign policy establishment, there had been several signs of the impending Soviet collapse when Bush was inaugurated on January 20, 1989. In December 1987, Premier Mikhail Gorbachev and President Ronald Reagan had signed a treaty limiting intermediate-range nuclear weapons and, five days before Bush was sworn in, Gorbachev had removed all Soviet troops from Afghanistan, ending a Cold War crisis that began in 1979. At a Vienna meeting the day before Bush's inaugural, thirty-five Communist and democratic nations, including the USSR, approved a significant follow-up to the 1975 Helsinki agreements. These accords committed these nations to respect an individual's freedom of information, religion, travel and privacy; to reduce the conventional armed forces of the Warsaw Pact and North Atlantic Treaty Organization; and to plan the institutionalization of the Conference on Security and Cooperation in Europe.

A temporary and uneasy consensus on global security issues was achieved at the UN Security Council, first with the expulsion of Iraq from Kuwait in 1991 and then with action to resolve civil wars in Somalia and Cambodia. Following quickly after the euphoria of Operation Desert Storm in Kuwait, Somalia was a bitter lesson for the United States, whose willingness to assume leadership roles in UN-sponsored interventions subsequently wavered. There had been no major European war after 1945, but tens of thousands of Europeans were still dying as a consequence of political violence in the former Yugoslavia and in Croatia and Bosnia-Herzegovina.

Mary Kaldor wrote in *New and Old Wars* (1999) of a new kind of conflict that would dominate the global agenda in the twenty-first century. Drawing upon the breakup of the former Yugoslavia and conflicts erupting throughout the former USSR, Kaldor argued that a new generation of warfare had emerged in which wars were fought not between but within nation-states, between the state and groups defined by a shared sense of

---

AN AGENDA FOR PEACE

Our aims must be:

- To seek to identify at the earliest possible stage situations that could produce conflict, and to try through diplomacy to remove the sources of danger before violence results;
- Where conflict erupts, to engage in peacemaking aimed at resolving the issues that have led to conflict;
- Through peace-keeping, to work to preserve peace, however fragile, where fighting has been halted and to assist in implementing agreements achieved by the peacemakers;
- To stand ready to assist in peace-building in its differing contexts: rebuilding the institutions and infrastructures of nations torn by civil war and strife; and building bonds of peaceful mutual benefit among nations formerly at war;
- And in the largest sense, to address the deepest causes of conflict: economic despair, social injustice and political oppression. It is possible to discern an increasingly common moral perception that spans the world's nations and peoples, and which is finding expression in international laws, many owing their genesis to the work of this Organization.

Source: Boutros Boutros-Ghali, *An Agenda for Peace: Preventive Diplomacy, Peacemaking, and Peace-Keeping*, 1992.

---

cultural identity and a politically manufactured sense of common grievance that "their" interests are not served by centralized authority. This, she argued, was a consequence of globalization stripping away the protective layer of international stability provided by the Cold War bipolar balance and the diminution of state control by the inexorable processes of economic globalization.[11]

Religion emerged as a potent source of political opposition to the liberal project. Revolution in Iran in 1979 transformed the country from secular autocracy to Islamic theocracy, giving added impetus to the rising tide of Islamic fundamentalism across the Middle East. Islam was the common denominator for the broad front of Afghan mujahideen fighting against Soviet troops in Afghanistan from among whose ranks emerged Islamist militants bent on attacking the foundations of U.S. power and halting the spread of liberal capitalism. Religious extremism and the bitter experience of war and deprivation spawned a global Islamist movement that fed off popular resentment toward the West in the developing world.

Following 9/11, the United States aggressively prosecuted a new form of realpolitik predicated on a presumed monolithic terror threat to the United States and its interests abroad. Pursuing Osama Bin Laden and his Al Qaeda organization into Afghanistan, U.S. forces were decisive in bringing about the removal of the Taliban Islamist regime in 2002. Although approved by the UN Security Council and supported by America's European NATO allies and Pacific allies Australia and Japan, the occupations of Afghanistan and Iraq are first and foremost U.S. military operations and representative of a strategic doctrine that regards military force as the principal agent by which American liberal democratic values can be exported to the Islamic world.

At the beginning of the twenty-first century the United States lost patience with the system it had largely created and wrote the UN out of its 2002 *National Security Strategy*. At the alleged insistence of British prime minister Tony Blair, the Bush administration campaigned for an enabling resolution at the UN Security Council before launching its invasion of Iraq. But it was evident that Washington viewed the UN as an institution that had lost its way, that was hostage to factionalism, stymied by diplomatic trade-offs, bloated, bureaucratic and quite possibly riddled by corruption. Smarting from sustained international condemnation for the foreign policy debacle in Iraq, President George W. Bush reminded the UN members of their responsibilities. Referring to the Universal Declaration of Human Rights in a speech to the General Assembly in September 2007, President Bush appealed to the legacy of Wilson and Roosevelt:

> Achieving the promise of the Declaration requires confronting long-term threats; it also requires answering the immediate needs of today. The nations in this chamber have our differences, yet there are some areas where we can all agree. When innocent people are trapped in a life of murder and fear, the Declaration is not being upheld. When millions of children starve to death or perish from a mosquito bite, we're not doing our duty in the world. When whole societies are cut off from the prosperity of the global economy, we're all worse off. . . .
>
> This great institution must work for great purposes—to free people from tyranny and violence, hunger and disease, illiteracy and ignorance, and poverty and despair. Every member of the United Nations must join in this mission of liberation.[12]

The speech was also a clear indication that the United States was looking to other countries to share the burden of world ordering. As George Bush spoke, 168,000 U.S. troops were deployed in Iraq, with a further 24,000 in Afghanistan and rising. By the end of 2007 the number of U.S. military deaths in Iraq was climbing inexorably toward 4,000, while the financial costs were expected to exceed US$3 trillion. Not since the Vietnam War (1965–1975), which cost the lives of 50,000 U.S. soldiers, had the United States borne such heavy human and financial war losses. Analysts such as Robert Keohane argue that the financial burdens of war and of underwriting the liberal international economic order that it had created at Bretton Woods severely eroded the capacity of the United States to direct global economic and strategic affairs after 1971.[13] Three decades on, a similar set of circumstances appears to be marking the end of another phase in U.S. hegemonic decline. Despite its unrivaled technological edge and the size of its economy, the United States confronts leadership challenges from China and a resurgent Russia, both of which have, like the United States, demonstrated their disregard for international principles enshrined in the UN system.

TOWARD A HUMAN SECURITY AGENDA

Human security challenges or "risks" elude easy categorization. A defining feature of twentieth-century globalization is the increasing complexity of global relations and the rapidity with which information ricochets around the world. Globalization has rendered the world more sensitive to sudden financial or strategic shocks, however localized they might at first appear.

The shifting terrain of global relations also ensures that security issues of any kind can appear unexpectedly and rapidly change in shape and scope. Human security risks can usefully be thought of as "polymorphous" in that at any one moment in time, people and their communities can be subject to political violence or environmental scarcities, which individually can generate a host of future dangers: food shortages, economic hardship, crime, disease and human rights abuses. To define a security crisis as military, environmental, societal or financial is to downplay the strings or threads of interconnected happenings, decisions, ideas and beliefs that shape trajectories of risk.

COMPLEX CRISES

Human security crises cluster around interconnected domains of risk. The arbitrary categorization of risks aids analysis, but without an appreciation of the dynamics of interaction between risk factors, human security risk analysis falters. Drug trafficking and drug addiction create a temporal link between the fates of communities in the developed and developing worlds, even if the numbers of persons involved are quite small. According to the UN Office of Drug Control (UNODC), over a twelve-month period spanning 2005 and 2006, an estimated two hundred million persons used drugs illegally out of a global population of 6.475 billion. Of these, 110 million used drugs on a monthly basis, of which twenty-five million, or 0.6 percent of the global working age population (15–64), were classed as "problem drug users."[14] Yet the total annual U.S. drug control budget stood at US$12.5 billion in 2004, more than four times the value of total U.S. contributions to the United Nations.[15] This is a measure of the scale of the drug "problem" in the United States, which extends far beyond the number of addicts to the corrosive influence of traffickers and the webs of criminal activity that envelop the addicted. Corruption in police ranks and among government officials corrodes law enforcement and public confidence in government institutions. At the regional level, drug production in Latin America destabilizes legitimate governments and creates de facto "narco-states" in territory beyond central government control.

According to World Health Organization statistics, over fifty-seven million people died from preventable diseases in 2006, more disease-related deaths in one year than the combined total of combat deaths in World War One and World War Two. UNAIDS estimates thirty-three million people worldwide are infected with the human immunodeficiency virus (HIV), the vast majority located in sub-Saharan Africa, which accounts for 22.5 million or 68 percent of all infections. Of those diagnosed with the virus, only a small proportion have succumbed to acquired immunodeficiency syndrome (AIDS), in which the immune system is gradually destroyed. Two million people died from HIV/AIDS in 2006, just over 1 percent of all disease-related deaths. But while diseases such as tuberculosis, cholera and malaria can be treated and cured, the HIV/AIDS virus is arrested with anti-retroviral drugs (ARVs) but remains—for the present—incurable.[16]

The search for a cure involves not just the pursuit of a wonder drug that can destroy the virus, but the reshaping of socioeconomic environments in which the virus is known to thrive.

Conflict, in addition to its political, social, economic and even cultural roots, can also be linked to radical changes in the natural environment. According to Jared Diamond, the underlying causes of the Rwandan genocide that claimed the lives of an estimated 800,000 people in 1994 were land degradation and attendant population pressures, which destabilized

---

HUMAN SECURITY AT RISK

At the global level human security no longer means careful constructed safeguards against the threat of nuclear holocaust—a likelihood greatly reduced by the end of the cold war. Instead it means responding to the threat of global poverty traveling across international borders in the form of drugs, HIV/AIDS, climate change, illegal migration and terrorism. The prospect of collective suicide through an impulsive resort to nuclear weapons was always exaggerated. But the threat of global poverty affecting all human lives—in rich nations and in poor—is real and persistent.

Source: UNDP, *Human Development Report*, 1994.

Rwandan society. Resource scarcity is likely to increase, and with it the likelihood of environmental refugees moving en masse across international boundaries.

Former World Bank economist Nicholas Stern lays out an alarming global scenario on the potential economic and social impacts of climate change. Synthesizing scientific data on climate change, Stern calibrates a sliding scale of natural and human disasters arising from the warming of the earth's atmosphere. A worst-case scenario was predicated on a five-degree Celsius increase in the earth's temperature, causing sea levels to rise, extensive inundation of low-lying coastal areas and widespread water stress threatening food security in India and China—effectively one-third of the world's population—with obvious consequences for economic and political security at the regional and global levels.[17] While these scenarios are increasingly accepted as plausible in even the most skeptical quarters, remedial steps have proved difficult to coordinate at the global level.

APPROACHING HUMAN SECURITY

As the Commission on Human Security argues in its 2003 report, conflict prevention, disease eradication, poverty alleviation, sustainable economic development, food security and the promotion of human rights are interlinked security concerns. The scope of human security so defined fitted well with objectives outlined in the UN's Millennium Development Goals (MDGs).

A DECLARATION OF INTENT

A. Freedom from Want

- Halve poverty by 2015.
- Make primary education universal by 2015.
- Improve educational opportunities for young girls.
- Arrest the spread of HIV/AIDS by 2015.
- Increase Internet and telecommunications access in the developing world.

B. Freedom from Fear

- "Strengthen respect" for human rights and international arms control treaties.
- Improve the United Nations' peacekeeping capabilities.
- Target sanctions so as to minimize impact upon the innocent.
- Reduce and, where possible, eliminate illegal arms trading.

C. A Sustainable Future

- Ratify Kyoto Protocol on Climate Change by 2002.
- Encourage member states to integrate environmental considerations into national accounts calculations.
- Conduct the Millennium Ecosystem Assessment.

D. Renewing the United Nations

- Enhance the legitimacy of the UN Security Council.
- Ensure that the UN is adequately funded.
- Increase opportunities for nongovernmental organizations to contribute to UN decision making and programs.

Source: Kofi Annan, *"We the Peoples,"* 2000.

Set forth at the 2000 Millennium Summit, these MDGs are *inter alia*: poverty eradication and food security; universal primary education; an end to gender discrimination; a two-thirds reduction in mortality under the age of five; substantial reductions in maternal mortality; lifting the burden of disease, especially HIV/AIDS and malaria; environmentally sustainable development; and the removal of financial impediments to growth by fostering a global partnership for development.[18] Indicative of the careful structuring of the UN's message, these goals were grouped for rhetorical effect by Kofi Annan to resonate with the ideals of Wilson and Roosevelt.

Although presented in the neutral language of public policy, each of these goals, to be achieved, requires that significant local cultural and political challenges be overcome. The MDGs rest on an overwhelming empirical case made by Amartya Sen as to the critical importance to human well-being of education, health care, gender equity, economic opportunity, and respect for human rights.[19]

The achievement of gender equity is today widely regarded as pivotal to sustainable human development. "Women's agency," writes Sen, where permitted in the development process, leads to the more effective utilization of natural and human resources because women tend to ensure that resources introduced into the community are shared equitably and that development lessons are learned and passed on to the next generation. Yet gender equity advocates confront strong opposition in societies where women are barred from higher levels of education and from joining the professions. In many parts of the world "traditional values" are used to justify the exclusion of women. This is not a question of religious conservatism versus secular modernity. In many modern Islamic countries, Malaysia being a good example, young women comprise a majority of tertiary students. Rather, it is a question of entrenched custom, patriarchal dominance and economic underdevelopment—systemic factors that can take decades to break down.

According to Roland Paris, the sheer scope of issues encompassed by the UN's broad conception of human security carries the risk of being too cumbersome to serve as an operational definition.[20] Narrowing their focus, researchers at the Canadian Human Security Centre at the University of British Columbia in their *Human Security Report 2006* limit the scope of human security to the study of the "incidence, severity, causes and consequences of global violence."[21] Placing human security squarely within the orbit of conflict studies, their approach attached the greatest importance to humanitarian assistance for victims of war and to the conditions that promote peace within and among states. Paradoxically, and unintentionally, they ensure that war remains at the top of the international security agenda. Further, by narrowing our focus to the immediate causes and consequences of conflict, we lose sight of the long-term trajectories of risk that can culminate in societal collapse.

Limiting definitions of war and conflict to statistical criteria also distorts our reading of the health of the contemporary global system. According to data provided by researchers from the Uppsala Conflict Data Program, the scale or intensity of conflict differs from that of war in the annual number of "battle-related deaths": twenty-five such fatalities per year, including civilian casualties, for political violence to be categorized as armed conflict, and 1,000 combatant and noncombatant battle-related deaths per year for political violence to be categorized as a war.[22] Applying these criteria, human security analysts claim that the incidence of war is declining and that, consequently, the world is becoming a safer place. However, shots do not need to be exchanged for the conditions of war or armed conflict to exist. In order to assess the potential for political violence to erupt and to escalate into war, we need to appreciate the diverse reasons people resort to violence and why states make war on one another. Rather than concentrate upon the immediacy of violence and its consequences, we should look to the early warning signs of conflict or war in an effort to limit the resort to political violence.

In "latent conflict" situations, a cease-fire or even a formal treaty might well exist between rival parties but where the grievances and suspicions that ignited political violence have yet to subside. Indian and Pakistani troops stare at each other across the disputed line of division in Kashmir, occasionally exchanging shells and rifle shots while militant groups sponsored by both sides engage in terrorist violence on both sides of the border. In Sri Lanka a 2001 cease-fire between the government and the Tamil Tigers fighting for an independent homeland in the north and east of the island state broke down in 2005 when both parties resumed their twenty-year struggle. Ironically, while the cease-fire remains theoretically intact, an estimated 4,000 people have since died in renewed fighting. Instances of periodic but persistent deadly violence can be found throughout Africa, Asia and Latin America.

THE SECURITY SPECTRUM

For a definition of human security to have explanatory force and to appeal to decision makers and researchers alike, it must establish a conceptual link with notions of world order. To put it another way, decision makers need the intellectual equipment and disposition to see the "full spectrum" of security in order to identify security risks and preventive measures that do not escalate into the use of force. Further, to be serviceable at a policy level such a definition must be anchored to a realization of the limitations imposed by an imperfect "anarchic" interstate system. This inevitably leads to compromises in the prioritization of human security issues—and to tensions between those disposed toward morality and ethics in international affairs and those who see the world in terms of power politics.

Human security was presaged in the policies of small to medium powers. Without employing the term, the Australian government incorporated a prototypical human security framework into Australian foreign and defense policy in the late 1980s. The 1989 *Statement on Australia's Regional Security* drew attention to the interconnections between traditional and nontraditional risks confronting Australia and the Asian region, from underdevelopment to drug trafficking to HIV/AIDS. Importantly, the policy prescription envisaged a positive multidimensional response incorporating military, diplomatic, economic and technical cooperation, thus linking Australian security to the security of its immediate neighbours.[23] More recently, Canada adopted an explicit and comprehensive human security agenda, as did Japan and other member states of the Human Security Network. Encompassing institutional, individual and systemic considerations, Canada defines human security in broad terms as

> in essence, an effort to construct a global society where the safety of the individual is at the centre of international priorities and a motivating force for international action; where international humanitarian standards and the rule of law are advanced and woven into a coherent web protecting the individual; where those who violate these standards are held fully accountable; and where our global, regional and bilateral institutions—present and future—are built and equipped to enhance and enforce these standards.[24]

SYSTEM-LEVEL GOVERNANCE

In shifting the locus of security away from states and the pursuit of military power to the security of people or individuals, the human security debate opens opportunities for a more comprehensive and flexible definition of security in which local and global levels of analysis are distinguished. Even if, as globalization theory maintains, place is diminishing in its significance as global economic relations transcend "time and space," attachments to place, identity and nation remain salient and potent realities. In 1945 five states—Britain, the United States, China, the USSR and France—set the agenda for the United Nations organization. As of 2008 there were 192 UN member states out of a total of 202 nation-states worldwide. The five permanent members still wield enormous influence, but they must do so in a more complex environment in which attachments to national political space, real or imagined, have not subsided.

According to Jim Whitman, "The weight of evidence is that our capacity to produce unwanted and sometimes dangerous conditions on a global scale is running greatly in excess of our deliberative and control mechanisms."[25] Human societies are manufacturing new global security risks at a faster rate than existing institutions can cope. Adopting the language of neoliberal management, Annan argued the new millennium thus needed a new method of global problem solving, one that placed emphasis upon "integration," "coherence," "flexibility" and "informational capacity" across governmental, nongovernmental and intergovernmental sectors.[26] Institutional reform and reforms to international rules were essential to the pursuit of human security.

The UN's Millennium Development Goals established policy priorities for the international community, but their realization depends upon the

GLOBAL NETWORK GOVERNANCE

Formal institutional arrangements may often lack the scope, speed and informational capacity to keep up with the rapidly changing global agenda. Mobilizing the skills and other resources of diverse global actors, therefore, may increasingly involve forming loose and temporary policy networks that cut across national, institutional and disciplinary lines. The United Nations is well positioned to nurture such "coalitions for change" across our various areas of responsibility.

The more integrated global context also demands a new degree of policy coherence, while important gaps must be filled. The international financial architecture needs strengthening, as does the multinational trade regime. Greater consistency must be achieved among macroeconomic, trade, aid, financial and environmental policies, so that all support our common aim of expanding the benefits of globalization. Conflict prevention, post-conflict peace-building, humanitarian assistance and development policies need to become more effectively integrated.

Source: Kofi Annan, "*We the Peoples*," 2000.

mobilization of a "plurality" of institutions and people. Human security cannot be achieved without firm economic and political foundations that secure basic needs and offer more than just the promise that aspirations for a better life lie within reach of "ordinary" people. Between the individual and the international community stand states that may or may not hold the well-being of their citizens as a paramount national interest and either persecute or make war against them. In the absence of a global sovereign, the advancement of a human security agenda requires international interventions ranging from development assistance to the deployment of peacekeepers. Governance thus becomes the challenge of brokering solutions to a dazzling array of security challenges.

In the absence of a genuinely participatory system of global government, states alone offer the tangible prospect for the kind of liberal democracy lauded by those who decry the state for meddling in economic affairs. Effective national-level governance is an essential complement to the advancement of human security, but as the Commission for Africa recognized, African underdevelopment is a direct consequence of governmental failures spanning forty years. The "weakness of government and the absence of an effective state," it concluded, was manifest in the "inability of government and the public services to create the right economic, social and legal framework which will encourage economic growth and allow poor people to participate in it."[27]

Similarly, the cosmopolitan ideal of a world without political boundaries can be realized only with some other political machinery by which decisions can be made and differences resolved at the local and global levels. States remain the essential building blocks of global order, and there are serious questions as to whether the dynamics of interstate relations have evolved to the extent that military forces can be decommissioned. While power is becoming more diffuse in the international system and governance networks more sophisticated and extensive, people and states continue to pursue or wield power for the most self-interested and nefarious of purposes. The explosion of nonstate actors in the late twentieth century broadened the scope of normative action on a global scale from environmental activism to human rights advocacy, but at the same time, and by the same means, the same transnational processes broadened the scope for anticosmopolitan and criminal activity.

THE EMERGENCE OF CIVIL SOCIETY ORGANIZATIONS

Nongovernmental organizations (NGOs) and international nongovernmental organizations (INGOs) have a significant role in filling service gaps in the provision of education, health and welfare, disaster relief and small-scale infrastructure development left by governments with insufficient resources or insufficient political will. But the roles of these organizations are much more varied. Also referred to as "civil society organizations" (CSOs), they pursue humanitarian missions and are distinct, in theory, from purely political or economic associations or organizations. Differentiated from protest movements, social clubs, and criminal gangs by virtue of their noneconomic and humanitarian social objectives, these nonstate actors have attracted significant attention because of their capacity to influence and mobilize social networks.[28] Manuel Costoya's typology of CSOs distinguishes between highly structured actors that warrant the title *organization* and more amorphous *movements*. Organized CSOs have decision-making structures, delegated responsibilities, budgets and programs. By contrast, social movements, such as the World Social Forum, at which people gather for dialogue and exchange of ideas about matters of common concern, are fluid, inchoate, volatile in the sense that they ebb and flow in tandem with global issues and the shifting priorities of those who organize them.[29]

According to the UN Commission on Global Governance, a nongovernmental organization is classed as international when it operates in three or more countries. Based upon this definition, there were 28,900 identifiable international NGOs in 1993 compared with a mere 176 in 1909.[30] More recent analysis suggests a much smaller number of 6,000 INGOs circa 2001, although this reflects more exclusive criteria. There were an estimated 2,500 northern INGOs in 1990, suggesting that the majority of INGOs are located in the developing world, although this would include affiliates of the major northern organizations such as World Vision, Oxfam, CARE, Friends of the Earth and more.[31] Whatever the accurate number, these transnational actors have, in the areas of service delivery, won increased credence at the UN and the multilateral banks (the World Bank and regional development banks) that rely upon NGO/CSO assistance to implement development projects and gather "local" information.

Table 1.1. I/NGO Categories

	I/NGO	Social Movement
Service-oriented	Oxfam, PLAN, World Vision	HIV/AIDS awareness
Reform-oriented	Amnesty, IRC, TI, PRI	Anti-Corruption, Make Poverty History
Transformative	Global South	World Social Forum

Source: Based upon analytical categories by Costoya 2007.

The end to the Cold War generated humanitarian crises in parts of the world previously inaccessible to Western governments and multilateral institutions. I/NGOs could draw upon long-established social networks, were mobile, and with avowedly neutral agencies such as the International Red Cross and Médecins Sans Frontières, were able to operate in war zones. Added to this was an increase in development funds available to NGOs—from the World Bank especially—but also from public donations.[32] Simply, transnational service and advocacy organizations complemented international development objectives at a time when the development agenda was lengthening.

TRANSNATIONAL CORPORATIONS

Transnational corporations and corporations in general are viewed with suspicion in development circles. Transnational corporations (TNCs) are companies engaged in production across two or more international boundaries. Benefiting from the relatively open and stable international business environment in the West and industrializing Asia after 1945, TNCs grew rapidly in number and scale. By 2006 there were an estimated 78,000 such corporations headquartered predominantly in Western Europe, North America and East Asia. Transnational companies routinely transfer materials, components and finished products across national boundaries, and these "internal" transfers account for a substantial proportion of world trade. Larger entities operate on an intercontinental scale, like the Shell Corporation, which manages its upstream and downstream energy operations across more than 130 countries. Motor vehicle manufacturers such as Honda, Toyota, Ford and General Motors manufacture and assemble motor vehicles in close proximity to major regional markets in Europe and Asia.[33] Comparisons between national productivity and corporate sales revenues reveal that many of the world's major TNCs are as significant economic actors as many medium-sized countries. Their investments are eagerly sought after by national governments for whom foreign direct investment equates to new employment and increased tax revenues. Corporations can thus extract "regulatory arbitrage" and exploit the weakened bargaining position of individual states competing with each other to attract lucrative investment dollars.

Foreign direct investment, from the West and from Japan and Korea, was a major factor in Asia's rapid late-twentieth-century economic growth. However, corporations stand accused by development, environmental and human rights groups of engaging in practices detrimental to the well-being of people and communities across the developing world. To a limited extent, the *OECD Convention on the Bribery of Foreign Officials* drew attention within the global private sector to the damaging effects of corruption and the potential costs of bribery by companies headquartered in countries that are signatories to the convention. International efforts to bring to account companies that perpetrate or are complicit in environmental destruction, child labor exploitation and political violence meet with stiff opposition from within the business community. Yet without cooperation from the transnational private sector, it is difficult to see how the UN Millennium Development Goals can be achieved.

During Annan's tenure as secretary-general, the UN embarked upon a program of business consultations under the umbrella of the "Global Compact." The considerable human and financial resources of transnational corporate actors and their undoubted influence could, it was thought, be harnessed toward the achievement of humanitarian objectives. Yet the degree to which corporations or private enterprise of any kind can subscribe to such efforts is paradoxically limited by the nature of business competition. Free-market advocates such as economist Milton Friedman argue that the social responsibility of business is to be profitable, because from profits come employment, government revenues, and rising consumption. Yet when the corrupt activities of corporations undermine United Nations programs, such as the UN's celebrated Iraq Oil-for-Food Programme, or subscribe to brutal regimes in return for access to natural resources, not only do they contravene international law, they undermine long-term human and global security.

REGIONAL ORGANIZATIONS

When the UN was founded there were no significant regional institutions that could serve as a bridge between the global and the local. In terms of mediating global programs for regional security, regional institutions are beginning to play a pivotal role in global governance. The region in which supranational institutional development is most advanced is Europe. Beginning with the European Coal and Steel Community, mutual gain through economic cooperation was the central dynamic in the formation first of the European Economic Community, then European Community and now the European Union (EU). Since the European Union's formation in 1993, membership has expanded from twelve to twenty-five, with more countries applying to join. Enlargement, once laughed at by detractors, demonstrated the attraction of economic security in numbers—especially for the smaller European states.

The European Council of Ministers, European Commission and Parliament have acquired some of the sovereign functions of member states. The EU can enact binding laws with regard to welfare provision, human rights, minimum wages, environmental standards, food safety standards and more. After failing at its formation in 1993 to deal effectively with the breakup of the former Yugoslavia, the EU has matured as a regional security actor. The EU is moving toward a "security community" in Europe in which the Union rather than member states acting as sovereign entities pursues a European foreign policy and, increasingly, a security role. Marking this new "self-awareness," an EU peacekeeping force was stationed in the Former Yugoslav Republic of Macedonia in 2003 to stabilize the country after a brief civil war in 2001. A measure of the resolve to assert "European" security interests, the EU now maintains two 1,500-strong multinational "rapid response" battlegroups to deal with strategic and humanitarian crises—in Europe but also in northern and sub-Saharan Africa.

Regional organizations are becoming increasingly active, perhaps in recognition that an underresourced UN system needs assistance to implement its security mandate at the regional and national levels. The lesser-known but influential Organization for Security and Co-operation in Europe (OSCE) is, write Nina Graeger and Alexandra Novosseloff, the most extensive European security organization because it brings together Russia as the successor to the Soviet Union with the North Atlantic Treaty Organization (NATO) incorporating the United States and most EU members. International institutions exist to foster shared norms or rules upon which confidence and cooperation can be built. As the EU's evolution demonstrates, regional organizations can help to generalize norms across state boundaries and bridge regional divisions. The OSCE's mission is similarly evolving from that of a facilitator of security dialogue and democratization to active participant in the business of peacekeeping. According to Graeger and Novosseloff, the organization "is the most important norm-building organization in Europe," but this effectiveness is limited by renewed geostrategic rivalry between the United States and Russia.[34]

THE DETERRITORIALIZATION OF SECURITY

Globalization increases the potency of transnational linkages and exposes national societies to a greater array of international shocks and security risks. Internally, many new states face the twin challenges of developing viable political institutions while competing for survival in a hyperglobalizing global economy. This is a challenge not just for the Global South but for the developed world—in short, it is a global human security challenge. This globalization of security demands a new framework of analysis and a new approach to governing these challenges, but there are questions as to the serviceability of human security as constructed by the UN. This chapter has argued that the security challenges confronting human societies are of such a scale that no one state, however large, can address them in isolation. Yet the scope for debate about appropriate governance responses seems unlimited.

Analysis of the idea of human security and of UN and regional human security agendas would be incomplete without first canvassing crucial theoretical starting points and perspectives with which to frame international and global social relations. The next chapter therefore explores the possible meanings of human security in theory and practice. Pursuing an eclectic approach, this chapter proposes that human security can best be conceived as a creative synthesis reflecting a diversity of ideas organized around common questions and shared concerns.

Chapter 2

THE ALCHEMY OF PEACE:
ELEMENTARY STUDIES ON
HUMANS AND SECURITY

Wars and different kinds of fighting have always occurred in the world since God created it. . . . It is something natural among human beings. No nation and no race (generation) is free from it.

—Ibn Khaldun

We seek peace—enduring peace. More than an end to war, we want an end to the beginning of all wars—yes, an end to this brutal, inhuman and thoroughly impractical method of settling differences. The once powerful, malignant Nazi state is crumbling, the Japanese warlords are receiving, in their own homeland, the retribution for which they asked when they attacked Pearl Harbor. But the mere conquest of our enemies in not enough. We must go on to do all in our power to conquer the

doubts and the fears, the ignorance and the greed, which made
this horror possible.

—Franklin D. Roosevelt

Without lasting peace, the basic infrastructure of human well-being cannot be put in place and secured. Despite reasoned argument against conflict, however, the idea that war is endemic to human society is deeply
embedded in the intellectual history of humankind. So too is the notion
that humans are instinctively aggressive and that human aggression can be
restrained or defeated only by overwhelming power. From a normative
view, political violence is caused by the absence of economic justice and
human rights, while from a materialist view, the nature of the real world
works against the realization of ideals. The essential building blocks of political stability are widely known, but geography, historical experience and
historical accident conspire against the dream of lasting peace. And while
there are increasing constraints upon the threat and use of force, there is
no single or simple prescription for lasting peace both within and between
states.

There is wide disagreement between different schools of thought as to
how durable peace can be achieved and preserved at the local and international level. Distinctions between realism and idealism place idealists at a
disadvantage because the default assumption in international affairs is that
realists are in tune with the world as it is while idealists naively pursue an
unattainable utopian future.[1] The dichotomy is misleading because realists
are not devoid of ideals and many idealists believe their ideals to be very
practical. The search for a theoretical basis for human security is thus not
a matter of negating realism or idealism but of seeking agreement between
scholars and practitioners as to how the goal of enduring peace can be
achieved in practice.

BETWEEN REALISM AND IDEALISM

In the stark logic of traditional or realist security studies, peace is interpreted as the absence of armed conflict or war and can only be sustained if
states maintain sufficient armed force to deter or repulse an attack by one
or more hostile powers. This realist view of the nature of international relations spans both international relations theory and foreign policy practice.
As Henry Kissinger, former U.S. secretary of state and national security

adviser in the Nixon and Ford administrations, writes in his landmark study of twentieth-century history, *Diplomacy* (1995),

> Nations have pursued self-interest more frequently than high-minded principle, and have competed more than they have cooperated. There is little evidence to suggest that this age-old mode of behavior has changed, or that it is likely to change in the decades ahead.[2]

Wilson and Kissinger were not, however, so far apart in their reading of international affairs. Wilson's Fourteen Points emphasize the role of morality, fair dealing and justice in relations between states. Though referring to events and issues long forgotten, his prescriptions can be distilled for contemporary relevance. Point one argues for transparency in diplomatic dealings; points two and three call for freedom of movement and for trade between nations to be free. Point four, recognizing the role of arms races in fostering suspicion and mistrust, calls for arms limitation. Points five through thirteen specify self-determination as the basis of political legitimacy within states and that state boundaries should be so arranged as to reflect the popular will. The fourteenth point sets out a case of the League of Nations, which, as discussed in chapter 1, proved largely ineffectual.

Kissinger argues that the United States was a moral force for good in the world, and responsibility fell to it for establishing and maintaining international order after 1945. The old European imperial order, he argues, was built upon the amoral principles of realpolitik, which defines security as a simple compound: power plus interest. The consequence of cumulative calculations of interest was a breakdown in the European balance of power that propelled Europe's descent into war. Wilson thought his prescription would modify an international system that was all but destroyed by the crude exercise of power. Against this backdrop of European failings, Kissinger portrays U.S. foreign policy during the Cold War as an attempt to balance moral considerations with the dictates of strategic and political reality—an uneasy but necessary compromise. Though ambivalent about Wilsonian idealism, which, he alleges, created a tension between the application of principle and the exercise of power that constrained U.S. foreign policy and that favored the *status quo*, Kissinger remains convinced that a moral foreign policy is both possible and necessary.

Kissinger is condemned by his critics as an arch-realist and for being as amoral as the diplomats of the "Old Europe" he condemns. Among those who brook no compromise between legal and moral considerations and the politics of self-interest, Kissinger is a war criminal who will never be brought to trial for the death and suffering allegedly caused by the exercise of American power across the developing world. International human rights lawyer and advocate Geoffrey Robertson in his book, *Crimes against Humanity* (2002), declares diplomacy, the craft at which Kissinger excelled, "the antithesis of justice."[3] Looking into the dawn of a new era of liberal internationalism, Fukuyama paints Kissinger as yesterday's statesman whose ideas had conditioned a generation of State Department and Defense Department officials to the detriment of U.S. interests in a world of rising economic interdependence. Yet economics has not displaced politics in the way that liberal internationalists had hoped. As discussed in chapter 1, the conditions for lasting peace are absent in many parts of the globe. "Great power rivalry" also did not dissipate with the collapse of the Soviet Union but has re-emerged in a new multipolar world.

Realism and neorealism flourished in the United States during the Cold War, but the realist worldview was stated definitively before the end of the Second World War by Hans Morgenthau in his classic *Politics among Nations: The Struggle for Power and Peace*, first published in 1945. Addressing both liberal and Marxist interpretations of international affairs, Morgenthau asserts that politics must be treated as an "autonomous" area of study, separate from economics or law, because politics operates according to the objective law of political self-interest to which economic and legal concerns are peripheral. Distinguishing the academic study of realism from the realities of international diplomacy, Morgenthau stresses that international order is not served by one nation asserting the universality of its national values as the United States was then doing. His first principle of political realism, however, that interest equals power, by reducing politics to a simple power/interest calculation, leaves much scope for interpretation and abuse.

In the logic of post-1945 U.S. foreign policy, if U.S. power could be used to make the world more secure, then this world should reflect American values. International security was thus linked directly to proselytizing liberal ideology, and, as discussed, a set of institutions was created that embodied American ideals cast as universal values. Realists, however, and historical realists in particular, are instinctively skeptical about the prospects for achieving durable peace through international cooperation of any kind beyond temporary alliances of convenience. "International politics," Morgenthau believes, "cannot be reduced to legal rules and institutions." According to this logic of international relations, rules and institutions, when needs dictate, should be set aside in the interests of national secur-

REALISMS OLD AND NEW

Realism and National Security

- Humans are naturally predisposed to use violence to achieve political ends.
- All politics is fundamentally about the pursuit of power.
- In international relations the national interest equals power.
- The state is the fundamental unit of international relations.
- States are rational actors and can be expected to act rationally when statesmen pursue their national interests.
- War is a rational instrument of state policy.
- States maximize their chances of survival through military alliances and the accumulation of military power.

Neorealism and World Order

- The international system comprises self-interested states.
- Anarchy is the defining feature of this system.
- States seek to maximize their security through the accumulation of power.
- Power derives from the possession of superior material capabilities.
- The balance of power constrains state behavior and sustains a measure of structure and stability in the interstate system.
- War is a corrective mechanism by which power imbalances are rectified.
- A general war is least likely when one state, a hegemon, achieves a preponderance of power but does not seek world dominion.

ity—which is what the United States has chosen to do throughout the era of American hegemony to the present day.

Realism's moral force depends upon an image of international environment cast negatively as a source of potential harm against which states must frame their security policies and act individually or through strategic alliances to reduce the risk of attack. Peace through strength is the realist dictum that dominated the study of international relations after World War Two. In this Darwinian struggle for survival, security is gained through the accumulation of strength measured as tangible military assets, with varying degrees of importance attached to a nation's economic base. In *Theories of International Relations* (1979), Kenneth Waltz argues that the nuclear balance between the USSR and the United States, rather than being a source of global insecurity, was responsible for the avoidance of superpower military confrontation. Accepting the liberal premise that human society had evolved to a point where war was counterproductive, Waltz believes that the prospect of species extinction focused the minds of decision makers more so than concern for international laws or humanitarian principles. Peace ensues from an orderly system or society of sovereign states where stability is preserved by overlapping and often interlocking global and regional power balances of limited durability. The creation of a world state, he surmises, is unlikely, and any move to create such a state would be accompanied by a global civil war as interests compete to control the vast power resources concentrated at the center.[4]

Realism and structural realism, or neorealism, leave us with few pointers as to how human security objectives might be achieved without subordinating human security to national security and to global stability conceived as a rough equivalence of material power. The use of military force conceived by realists and neorealists alike as a rational instrument of policy is an essential corrective to aggression by states seeking to overturn the interstate system. Yet an interstate system populated with rational state actors behaving according to rational calculations of self-interest is no guarantee of human survival in an era of nuclear proliferation. Nineteenth-century German military strategist Karl von Clausewitz is famous for the dictum that war is "an act of policy" and "merely the continuation of policy by other means."[5]

Yet World War One demonstrated how states acting rationally according to the rules of the European balance of power system could launch themselves into a grinding war of attrition that proved a costly and, for the most part, futile exercise. The creative potential of an entire generation of Europeans was squandered. Military historian John Keegan writes in *A History of Warfare* (1991), "the First World War was . . . an extraordinary, a monstrous cultural aberration, an unwitting decision by Europeans . . . to turn Europe into a warrior society."[6] The origins of the Great War are thus to be found not merely in shifting power balances but in the cultures of European states that spent the preceding decade preparing for the inevitable.

SUBJECTIVE SECURITY

The realist notion that security is contingent on the favorable workings of power relations between states downplays the crucial role of ideas in shaping international policy. What we know as international or global affairs is constituted by states and institutions, but these structures are populated by human beings who make decisions based upon imperfect information and who are subject to an array of human and social pressures. Realist historians admit that psychological factors have an important part to play in shaping official actions. Wars, according to historian Geoffrey Blainey, occur simply because one state miscalculates its relative military power and presses an assumed strategic advantage over a perceived enemy. War determines the accuracy of power perceptions.[7]

Writing before postmodernism burst onto the intellectual scene, Robert Jervis examined the role of subjectivity in international affairs, focusing on the thinking processes of political decision makers in his landmark *Perception and Misperception in International Politics* (1976). Jervis argues that we are predisposed to view the world in terms of our own experiences and to assimilate new information into our existing views and beliefs. A pessimistic view of human nature and entrenched suspicions of peoples with differing value systems creates the danger that unnecessary force might be used to resolve a dispute or head off an anticipated challenge to a state's interests, whether or not such a challenge is likely. Decision makers in an anarchic system assume the worst, leading to misreading of others' intentions with regard to security and military affairs. An arms buildup by one state is automatically inferred by onlookers to have damaging implications and is read as an intention to wage war. This is the classic security dilemma in which the "imperatives" of military strategy create their own strategic momentum leading to war—as occurred in August 1914.[8] Subjective human conceptions of external reality thus, ironically, "construct" the threat against which national resources are mobilized and transform prediction into self-fulfilling prophecy.

U.S.-led interventions in Iraq and Afghanistan were predicated on one paradoxical element of realist logic—that in an imperfect world, force is necessary to restrain aggression. After 9/11, the Bush administration conceived a global terror threat constituted by a world of interlocking Islamist terror groups guided by Osama Bin Laden and sponsored by rogue states: Iran, Iraq and North Korea, dubbed the "Axis of Evil" in an allusion to the alliance of Nazi Germany, Italy and Japan in World War Two. The solution to the threat was to transform the Middle East by turning Iraq into a model Arab democracy and by working with friendly governments to defeat Islamist groups operating across the region and into North Africa. In casting this campaign as a struggle between good and evil, the U.S. government ignored the myriad local political circumstances that fueled sectarian and ethnic conflicts and that created a groundswell of popular support for Islamists. In casting the war on terror as a fundamental struggle between good and evil, the United States missed opportunities to minimize the influence of Islamists in an otherwise moderate Islamic world and ignored the underlying causes of political discontent and violence.[9]

Security is a battleground of ideas where the principles of human security set out by the United Nations Development Programme (UNDP) meet with hostile reception. The metaphor of the battleground is entirely appropriate as, in times of national crisis such as 9/11 and after in the United States, opponents of the ill-conceived use of force against Iraq were pilloried in the public domain. Barry Buzan argues that rival conceptions of security reflect tensions between idealist and realist worldviews.[10] But is there an unbridgeable gulf between idealist and realist conceptions of security? Realists (materialists) and idealists (constructivists) differ according to the priorities by which they order international politics. As Alexander Wendt argues, "Materialists and idealists tend to understand the impact of ideas differently. Materialists privilege causal relationships, effects, and questions; idealists privilege constitutive relationships, effects, and questions."[11] However, it is useful to consider a further distinction between philosophical idealists (constructivists) concerned with the construction of reality and moral idealists who assert objective rights and wrongs. To view realism and idealism as polar opposites denies the capacity of realists to express ideals and reinforces the orthodox view in international relations that idealists are unrealistic. Idealism with a capital I refers specifically to a movement in international relations that traces its policy origins to Wilson and its intellectual origins to the ideas of eighteenth-century Prussian philosopher Immanuel Kant. Kant's views on "perpetual peace," what we might understand today as durable security, were a pragmatic compromise between the harsh realities of relations between states and the constitutive elements of peace. Paradoxes abound when seeking to compare and contrast idealist and realist positions.

If life, as seventeenth-century English philosopher Thomas Hobbes wrote, "is nasty, brutish and short," we might surmise that war arises from

KANT'S PRINCIPLES OF PERPETUAL PEACE

1. No treaty of peace shall be held valid in which there is tacitly reserved matter for a future war.
2. No independent states, large or small, shall come under the dominion of another state by inheritance, exchange, purchase or donation.
3. Standing armies (*miles perpetuus*) shall in time be totally abolished.
4. National debts shall not be contracted with a view to the external friction of states.
5. No state shall by force interfere with the constitution or government of another state.
6. No state shall, during war, permit such acts of hostility which would make mutual confidence in the subsequent peace impossible: such are the employment of assassins (*percussores*), poisoners (*venefici*), breach of capitulation, and incitement to treason (*perduellio*) in the opposing state.

First Definitive Article for Perpetual Peace

The civil constitution of every state should be republican.

Second Definitive Article for a Perpetual Peace

The law of nations shall be founded on a federation of free states.

Third Definitive Article for a Perpetual Peace

The law of world citizenship shall be limited to conditions of universal hospitality.

---

the innate tendency of humans to fight each other rather than cooperate. According to Hobbes, war was the natural condition of human relations, altered only by the threat of greater force at the hands of the state.[12] Yet this is not so far removed from Immanuel Kant's argument that "the state of peace among men living side by side is not the natural state (*status naturalis*); the natural state is one of war." While conflict is interspersed with periods of peace, there is always, says Kant, the "unceasing threat of war." Consequently, without a political order of some form there can be no hope of peace between people or states. The point of difference, however, is in the basis of order. The Hobbesian materialist view is that peace can be achieved only by the restraining threat of countervailing force—the classic realist position. Kant the moral philosopher thought a world government impossible and instead favored a world federation of states in which governments agreed to set aside differences and to abide by a common set of moral principles.[13]

CONDITIONAL PEACE

Human security is a concept framed in opposition to traditional or realist notions of state-centric security but which, in its manifestations in official policy, is drawn inexorably toward neorealist prescriptions. Indeed, human security in practice tends, argues Mohammed Nuruzzaman, to follow a neorealist "problem-solving" and reform-oriented path.[14] Yet this is done in the interests of promoting justice and enhancing order rather than to maintain a barely tolerable *status quo*. Kant attempted to reconcile ideas and ideals with material realities to argue a pragmatic case for a gradual reshaping of international order. Pragmatism need not therefore be treated as a dirty word by idealists any more than idealism should be treated as nonsense by political realists. In a practical sense, human security can be said to derive from certain structural and normative conditions. For Kant, the nature of states, their system of government, and orientation toward the outside world were crucial factors affecting international peace. From a normative perspective, Kant argued that fair dealing, trust and respect for the dignity of humans were enabling values that increased the prospects for peaceful relations between states.

Getting the "right" form of government at the nation-state level remains a significant challenge in much of the contemporary world. There are myriad factors that shape the internal security environment—including transnational security linkages. States are not unitary in that they predominantly comprise ethnically and culturally diverse peoples, and, as Buzan argues, cultural communities can form identity groups that span state borders and that can be both a security challenge to the state and a focus for state oppression.[15] This is not to argue that ethnic diversity is a source of political weakness or to suggest therefore that states should abandon multiculturalism or feel emboldened in assimilating "troublesome" minorities. In developing countries where the "idea of that state" is challenged, large economic inequalities easily become a source of friction between the state and those on the margins. Where economic resources are poor or underexploited, and where political divisions are deepened by competition over land, the potential for rivalry to escalate into armed conflict is increased. An unraveling of the consensus that brought the state together in the first place leads, in the worst cases such as Sudan, Burma and Colombia, to endemic conflict.

There are empirical connections between the prevalence of poverty, disease, lawlessness, illiteracy and poor nutrition, environmental degradation and lack of access to modern communications technologies on the one hand, and authoritarian or brutal totalitarian regimes, war, political oppression and genocide on the other. The State Failure Task Force lists a series of conditions or factors that can lead, in combination, to state failure occasioned by political violence.[16] However useful such measurements in framing our understanding of complex causality and in providing early warnings of impending conflict, the construct "state failure" is open to

---

THE RISK OF ARMED CONFLICT

The risk of political violence is increased within states where there is:

- An authoritarian or repressive government in power.
- Sustained political and economic discrimination against distinct social groups.
- Regular and severe use of force by the state against its political opponents.
- A strong sense of group identity among the victims of discrimination and state-sanctioned violence.
- Cohesiveness within and even among groups suffering discrimination.

Source: Barbara Harff and Ted Gurr, *Ethnic Conflict in World Politics*, 2004.

Risk variables for political violence include:

- Low quality of life measured by child and maternal mortality rates.
- High population density leading to intense resource competition.
- Partial democratic or full democratic government.
- Limited engagement with the international economy.
- Proximity to violent conflicts.

Source: Ted Gurr et al., *State Failure Task Force: Phase III Findings*, 2000.

abuse—for example, when used to justify preemptive intervention either by the international community or by neighboring states when failure is far from imminent. Strategic necessity was used by the United States to justify military interventions in Central America to eliminate socialist regimes during the Cold War. Indonesia's invasion of East Timor in 1975 was similarly justified by claims that political trends indicated a high risk that the country was falling into Communist hands after Portugal's sudden withdrawal. State failure is not free from the risk of selective interpretation.

One difficulty with the *State Failure Task Force Report* (2000) is its measurement of "ethnic war." The category "ethnic war" implies that fault lines in ethnically diverse states affected by internal conflict reflect the boundaries of ethnic identity. Yet ethnic identity and ethnic solidarity are not necessarily one and the same. Some of the fiercest wars of the past two centuries were fought between peoples for whom similarities outweighed differences.[17] World War One might be interpreted as a European civil war fought between countries with a shared cultural, religious and political heritage and linked by royal marriage. The genocide of an estimated 800,000 Tutsi Rwandans was perpetrated by people of the same ethnicity but taught to identify themselves as Hutu under Belgian colonial rule. The long-running war of secession between the Karen National Union (KNU) and the Burmese state is complicated by the split between the separatist Christian KNU and the Democratic Buddhist Karen Army (DBKA) fighting for the government (see chapter 4).

In time of national crisis, appeals to particularistic ethnic identity cast as national identity can have mass appeal. Former Serbian president Slobodan Milošević exploited ethnic rivalries and historical memory to win and hold onto political power. During the 1990s, atrocities in the Balkans were commonly attributed to historic ethnic hatreds. But, as Valere Philip Gagnon found in his study of wars of secession from the former Yugoslavia, many Serbs refused to be conscripted to fight on behalf of Serb minorities in Croatia and Bosnia.[18] To argue that solidarity is a function of shared ethnicity is to glaze over the machinations of ambitious and unscrupulous politicians or the catalytic influence of racially motivated state-sanctioned violence. It is the absence or failure of mechanisms by which to resolve identity differences and ensure equity across ethnic boundaries that often propels competitors toward armed confrontation, or, as Gagnon puts it, the real struggle in so-called ethnic conflicts is the struggle for "homogenous political space" driven by the dominant model of political organization: the sovereign territorial nation-state.[19]

Thus the international community faces a dilemma: to intervene or not to intervene when a security crisis looms. Intrastate conflicts have the potential, like wildfires, to jump across borders into neighboring states. Buzan's analysis of "security complexes" explains how the movement of insurgent groups across state borders or the deliberate mobilization of transborder minorities to wage war by antagonistic governments or insurgent movements increases the likelihood of interstate conflict. Even the mere existence of armed conflicts among regional neighbors can heighten the level of conflict risk sensitivity. Thus geographically distant conflicts have the potential to spread and engulf entire regions unless corrective measures are taken either by states bordering on conflict zones or by the international community. The term *security community* connotes a group of neighboring states whose security interests are indistinguishable because the insecurity of one state affects all others. For such a community to function, there needs to be some agreed basis upon which neighbors are empowered to act to prevent the "contagion" of war from spreading.

Realists argue that stability at the national or regional level is no guarantee of peace. According to Waltz, "Saying that stable states make for a stable world amounts to no more than saying that order prevails if most states are orderly. But even if every state were stable, the world of states might not be."[20] The twentieth century offers cautionary notes for peace and development studies analysts assessing the complexities of conflict. While the risk factors detailed above do much to explain the persistence of conflict in the developing world, it should be remembered that World War One and World War Two were fought between economically advanced countries with relatively high standards of literacy and life expectancy. Germany was a major industrial power by 1914 but one that had been turned into a military camp by decades of militarization. It should also be remembered that Adolf Hitler and the German National Socialist Party were electorally popular and, though never winning a majority, secured the largest number of votes at elections in 1932 and 1933. Hitler and the Nazis then subverted parliamentary processes to seize absolute power in 1934. Even in countries that score highly on all or most development indicators, the possibility of a lapse into armed aggression cannot be eliminated entirely.

Globalization alters the landscape of conflict and amplifies internal struggles within states. Soviet disintegration flattened out temporarily a downward trend in the incidence of armed conflicts since the end of the Cold War. International interventions contained conflicts in the former Yu-

goslavia in the 1990s, and preemptive peaceful intervention saved the Former Yugoslav Republic of Macedonia from the fate of its neighbors,
Croatia, Bosnia and Serbia. This much gave cause for optimism in that,
because we live in a globalizing interconnected, even interdependent,
world, the desire for peace is stronger. Yet there are many seemingly intractable conflicts that predate the Cold War and are not new, despite sharing
many of the characteristics of Mary Kaldor's new wars. The origins of civil
wars, secessionist struggles, intracommunal wars and intercommunal wars
across Africa and Asia can be traced to the arbitrary formation of colonial
states and fundamental disagreement over the terms of decolonization.
Kaldor, looking back at the tragedies of Eastern Europe in the 1990s, concedes that war remains an ever-present risk. Qualifying the optimistic view
that war can be limited—even controlled—she warns that "war, like slav-
ery can always be reinvented."[21] Reviewing the history of war, Keegan concludes that "the effort at peacemaking is motivated not by calculation of
political interest but by repulsion from the spectacle of what war does."[22]
For historical realists such as Blainey, this psychological truism ensures
that peace remains a "wasting asset."

THE ECONOMICS OF PEACEFUL COEXISTENCE

The search for a workable formula for human security must, despite the
objections of realists, consider the real intersections of economics and politics. A major element of 1990s liberal triumphalism was the idea that economics had supplanted politics. Yet for liberals and Marxists, economics
and politics have always been two sides of the same coin. Norman Angell,
author of the controversial and frequently misconstrued book, *The Great
Illusion* (1912), argued that the use of military power in an economically
"interdependent" world was irrational. His conclusions have since been
frequently derided by realists who assert that World War One negated
Angell's thesis. Yet, as Angell himself makes clear, his book was "not a plea
for the impossibility of war . . . but for its futility."[23] Angell makes the reasonable evolutionary point that given the level of interdependence already
in evidence between Britain, France and Germany, war threatened to destroy rather than enhance the economic interests of each. Subsequent
events did not disprove this observation. Two world wars eroded the foundations of the European imperial order, weakened the British Empire, destroyed Germany's economy twice, and brought destruction and
humiliation upon Japan in 1945.

Advancing the nineteenth-century Cobdenite view that free trade would reduce the likelihood of war between nations, Angell was sanguine about the human capacity to learn from past mistakes and to evolve toward pacifism. For Marxist thinkers, however, free trade meant only the continuation of capitalism to some future point when the world's working classes would rise up against the owners of capital and bring about a revolutionary proletarian state. A global class war was inevitable, wrote Karl Marx and Friedrich Engels in *The Communist Manifesto* (1848). "Freedom of commerce" would create a world market in which national differences would dissolve, leaving only class as the line of division. Marx's materialist reading of history treated observable historical trends as predictive measures of the future. Hence the assumption of inevitable class war on a global scale that would conclude with the negation of war once and for all. Here was a teleological argument that human history was driven by a struggle between classes for supremacy. Proletarian revolution would result in the "dictatorship of the proletariat," at which point class struggle would cease.[24]

For Marx and the Marxists, war is a necessary feature of capitalist interstate relations. States are the "agents of capital" and wage war to secure economic advantage for their capitalist sponsors. Wars and financial crises are symptomatic of contradictions within capitalism and a portent of capitalism's demise. But, wrote Vladimir Lenin, some forms of war were "progressive"—where they advanced the historical movement of class struggle. Wars of colonization and wars between the most powerful states for control of the world economy were wars of imperialism—nothing more.[25]

Marxism manifested in its most aggressive, some would say perverted, form in Soviet Russia and China, where Communist states waged wars against their own people to root out capitalism and implant socialism. Marxism also gained credence as a reform agenda rather than a revolutionary ideology in the late 1940s. Raúl Prebisch, an economist at the UN Economic and Social Commission for Latin America (ESCLA) and from 1948 its director, developed an explanation as to why Latin American countries, despite over a century of independence, had not modernized their economies but remained heavily dependent upon raw materials exports to and investment from their former colonial overlords: Portugal for Brazil and Spain for the remainder. While former colonial states enjoyed formal political independence, in economic terms they were still "dependent" upon their former colonial overlords for capital and markets. "Structural" economic inequalities in the international system were a consequence of neocolonialism, in which former colonies were trapped in a pattern of commodity-dependent development. *Dependencia*, dependency theory in the West, fit naturally into a Marxist worldview but became influential in economic policy formulation across the developing world through the UN Conference on Trade and Development (UNCTAD), of which Prebisch became secretary-general in 1964.

Ranged against neo-Marxist critiques of capitalism and Marxism-informed development theory, Walt Whitman Rostow's *The Stages of Economic Growth: A Non-Communist Manifesto* (1960) set out a case for liberal modernization. Rostow argues that subsistence agricultural societies can be transformed in market-oriented meritocracies though the abandonment of tradition and the promotion of individualist economic competition.[26]

Underdevelopment is a consequence of the failure to adopt the liberal capitalist model and not a consequence of capitalist exploitation. Paralleling Rostow's model of economic modernization, the American political scientist Samuel P. Huntington plots a path to political modernity. In *Political Order in Changing Societies* (1968) he maps out the stages of political growth or modernization. Theocracies occupy the lowest stage from which societies escape by virtue of rising political participation, the development of parliaments and the emergence of civil society. Importantly, however, Huntington argues that democracy is neither a precondition nor an inevitable consequence of economic development.[27] Despite this fine distinction between Huntington and Rostow, the discourse of liberalism has synthesized both positions into a template of desirable economic and political transformation as manifest in the work of Fukuyama.

Claiming the authority of history, both Rostow and Huntington draw lessons from nineteenth-century industrial Britain and the emergence of parliamentary systems in Europe—but then again, so too did Marx. And like Marxism, liberalism could not easily be transposed onto non-European societies in practice. Marxism and liberal capitalism appeared in many guises in the twentieth century. Mao became the Asian Marx after adopting Marxist ideology to a social context with no urban proletariat. In post-1945 Japan and the industrializing states of East and Southeast Asia, capitalism was managed through alliances between government and big business. Politics tended to be monopolized by one or two large political parties, which used the resources of state to entrench their domestic power. Dubbed "the Asian Way," this model of economic development fed off highly personalized power networks, industrial policies that favored bigger players and compliant labor movements. State-led industrialization became the target of scathing Western critiques following the Asian crisis of 1997, seen largely to be the result of corrupt government–business relationships, and yet the Asian model, with its emphasis upon social order and hierarchy, had proven enormously successful until that time.

Former World Bank adviser Joseph Stiglitz is scathing in his assessment of the fiscal remedies meted out by the International Monetary Fund to countries in economic difficulty. Stiglitz blames the IMF for the severity of the Asian crisis and for the virtual collapse of the Russian economy in 1998. In *Globalization and Its Discontents* (2001), he lays out how the ideology of free markets fails in practice because executives in New York and Washington, London and Paris fail to take account of local circumstances and instead presume that the adoption of universally "correct" economic prescriptions will ensure economic stability leading to growth in the long run. Stiglitz, like all liberal economists, believes that imperfections in global economic governance can be ironed out by the correct application of liberal principles.

Capitalism could be made to work if capitalism—the pursuit of economic self-interest to be more specific—were both rule governed and governed by independent institutions. Yet, as Stiglitz acknowledges, the groundswell of antiglobal, anticapitalist protest manifest against the World Economic Forum from Seattle to Melbourne and Cancun demonstrates the depth of public suspicion toward the world's richest nations and the super-rich.

HEGEMONY AND COUNTER-HEGEMONY

Richard Falk rehabilitates the Marxist idea of dialectical materialism, placing it front and center of his analysis of global order in *Predatory Globalization* (1999). Falk observes the evolution of grassroots protest movements into a transnational groundswell of demands for global political change. Protest movements and localized resistance to transnational corporations across Asia, Africa and Latin America, despite variations of circumstance and motives, reflect common themes, namely, opposition to the operations of transnational capital and attendant abuses of human rights. "Global civil society" thus exists as a counter-hegemonic response to, in Falk's words, "predatory globalization from above": led by the Western governments, TNCs, the World Bank, and the IMF. In this "global dialectic" the agents of "globalization from below" make use of new communications technologies to build transnational alliances to challenge the power of governments, corporations and international institutions. The aim of global civil society actors, according to Falk and other radical thinkers, must be to force liberals and liberal institutions to "implement their rhetoric," that is, to be accountable for actions that run contrary to the principles of democracy, freedom, rights and justice.[28]

Yet system shifts and system transformations are historically accompanied by conflict. Political economist Robert Gilpin argues that extended periods of world peace have been accompanied by the predominance of one powerful state, a hegemon, committed to the preservation of international order. When the hegemon's power declines to a level where it cannot maintain the established order, wars ensue to determine which state will emerge to take its place.[29] Revolutionary transformations led by fanatical "fantasists," as Paul Berman points out in his extended essay *Power and the Idealists* (2005), can culminate in a cycle of violence and repression as radicals seize the power of the state to make inroads into all facets of public and private life.[30] Hegemonic and revolutionary changes are, as stressed in chapter 1, thus often violent and traumatic processes that overturn established value systems, causing massive societal dislocation.

Counter-hegemonists are prepared to tolerate necessary evils—political violence, revolutionary war, subversion of established values and enforcement of new, "alien" values—in pursuit of their utopian goals. The dissolution of an evil capitalist system, Marx believed, justified "despotic" actions such as the seizure of private property.[31] Ultraradical polemics such as Michael Hardt and Antonio Negri's book, *Empire* (2000), offer no alternative to the wholesale dismantling of capitalism—by violence if necessary. Sharing the same historic sense of moment and movement, the authors celebrate revolutionary militancy with almost messianic fervor. From this perspective the prescriptions for human security set down by the UN run counter to the true nature of human security, which can only be realized in a postcapitalist world. Development interventions, human rights regimes, indeed the entire edifice of global order, are merely imperialist measures designed to aid the survival of the "empire" and delay the historic movement toward world revolution.[32] Class war for the Marxists is both morally just and historically inevitable.

The language of counter-hegemony should not, however, be read simply as the language of liberation. We should be careful not to presume that realists are more prone to undermine the pursuit of global goods than those espousing universal ideals. The latter point is made by Berman, who draws explicit parallels between the revolutionary idealism of the European left in the 1970s, the zeal of Islamic idealists in Iran after the revolution of 1979 and the totalitarianism of Nazi Germany in the 1930s. When idealists become Berman's "fantasists" driven by visions of a perfectible future, political violence becomes justified to achieve utopian ends, and opponents can be hurt or killed.

Where ideological extremists achieve control over the state, warns Berman, people die in large numbers in the name of the revolution or justice or God.[33] Power can be a catalyst for an uncertain chain of political reactions, and peace might be the least likely outcome from the violent pursuit of ideological ends.

Many nonstate organizations mobilized around local and global agendas today do not advocate sentiments that accord with Falk's ideals. If Islamism is, as Tariq Ali argues in *Clash of Fundamentalisms* (2002), an understandable revolt against the evils of the American empire, then Islamist militants form a violent wing of the same global counter-hegemonic movement against capitalist imperialism. Harakat al-Muqawama al-Islami-yya (the Islamic Resistance Movement), or Hamas for short, engages in social, political, military and terrorist activities. It is estimated that between 90 and 95 percent of the organization's funding and activities are devoted to social programs in the Palestinian Territories—Gaza and West Bank—but the remainder is of greatest international concern.[34] Hamas is committed to the eradication of the state of Israel and prosecutes this mission through its Izz a-Din al-Qassam Brigades. Despite ambiguously stepping back from this position after winning power in the Palestinian elections in 2006, Hamas remains linked to Islamist militants and to suicide attacks against Israeli civilians.

REVOLUTIONARY MILITANCY

Militancy today is a positive, constructive, and innovative activity. . . . This is the form in which we and all those who revolt against the rule of capital recognize ourselves as militants today. Here is the strong novelty of militancy today: it repeats the virtues of insurrectional action of two hundred years of subversive experience. . . . This militancy makes resistance into counterpower and makes rebellion into a project of love.

Source: Michael Hardt and Antonio Negri, *Empire*, 2000.

Hate and terror networks and transnational criminal organizations weave the world together in uncivil ways that make us uncomfortable and that do not presage the birth of global civil society. Laskar e-toiba, Laskar Jihad, Harkat-ul-Mujahideen, Aussie Freedom Scouts, the Ku Klux Klan, to name but a few, are antiliberal and paradoxically anticosmopolitan transnational social and political movements. Preaching doctrines of religious and racial intolerance, they exploit international networks, use the Internet to mobilize funding and support and could conceivably be thought of as the dark side of global civil society.

As Moises Naim explains in *Illicit* (2005), many transnational nonstate actors are exceedingly "uncivil." The explosion in global crime exposes many contradictions thrown up by the double-edged nature of globalization. Though accounting for only a fraction of legal cross-border mobility, these illegal or "illicit" movements are a direct corollary of the very technological advances lauded by globalists and need to be recognized as market-oriented activities. For those engaged in the illicit movement of people, involvement is not a matter of criminality, but rather, as Mark Findlay argues, of market choice. In the same way that we might look at membership of Islamist militant organizations as a decision made in a context where there are few other options for social progression or few alternative views to counter the appeal of extremism, criminal activities are often a rational response to desperate financial circumstances.

"Uncivil society" poses a challenge not only to the theories and aspirations of radical idealists, but to the functioning of the global liberal economy. Crime syndicates and gangs undermine political and public institutions in countries where the roots of democratic governance are still shallow or where deep-seated political divisions create opportunities for criminals to buy influence and prosper from intrasocietal conflict. Colombia in Latin America is a case in point, where coca production flourishes in a country embroiled in a revolutionary war.[35] Where people are denied basic economic and social rights by virtue of government policy or as a consequence of official corruption, the likelihood increases that some will opt for a life of crime as a trafficker or money launderer, for example.[36]

Prescriptions for the threat of transnational or simply local crime bear strong similarities to the structuralism of peace studies. Mark Findlay's *The Globalization of Crime* (1999) specified causal connections between poverty, extreme inequality, lack of legitimate economic opportunity, frustration and seismic regime shifts as *criminogenic* factors. Where there is a sufficient gap between rich and poor to make the rewards of illicit activity attractive to those on or near the bottom of the social scale or indeed where "revolutionary cause" justifies the trafficking of narcotics or people to fund "the struggle," then people will make the "rational choice" to engage in illicit activities. When regimes change sharply, such as the former Soviet Union is changing, the trauma of the transition to a new set of values undermines learned values of right and wrong behavior, leaving people at risk of being drawn into criminal networks.[37] Conflict zones are extreme cases of social distress and unsurprisingly are breeding grounds for illicit business, from looting to the trafficking of persons. Conflict avoidance and crime prevention thus share a common "solution" in the form of sustainable economic development. But what level of equity and what measure of justice makes development sustainable?

THE LANGUAGE OF SECURITY

Taking an ontological leap beyond Buzan's efforts to broaden the definition of security, the work of Michael Shapiro and Hayward Alker explores the subjectivity of our interpretations of the world around us and the hegemonic possibilities present in all-consuming "grand narratives" of security.[38] This constructivist/philosophical idealist critique of security studies makes plain the role of culture and theory in constructing our social and political reality. While expanding the definitions of security to encompass humanitarian issues is a step in the right direction, conceptual gaps remain, especially in relation to gender.[39] The index to the UN commission's report reads like an item list for a standard development project: conflict resolution, education, poverty alleviation, refugee movements, health and governance are long-standing UN concerns, but ironically, in addition to the glaring omission of environmental issues, there is a lack of emphasis upon the gender dimension of security.

If reality is what we choose to see, feminist writers are aware that gender issues receive little attention in both liberal and unreconstructed Marxist worldviews. Within feminism, by no means a homogenous field of scholarly inquiry, there is utter frustration with the construction and discussion of an international agenda defined almost entirely by male politicians, policy professionals and academics. Feminist writers on human security foreground this gender dimension and draw attention to the greater exposure of women to security risks ranging from systematic political violence, systemic oppression and sexual exploitation.[40]

For the purpose of discussion, feminists are referred to collectively and feminism used to denote a view of international relations in which women as opposed to humans are the referent of security. The feminist view is concerned with development, justice, democracy and freedom, and feminists are at pains to argue how the realist worldview ignores much of what constitutes international relations. Morgenthau's definition of power as "man's control over the minds and actions of other men," for example, encapsulates the chauvinism of political realism. Power in Morgenthau's eyes means political power embodied in the control of the state and the capacity to apply overwhelming military force. Yet there are many forms of power. Affiliative power is the power to organize and to build relationships, to mobilize social movements, and to organize protest or resistance. "Empowerment" means the development of human capacities through education, through the opportunity of employment, by lifting self-esteem, through political awareness raising and by possession of the means to communicate across distances.[41] Counterpower in a feminist sense incorporates nonviolent protest and information sharing across borders, by which power as control can be circumvented and undermined.

Feminists highlight the limitations of security analysis drawn from a narrow frame of reference and bring attention to the connections between different and additional levels of security encompassing gender, family and community. The language of power and security excludes questions of gender because, argues Cynthia Enloe, traditionally the field of international relations was exclusively a male domain, hence the priorities of the discipline are shaped by male priorities. In *Bananas, Beaches and Bases: Making Feminist Sense of International Politics* (1990), Enloe asserts, "International politics has been impervious to feminist ideas precisely because for so many centuries in so many cultures, it has been thought of as a typically 'masculine' sphere of life." This is not a matter of a woman's "chromosomes and menstrual cycle" but rather a consequence of "social processes and structures" of subordination and exclusion. Dominance of masculine views and values thus, she argues, leads to an acceptance of the inevitability of war justified by a masculine assumption that the world is a violent and volatile place against which people and states must be protected by whatever means. On the centrality of violence in the construction of gender roles and the gendered subjectivity of security risk, she argues,

> When it's a patriarchal world that is "dangerous", masculine men and feminine women are expected to react in opposite but complementary ways. A "real man" will become the protector of such a world. He will suppress his

own fears, brace himself and step forward to defend the weak, women and children. In the same "dangerous world" women will turn gratefully and expectantly to their fathers and husbands, real or surrogate. . . . Ideas of masculinity have to be perpetuated to justify foreign-policy risk-taking.[42]

Taking the idea of human security into the local community and home, Enloe points out how social constructions of gender roles ensure that women are typecast as "carers" and "nurturers" without any attendant recognition of the significant economic value of their unpaid work. The "international" is composed of many dimensions of human action, but the overpowering emphasis upon military security, economics and liberal institution building leaves most of the canvas of international affairs unexplored.[43] Feminist author Jan Pettman expresses the same concern about the impoverished language and hence logic of political realism and economic liberalism. Highlighting the gender dimension to international politics of cross-border movements, Pettman writes,

> Mainstream international relations usually fails to pursue migration including labor migration. . . . International relations and its international political economy brothers are even less likely to analyze other kinds of female work whose forms are increasingly internationalized. Women work on the streets or in bars in a sex industry that is international both in military and tourist prostitution and in the importation of "exotic" foreign women to work in the local scene.[44]

The edifice of international relations is deconstructed by L. H. M. Ling to reveal the persistence of masculinist worldviews in different and seemingly contradictory models of views of world order.[45] This is feminism cast in its most radical anticapitalist and antiliberal light. Fundamental to this radical view is the argument that liberal capitalism is inscribed with masculine individualism, ensuring that women's contributions, paid and unpaid, as workers and as nurturers in the home, remain grossly undervalued. The economic security of women thus depends upon a system-level transformation, but one that begins with a reconstitution of gendered power relations.

The neo-Marxist idea of a geographical division of labor retains explanatory force in a postcommunist, globalizing world. Irrespective of ideological position, women are doubly disadvantaged by geography, socioeconomic status and gendered social values. The exploitation of women as low-wage workers in modern electronics factories in Malaysia is encouraged by the Malaysian government's belief that women are much

---

FEMINISM AND IR THEORY

Realism removes ideology from its concept of power. States strive for hegemony for power's sake, realists argue, and that's why power reigns across time and space; it has nothing to do with ideas, beliefs, norms or identities. Liberalism makes an opposite move by deleting power from ideology. Liberal norms and institutions prevail, liberals tell us, because they merit such prominence and not because they happen to serve power interests. . . . Constructivism and IPE blinker us further by smuggling in Western hegemony while ostentatiously searching for "universal concepts" and processes.

Source: L. H. M. Ling, "Global Presumptions," 2006.

---

more dexterous than men, thus gendering assembly work as feminine.[46] In the Philippines, where guest worker remittances from Filipino workers overseas constitutes a significant foreign exchange inflow, the government consciously promotes an image of Filipina workers as malleable and obedient domestic and factory workers. Price "incentives" perpetuate the exploitation of women as cheap labor and commercial sex workers. According to the Coalition Against the Trafficking of Women (CATW), young village girls kidnapped or recruited from Burma or Thailand attract prices ranging between US$18,000 and US$40,000 per head in Japan. Women exploit women in many cases, but feminists argue the "benefits" of this exploitation flow substantially to men as customers or shareholders.

But if radical feminists are suspicious of the entire liberal project, what value should we attach to efforts to promote women's rights through international law? The UN is agent and instrument of the liberal international order, but without UN-sponsored research, awareness-raising campaigns and funded gender empowerment programs, the cause of women's rights would be much retarded. Feminist critiques of the "framing" of world order in the academy and beyond are directed in the main toward the West, transnational capital and the state as an agent of transnational capital. As with Falk, international institutions are seen as extensions of the state system and likewise committed to the promotion of liberal capitalism and masculine individualism. Feminism is thus a form of constructivism in which feminists call for a shift away from masculine framing of international issues that they claim will bring about a larger measure of justice for women. In this regard, global economic and social transformations benefit feminism by creating new spaces for argument and action. As Virginia Vargas argues, globalization offers the opportunity for women to negotiate new identities and to refashion social values in a world of flux.[47]

This, of course, assumes that women are empowered to negotiate. Radical feminism can be criticized for being as reductivist as political realism in, for example, reducing all forms of conflict to competitive male power relations. But war is gendered in that wars are perpetrated and fought largely by men. Rape is widely used as a weapon of war by armies substantially comprising men acting to exploit the vulnerability of women for strategic gain and sadistic enjoyment. The introduction of gender perspectives into readings of international relations or strategic studies thus draws attention to the nature of violence and of violence against women—which intuitively appears to be increasing. It also highlights how the dynamics of the international sphere impact differently according to gender and thus lends weight to demands that international law and governance be reformed to acknowledge the injustices suffered by women.

COSMOPOLITAN FUTURES

Feminism magnifies the discriminatory nature of national and international politics. With one notable exception, the corpus of traditional international relations is also silent on the issue of culture and cultural diversity in world affairs. Already socially and economically marginalized by their gender, women in oppressed cultural minorities endure a third degree of disadvantage. In the same vein that feminists challenge liberals and realists for assuming a gender-neutral universe, feminist writers but also progressive liberals such as David Held draw attention to issues of cultural identity, racism and discrimination.

Cosmopolitanism encapsulates ideas of a higher moral order prior to the state first expressed by ancient Greek philosophers. It encompasses not only teleological ideas of "cultural convergence" and the arrival of a "global village," but also the ideal of cultural diversity and the possibility of peaceful accommodation between people of different cultures. U.S. presidents since Wilson have voiced a cosmopolitan universalism founded upon universal values to which all societies irrespective of culture or religion are supposed to aspire. Assertions of the "indivisibility" of rights carry the implicit message that all societies irrespective of religion, language and tradition share certain basic human values and ideals.

Where cultural issues enter into the realm of political realism, as in Samuel Huntington's *The Clash of Civilizations* (1997), cultural differences are portrayed as impediments to regional and global cooperation. Indeed, Huntington offers an enlargement of the ethnic war thesis that ethnic identity cast as "civilizational" identity manifests primordial ties that cannot be diluted by rising economic interdependence. Defining the contours of a post–Cold War world order, Huntington proposes a "civilizational paradigm" to explain how states will in future coalesce not around political ideology but around "civilization." In this frame of thought, cultures are clearly bounded, permitting generalizations about "East" and "West" and distinctions between "Asian" and "Confucian." He argues that, "For the first time in history, global politics has become multipolar *and* multicivilizational."[48] Huntington advances the neorealist view that globalization impels global economic integration but also the assertion of difference:

> People define themselves in terms of ancestry, religion, language, history, values, customs, and institutions. They identify with cultural groups: tribes, ethnic groups, religious communities, nations, and at the broadest level, civilizations.[49]

Cultural traditions thus generate "natural" political dividing lines—or so Huntington would have us believe. Culture leads economics and politics, hence "multicivilizational" regional groupings are doomed to fail—which means that efforts by Australia to integrate with its Asian neighbors, for example, are futile simply because Australia's core Anglo-Irish cultural traditions are incompatible with those of the Asian region. "The roots of economic cooperation," Huntington argues, "are in cultural commonality."[50]

Huntington took aim at economic liberals who, for reasons already discussed, secured the moral high ground in the 1990s. However, the pessimistic message in his work was that rivalry and conflict, not international cooperation, would drive relations between states in the post–Cold War world. Neorealist cosmopolitans of a liberal persuasion are more optimistic. As the foremost authority on international cooperation, Robert Keohane writes in *After Hegemony* (2005), "Despite the persistence of discord, world politics is not a state of war. States do have complementary interests, which make certain forms of cooperation potentially beneficial."[51] He goes on,

> If international politics were a state of war, institutionalized patterns of international agreement that we observe on issues as diverse as trade, finan-

cial relations, health, telecommunications, and environmental protection would be absent.[52]

There were over 300 intergovernmental organizations at the start of the twenty-first century, indicating a high level of agreement between states about common interests with regard to trade, investment, the environment and the regulation of an increasingly complex global economy. The extent to which this means the eventual disappearance of borders or global economic integration is debatable. Marx argued that capitalism was dissolving national barriers between the working and middle classes. Paradoxically, the liberal business analyst Kenichi Ohmae argued the same in his controversial book *The End of the Nation State* (1996). Where Keohane interprets the increasingly complex web of global and regional institutions, rules and laws as evidence that cooperation is possible in the midst of an anarchic system, market cosmopolitans like Ohmae disdain the role of governments and institutions. A classic example of the liberal cultural convergence thesis is the claim by Ohmae that capitalism is diluting cultural taste to create a world of global consumers with homogeneous consumer preferences defined by Western cultural and material brand names.[53]

For those who believe in the transformative potential of international politics, from radicals like Falk to political liberals like David Held, cultural differences can be overcome, not by economic forces, but by seeking common ground—or pragmatic compromise. Stephanie Lawson argues for a dilution of false cultural dichotomies and an end to unhelpful distinctions between universalism and relativism. In refashioning the ways in which we think and speak about culture it is possible to "transcend" but not to "negate" difference.[54] Held argues that states and international organizations must and can be transformed to become truly representative of a global public, more democratic and thus better equipped to govern in the interests of humankind. Resolving "accountability deficits" at the UN, World Bank, World Trade Organization and IMF—Held's primary concern—would be a step in the right direction. But so too would be the bridging of cultural divides: between East and West, Christian and Muslim, indigenous and nonindigenous. Cosmopolitanism for Held is a pursuit of better understanding across cultures in support of global rules and a global moral order. It is

> the capacity to mediate between national cultures, communities of fate and alternative styles of life. It aims to disclose the basis for dialogue with the traditions and discourses of others with the aim of expanding the horizons of one's own framework of meaning and prejudice.[55]

Material forces are, from a political cosmopolitan view, impelling states toward greater cooperation. Ulrich Beck (1999) and Anthony Giddens (1999) stress the pervasiveness of individual insecurity in a world where the pillars of modernity are crumbling, creating a new dynamic of transnational cooperation mobilized around shared perceptions of "manufactured" risk. "World risk society," wrote Beck, is a global society that coheres around the myriad uncertainties affecting our everyday lives, be they economic uncertainties arising from the insecurity of employment in a volatile global economy, uncertainty as to the safety of the food we eat or fears of global warming.[56] In a world of multiplying risks, most of which are created—hence Giddens's term *manufactured*—by humans, Beck argues that self-interest is directly aligned with the global common interest and that this dynamic can transform global governance:

> At the start of the third millennium the maxim of realpolitik—that national interests must be pursued by national means—needs to be replaced by the maxim of cosmopolitan realpolitik, namely "the more cosmopolitan our political life, the more national and successful it will be." Only a politics that is multilateral is capable of opening up unilateral options for action. If global problems did not exist, *they would have to be invented* [emphasis added], as they create a common transnational context.[57]

Prescriptions for human security thus differ markedly according to ideology or values. In practical and immediate terms, if security for people is to be achieved, then compromises must be made. In the spirit of cultural cosmopolitanism, this involves reviving the Aristotelian "doctrine of the golden mean" or the Buddhist "middle path" to navigate between extreme positions about the nature of and remedies for human insecurity. No single position on the nature of order or security is beyond criticism. Liberal populists either ignore or downplay the persistence of inequality in the global system, while neo-Marxists and feminists hide the potential human costs of a sudden and radical transformation of international relations. International cooperation is a reality, but we should not invest too many hopes in international organizations because, as recent history reminds us, these organizations are often conduits for the pursuit of particular state interests. Liberal internationalists are concerned with the design and application of international laws to achieve realistic goals of universal human rights and equitable global economic growth. But the power politics continues on every continent, as do political struggles over ideology, religion and money.

As Keohane argues, political analysis should proceed with due recognition of the role of power in political affairs and the weaknesses of human nature which "serve as barriers against wishful thinking."[58] Cautioning against blind liberal optimism, critics of market liberalism and liberal institutionalism such as John Gray warn that the policy underpinnings of global capitalism, defined by the Washington Consensus, are struggling in the face of resurgent realpolitik. In this less-benign international context, free markets appear as naive, unattainable—perhaps utopian—ideals. While market liberals have from the time of Smith hungered for an economy with minimal government interference, the myriad challenges to the post–World War Two liberal international order demand political as much as economic solutions.

POWER AND GLOBALIZATION

In attacking the intellectual foundations of realism, constructivists tend to treat power as a universal and uniform concept. The nature of power is perceived differently in many parts of the world. Asian concepts of power, for instance, treat it as an amoral force existing in the natural environment—as tangible and as natural as the wind and the rain. Sun Tzu's *The Art of War* remains a key text for students of strategic studies and international business in North America, Europe and Asia, yet the idea of power upon which it is based is quite alien to Western societies. The goal of military strategy in ancient China was to harness natural forces and to turn these against one's enemies. In drawing a distinction between Chinese and Japanese concepts of power, Lucian Pye notes that the art of Sun Tzu was to skillfully manipulate natural forces to outwit potential opponents and, where necessary, avoid direct confrontation where victory was not assured. In Japanese tradition, however, Pye argues, the spirit or "way of the warrior," *Bushido*, could be a decisive factor when fighting against seemingly overwhelming odds. The notion that one should avoid confrontation was thus allegedly alien to Japanese martial culture (see chapter 5).[59]

Pye observes these traditions at play in contemporary Chinese and Japanese business practices. If the ending of capitalist exploitation means the end or modification of capitalism, we must be clear which form of capitalism we mean. American transnational corporations are held up as exemplars of the worst form of capitalism. Yet the United States must contend with a world in which both China and Russia exercise enormous influence, largely without domestic scrutiny and without recognizable moral constraint. North American, European and Asian corporations compete in a global economy that rewards only the narrowest calculation of profit and loss. A latecomer to global capitalism, China opportunistically takes advantage of a particular world economic system to advance Chinese economic interests. Rather than this being a capitulation to neoliberalism and a subordination to global markets, China's economic strategies might be better understood as autonomous strategic choices made in pursuit of interests defined by international circumstances and opportunities—the prevailing balance of possibilities—and designed to maximize China's positional advantage.

The applicability of other Western ideas—democracy, equality, justice, human rights—is open to question when the context of debate shifts outside the Western sphere, but as Lawson and others remind us, there is scope for cross-cultural agreement on the meanings of these words. Yet in status-oriented societies, language entrenches social hierarchy and distance where separate vocabularies are used to mark social rank. If it is accepted that democracy is the "least worst" form of government, then it should also be accepted that democratic politics must derive from a process of political evolution specific to each cultural sphere. External imposition of an entire system of government cannot work without prolonged military occupation, allowing for the transformation of the underpinning cultural system. The United States was able to transform the Japanese state during its postwar occupation (1945–1952), but only because indigenous ideas of democratic practice were already incorporated into Japanese statecraft after the Meiji Restoration of 1868 before succumbing to extreme nationalism and militarism in the 1930s.

Realist interpretations dominate the discipline of international relations with tangible consequences for the framing and implementation of foreign and global policies. If security ensues "from the barrel of a gun," then investment in security goods will be skewed toward military assets, as it is in most countries—at the expense of health, education, natural and built environments and more. Then again, idealists of the peace studies movement advocate the use of just force to prevent or end genocide, while many realists aver the idea of humanitarian intervention. If we acknowledge that the seeds of many conflicts can be found in the disregard for human welfare, then human well-being should be treated as a tangible security concern. If human security is advanced through peaceful accommodation between states and peoples, then attention must be paid to those conditions most conducive to peaceful cooperation. But what grounds are there for intervention, and when should intervention be considered by the international community in the interests of human security?

CHAPTER 3

"BLACK HAWK DOWN": THE LIMITS TO INTERVENTION

The American people would be wise to reject the embryonic doctrine of humanitarian intervention as the new U.S. mission in the post–Cold War era. Although such a mission undoubtedly appeals to those who have an insatiable desire to correct all the ills of the planet and the hubris to assume that American power can achieve that utopian objective, it would inevitably entangle the United States in an array of bloody conflicts that have no relevance whatsoever to America's security interests.

—Ted Galen Carpenter

States have traditionally developed their military capabilities to defend against possible attack and to advance national interests abroad. Where national interest is defined simply as power, the only logical reason for intervention in the affairs of another state is as retaliation for an attack or to extinguish an imminent threat of attack. This view is ingrained in national security establishments and reflects the dominance of realist thought among military decision makers. Yet the new security crises that emerged in Africa and Eastern Europe after the collapse of Communism demanded an effective international response, even though no immediate threat to U.S. security was apparent. For forty years the ideological clash between totalitarianism and the free world had provided Americans with a reason to respond—either directly or indirectly—whenever the Communists sought to extend their influence. With this rationale gone, a new security doctrine was necessary—one that would deflect pressure for cuts to military spending and to return a peace dividend to the American public. Boutros-Ghali's *Agenda for Peace* had the potential to legitimate a new U.S. post–Cold War role, but this entailed possible open-ended commitments to UN peacekeeping operations and a commitment to humanitarian ends that lay beyond Washington's electoral mandate.

THE U.S. ROLE IN THE POST–COLD WAR ERA

By 1991, however, U.S. security planners found they needed to devise new strategies for dealing with future crises around the world. The costs of future responses to foreign crises, moreover, had to be reconciled with the U.S. national debt, which had increased from one trillion dollars in 1981 to over five trillion dollars by 1992. The lack of a definite U.S. post–Cold War policy became apparent after Bush called for a new "world order" at the end of the Iraqi war in March 1991. Problems in Somalia, Haiti, Yugoslavia and other regions quickly appeared, but neither Bush nor Bill Clinton was able to immediately devise strategies to meet these crises.

As the U.S. media, the public and politicians focused attention on domestic affairs, the evolving post–Cold War world became a critical issue for those concerned with international developments. Among individuals who dealt with world politics and economics, discussions regarding international policies for a world order congenial to the United States focused on four basic questions: Is isolationism possible? What polarity of power relations would evolve between nations? What type of future conflict is most likely? And when, where and how should the United States intervene?

RETURN TO ISOLATIONISM?

As early as 1990, Republican critic Patrick Buchanan proposed that with the Cold War ended, the nation could revive its earlier isolationist policies, and he campaigned for the presidency on that platform in 1992 and 1996. Buchanan's ideas on isolationism first appeared in a 1990 article in which he declared that Communist losses in Eastern Europe indicated the Soviet Union was no longer a military threat. The United States should now withdraw its armed forces from Europe and stop all foreign economic assistance. "Let us go back," he wrote, "to a time when the establishment wanted war but the American people did not want to fight," that is, to the 1930s, when the America First organization opposed U.S. intervention in Britain's war against Nazi Germany. Although Japan's attack on Pearl Harbor rallied the nation to war, most American soldiers were brought home by 1946 and remained there until the onset of the Cold War. Under Dwight Eisenhower, the Republicans adopted an internationalist policy against Communism, but with that battle won, Buchanan criticized Republicans who continued to advocate internationalism. He wanted to abolish foreign alliances such as NATO, adopt protectionist tariffs and end illegal immigration. Despite these explicated proposals, Buchanan floundered at the polls in both campaigns.[1]

In 1992 and 1996 domestic issues dominated the elections because, with the Soviet enemy gone, there was no serious international crisis. As pollster John Mueller explains, Americans held basic "common sense" concerns about international policy but paid attention only if a crisis impacted their lives or a conflict caused American deaths or casualties.[2] Yet the world of 1992 was not the world of 1941 as perceived by Buchanan. New communication technology linked continents together as never before in history. Therefore, unlike Buchanan, most commentators on foreign policy could not accept isolationism.

WORLD POWER POLARITY

Aside from isolationism, the major issue for the post–Cold War world was what would replace the Cold War's bipolar balance of power. The two general options most cited were (1) the United States should retain its present post–Cold War role as the "unipolar" global power, or (2) the United States should become part of a future tripolar or multipolar system.

Charles Krauthammer has defined the unipolar concept in which the United States should act alone in deciding most international questions. Desiring an activist U.S. foreign policy, Krauthammer rejects Buchanan's retreat to "fortress America" but admits the United States has lost the dominant economic position it had held until the 1960s. Nevertheless, he asserts, the United States remains the principal center of the world's economic production and could dominate world politics because it has the world's greatest military capability. Recognizing that in future generations the United States might simply be the largest partner in a multipolar world, he wants Washington to act as the superpower directing the world during the transitory era toward those future relationships. U.S. leadership could include intervention under collective security, as happened in the 1991 Iraq war that he calls an instance of "pseudo-multilateralism," because the United States controlled United Nations activity. In the post–Cold War interim, Krauthammer fears that the U.S. government might spend too much on social welfare programs and too little on the military. He concludes that, "Our best hope for safety is in American strength and will—the strength and will to lead a unipolar world, unashamedly laying down the rules of world order and being prepared to enforce them."[3]

Senator Jesse Helms and other Republicans favored Krauthammer's unipolar concepts, although Helms also wanted to restrict presidential prerogatives as commander-in-chief by foreclosing effective U.S. participation in UN peacekeeping operations. After the Republican congressional victory in 1994, Helms became the chair of the Senate Foreign Relations Committee and a constant irritant to Clinton's foreign policies. A staunch advocate of limiting or ending U.S. involvement in any UN peacekeeping operations, Helms wanted the United States to leave the UN unless it was "radically overhauled." He wanted to stop the UN's "encroachment" on state sovereignty, cut 50 percent of its bureaucracy, overhaul the UN budget process and limit its peacekeeping activities.[4]

A MULTIPOLAR WORLD?

Extensive literature about a multipolar world appeared after 1989, with two prominent authors representing different aspects of this perspective: Harvard professor Joseph Nye and University of London professor Lawrence Freedman. These authors envision a world power structure of three or more power centers in which the United States would be the strongest. Nye indicates that the unilateral hegemony of the United States is "unlikely because of the diffusion of power through transnational interdependence." Preferring the term *multilevels of power*, Nye wants to have a strong U.S. military but recognizes that the United States would not be able to control the economic and political centers in an interdependent world. Thus, the United States should work with like-minded nations to resolve such international problems as relations between world markets, small nations having unconventional but destructive weapons, the international drug trade, environmental dangers of technological society and diseases that can spread across continents.[5]

Similar to Nye's multipolarity, Freedman emphasizes how America's successful strengthening of democracy in Asia and Western Europe after 1945 created valuable political-military allies to rebuild the world's economic foundations, promote political democracy and play the crucial role in stopping Communist expansion. As a matter of course, U.S. allies also became able to compete with U.S. business for world trade and investments because these alliances encouraged European economic unity and a prosperous Pacific Rim. Freedman believed these European and Asian allies expected to have a greater post–Cold War role in international affairs and, if the United States accommodates their expectations, all parties will benefit by resolving economic and trade issues that could otherwise result in increased tensions or conflict.[6]

Both Freedman and Nye believe the areas peripheral to the U.S.-European-Japanese core blocs are the most likely ones of future warfare and threats to the core countries' stability. Most Cold War conflicts occurred in third-world regions, and controlling such conflicts would require cooperation between the multipolar powers. In fact, the breakup of the Soviet empire added to the number of peripheral underdeveloped nations where trouble broke out after 1989 and would continue to fester.

RETHINKING SOVEREIGNTY

The foreign policy consensus was that the post–Cold War era had significantly changed previous criteria for interventions, especially in the underdeveloped world. One important change was that which permitted intervention in a nation's internal affairs if *world security* required it. During the Cold War, international groups such as the UN would not intervene in a nation's *internal affairs* because national sovereignty was sacrosanct. The UN perceived itself as an impartial group excluded from intervention without the explicit request of a nation's government or of each nation involved in a dispute. Since 1989, this concept of sovereignty has been challenged because many small ethnic or cultural groups have claimed a right to secede from an existing government. These claims raised dormant questions about sovereignty because conflicts within some states called for external intervention without permission from an existing government or governments. Ted Robert Gurr's 1994 article listed fifty internal conflicts, thirteen of which had already resulted in the deaths of over 100,000 people each and caused the flight of thousands of refugees to neighboring states. These data seemed to justify some interventions, but they also indicated the difficulty in deciding which of fifty cases required intervention by the United States or other organizations.[7]

The existence of so many potential trouble spots led Robert D. Blackwell to propose that human rights violations would justify U.S. intervention *only if* the violations met certain criteria. They must (1) become public knowledge, (2) involve large numbers of people, (3) take place over a long period of time, and (4) affect a disproportionate number of helpless people, especially children. Blackwell's qualifications appeared to require extensive suffering preceding any intervention, whereas other observers, including Boutros-Ghali, searched for a means of "preventive intervention" that would forestall such human suffering.[8]

Although a variety of qualifications have been proposed to justify intervention in the post–Cold War era, this chapter focuses on the four criteria for intervention suggested by Josef Joffe:

- There is a moral imperative for action.
- There is a national interest involved, especially if military action is included.
- There is a reasonable chance of success.
- The intervening state has full domestic support.[9]

MORAL IMPERATIVE FOR ACTION

The moral imperative assumes that world security requires concerned nations to regulate the behavior of existing or evolving states when conflict erupts within or among them. Intervention may be necessary if the conflict violates human decency or affects the security of neighboring regions. To encourage democracy, Joffe believes the United States and other nations must protect human rights and civilized standards of moral behavior. Nevertheless, Joffe says "purely humanitarian" reasons for *military* intervention are insufficient unless the conflict threatens the perceived national interests of the United States or other states.

NATIONAL INTEREST INVOLVED

Broadly viewed, national interest may be involved if conflicts spill across borders into neighboring states, disrupt international order or endanger the supply of a natural resource such as oil. Because the geographic location of the United States separates it from the European, Asian and African continents, concepts of the U.S. national interest have depended on a broad or restricted view of the nation's place in the world. An isolationist's view of the national interest is usually limited to defending U.S. borders or the Western Hemisphere. Internationalists, however, divide into at least two groups in interpreting the national interest. One restricts the U.S. action in the post–Cold War world by expecting Europeans, Asians or Africans to be the principal actors in their region unless there is a clearly defined U.S. interest involved. A second wants the United States to be the world leader by asserting extensive U.S. influence and activity in all dangerous parts of the world. These three categories indicate the range of basic perceptions influencing national interest. In the final analysis, the president and his national security advisers (or congressional leaders) must relate their perceptions of the nation's foreign interests to its domestic interests when considering intervention. If the moral imperative and the national interest are positively ascertained, intervening should outweigh the consequences of *not* acting.

REASONABLE CHANCE OF SUCCESS

Estimating the chances of an intervention's success involves risky claims, but the prospects may be evaluated by weighing three major factors: the type of intervention to be undertaken, the target country's geographic location and military capabilities and the intervention's objective.

- The type of intervention may be a limited action such as an embargo or embargo enforcement, a more difficult act such as air strikes or naval bombardments, or a large-scale employment of combat forces. Obviously, the more complex and involved the intervention, the greater the risk.
- Second, the geography of the region and the opposition's anticipated military strength must be compared to the intervening force's capacity. In the 1991 Iraqi war, the region's geography and Iraq's conventional war capacity favored a military response. Under different conditions, however, intervention may face geographic obstacles ranging from jungles or deserts to vast plains or mountains, and the opposition's military capability may range from well-trained and

well-supplied conventional or guerrilla forces to demoralized para-military factions with incompetent, low-technology military units.

- Third and most vital, a mission's success depends on the political and/or military objectives expected to be fulfilled. General Colin Powell's description of the 1991 Iraqi campaign illustrates the connection between military and political objectives. Powell justified the president's decision to stop the war after 100 hours of ground combat without overthrowing Saddam Hussein by insisting that the U.S. objective was simply to liberate Kuwait. However, critics of this decision argue Bush's wartime rhetoric had enlarged the objective by demonizing Hussein and calling for a "new world order."

The gap between Bush's politically oriented world order, presumably including a passive, cooperative Iraq, and Powell's limited military objectives raised expectations of what the mission would accomplish and, therefore, has resulted in continued postwar frustrations. Stating objectives clearly is important in evaluating the chances for success, but, as Lawrence Freedman observes, determining an objective is especially difficult when conflicts concern politics within the target state, a situation that recurred in Somalia and later in Haiti and Bosnia. During a power struggle among competing groups, the intervening forces usually favor one group because they will be perceived to be victims and they are willing to cooperate with their new protectors. If the fundamental political issues of a conflict are not settled during the intervention, the original power struggle will probably be renewed when the intervening force pulls out.

With these difficulties in mind, the possible objectives for a political military intervention may be defined as (1) peacemaking to persuade all parties to agree to a cease-fire, (2) peacekeeping to maintain a cease-fire that all parties accept and to punish violators if necessary, (3) prevention to act before a conflict erupts, (4) coercion to change behavior of a government or group violating international behavior standards, (5) coercion to unseat an unacceptable government and help establish a new government and (6) providing protection to humanitarian aid providers while a conflict persists.

INTERVENING STATE HAS FULL DOMESTIC SUPPORT

Democratic governments require domestic support for interventions to be undertaken and to be sustained. On the positive side, Joseph Nye finds it axiomatic that democratic governments never war against each other because their leaders must first exhaust all means to find solutions to their differences short of war. On the negative side, a democratic leader's need for domestic support may make military intervention difficult unless there is a clear-cut threat to a vital national interest.

An important addendum to domestic backing is whether democratic leaders must have backing *before* intervening or may use their persuasive powers to *gain backing after* intervening. The timing of support was an American political concern because the "Vietnam syndrome" has blamed U.S. losses on the news media and public opinion. In 1983, President Reagan's Secretary of Defense, Caspar Weinberger, listed the need for "a reasonable assurance of public support" prior to any military intervention. Less attention was given to Secretary of State George Shultz, who responded that Weinberger's requirement of public support *prior to a presidential decision* was "hiding behind the skirts of public opinion." Shultz argued the president should make decisions and then articulate reasons to win and maintain public support.[10]

Two factors influencing U.S. policymakers' and public perceptions of foreign events are mass media reports and public opinion polls. Although the influence of transnational television reports, such as those of CNN, is controversial, the public's perception of world events is instantaneously updated because satellites quickly transmit pictures of human catastrophes. This capability can provide daily pictures of the hazards of intervening, but media sound-bites can seldom explain the complex causes involved in a conflict or the various reasons for presidential decisions.

Most polls after 1989 show that the U.S. public usually favors an active role in international affairs. Detailed annual polls by the Chicago Council on Foreign Relations have concluded that the public's distaste for foreign activity reached a low point of 54 percent in 1982 but reversed in 1992, when 62 percent approved an active U.S. role abroad.[11] In an extensive 1996 survey of the public's perceptions of foreign relations, Steven Kull and I. M. Destler found that most Americans lack accurate knowledge about international affairs. They report 74 percent of the public want the United States to promote peace cooperation and human welfare in the international arena yet believe the country should "not be the single world leader." However, in-depth questioning on foreign affairs indicates the public lacked basic information. Poll respondents thought the United States provided 40 percent of costs for all UN peacekeeping, whereas the

U.S. contribution was 2 percent and in terms of gross national product of industrial nations, "the United States gives the lowest percentage of all."

THE SOMALIA INTERVENTION

President George H. W. Bush's decision to intervene in Somalia in December 1992 may have been his final attempt to demonstrate U.S. support for a new world order. The method he chose, however, raised serious questions about his administration's criteria for intervention. Indeed, critics have denounced it as a formula for failure.

The disintegration of Somalia's government began with civil strife in 1988 and had reduced the state to political chaos by January 1991. For two years the United Nations tried, but failed, to obtain an effective cease-fire among the warring factions because starvation was causing the deaths of many children, women and elderly men. A moral imperative acceptable to the American public had become evident by November 1992, but because the administration perceived no national interest at stake in Somalia, President Bush seriously qualified the role of the U.S. mission. His adoption of a strictly humanitarian mission resulted in the proverbial wrong intervention, in the wrong place, at the wrong time. After the United States withdrew in October 1993, the UN mission would continue until March 1995. Although the combined UN-U.S. intervention may have temporarily saved many lives, fighting among Somali warring factions continued to cause food shortages and deaths long after they left.

SOMALIA'S IMPERIAL LEGACY

Throughout the nineteenth century, the European race for control of African territory created states with boundaries that ignored clan, family and tribal dominions, including Somali clans in northeastern Africa. Although Ethiopia often exerted political control over northeastern Africa, the pastoral regions along the Red Sea and Indian Ocean contained Somali clans that had converted to Islam in the eighth century and shared a language and culture based on complex clan and subclan relations. After 1850, France, Great Britain and Italy sought seaports on the Red Sea to control a waterway whose value greatly increased after the Suez Canal opened in 1869. When they resolved colonial claims, French Somaliland contained the port of Djibouti, British Somaliland comprised the northeastern triangle of the "horn" of Africa, and Italian Somaliland lay to the south, including Mogadishu's port. These divisions ignored Somali clan holdings as well as the So-malis in Kenya and the Ogaden province of Ethiopia.

In the 1950s, an African wave of rebellion did not affect the French in Djibouti, but the British and Italian colonies were united in 1960 as an independent state. On gaining independence, Somalia set up a republic with a president, prime minister and legislature in Mogadishu, although the British and Italians had done little to prepare them for nationhood. The state's pastoral economy supported a subsistence level of living, and clans and subclans were not ready for rule by a central government. Somalia's interclan relations had local ethical rules but lacked an overarching concept of law essential to a modern centralized nation.[12]

During the 1960s, the government misspent tax revenue and failed to build a transportation and communication infrastructure that would have united the entire country. Amid complaints about the government, military officers led by General Mohammed Siad Barre overthrew Somalia's president in 1969 and established a regime based on Communist slogans adopted from the Soviet Union's agents who backed the rebellion.

SOMALIA: KEY FIGURES

Aideed, Mohamed Farah: Leader of a strong military faction in Somalia, claiming to have overthrown Barre in 1991.

Aideed, Husein Mohamed: Former U.S. Marine and son of Mohamed Farah, who replaces his father in 1996.

Barre, Mohammed Siad: Military dictator of Somalia to 1991.

Bir, General Cervik: Muslim Turkish general and commander of UNO-SOM II forces; works with UN envoy U.S. Admiral Jonathan Howe from May to October 1993.

Hersi, Mohamed Siad ("Morgan"): An ally of Siad Barre and his clan.

Jess, Ahmad Omar: An ally of Aideed in southern Somalia.

Kittani, Ismat: UN envoy to Somalia who replaces Sahnoun in October 1992.

Mohamed, Ali Mahdi: Chief opponent of Aideed in Mogadishu; has the support of the Organization of African Unity.

Sahnoun, Mohamed: First UN envoy of UNOSOM I in Somalia; fired by Boutros-Ghali in October 1992.

General Barre's rule from 1969 to 1991 paralleled the Cold War. First the Soviets, and later the United States, extended him economic and military aid. After 1969, Moscow sought to expand its sphere of influence in northeastern Africa by moving into Ethiopia, but its plans went awry. The Soviets armed Ethiopian rebel Haile Mariam Mengistu, who subsequently ousted American ally Haile Selassie, but they ignored the fact that Somalia was at war with Ethiopia to "liberate" Somali clans in Ogaden—a province Ethiopia had controlled since the nineteenth century. Barre's war, which had begun against the U.S.-supported Selassie, was now waged against the Moscow-aided Mengistu. When Barre rejected Soviet orders to leave Ogaden, the Soviets sent additional military equipment to Mengistu and had Fidel Castro send 18,000 Cuban troops to expel the Somali troops. When Barre's forces reluctantly withdrew, some 300,000 Ogaden refugees followed. After this setback, Barre received aid from the United States, the UN and nongovernmental (NGO) humanitarian groups. Washington replaced Soviet influence in Somalia in 1980, opening a naval base on the Red Sea. President Ronald Reagan decreased U.S. economic aid from $36 million in 1983 to $8.7 million before canceling it in 1989, but the Pentagon's military aid continued until 1990, when rebel attacks weakened Barre's regime.

Journalist Jonathan Stevenson believes that the U.S.-UN food relief to Somalia over ten years had made the clans and refugees dependent on food imports and that the rebellion completely disrupted the food supply after 1988.[13]

UPRISINGS BRING ANARCHY

General Barre diverted vast funds to his war against Ethiopia and thus did not develop a sound economy for Somalia. Moreover, while the northern Somali clans' livestock provided the nation's principal export income, Barre passed these funds to corrupt friends. Governmental corruption plus the miserable conditions of Ogaden refugees prompted the uprisings against Barre in the spring of 1988.

Mohamed Sahnoun, a former official of the Organization of African Unity (OAU), identifies three missed opportunities between 1988 and 1992 when preventive intervention by the UN, the OAU, the League of Arab States or the United States might have deterred Somalia's descent into political anarchy. The first occurred in 1988, when the UN and the OAU gave only relief assistance despite reports by Amnesty International and Africa Watch of large-scale killing and human rights violations in Somalia.

Led by the Issaq clan, the Somalia National Movement (SNM) attacked northern towns located near the U.S. naval base at Berera before Barre ordered a full-scale military assault on the Issaq. Using aircraft and heavy artillery bombardments, the attack destroyed 70 percent of Hargeysa and other Issaq towns, killing 5,000 men, women and children.

Although the UN and NGOs sent humanitarian relief to northern Somalia, Washington suspended U.S. aid, an action that hurt Barre's regime but did not help his opponents. The Issaq's SNM continued its opposition and sought the backing of other disaffected Somali clans. With sporadic fighting disrupting Somalia, a second chance was missed in May 1990, when 144 prominent Somali physicians, scholars and other intellectuals promoted peace negotiations by signing a manifesto. Although the manifesto's signatories risked their lives by defying Barre, neither the UN, the OAU, the United States nor others helped them. Although Italy and Egypt sought a meeting of Somali opposition groups, clan leaders refused to attend.

The third and most critical missed chance to avoid wider fighting occurred on January 26, 1991, after rebels overthrew Barre. Unfortunately, the rebels' success occurred precisely at the same time that Washington's attention was diverted elsewhere—to a U.S.-led UN coalition attack on Iraq to liberate Kuwait. U.S. naval units on duty in the Red Sea rescued American, Soviet and other diplomatic personnel from Mogadishu. The UN also evacuated its Mogadishu relief headquarters and did not return until August 1991.[14]

INEFFECTIVE UN INTERVENTION

Barre's overthrow in January 1991 brought chaos to Somalia that a UN humanitarian effort could not contain. Somali clans that united against Barre had not developed plans for a new government and, consequently, at least thirteen clans and subclans subsequently fought for regional or national control. While humanitarian agencies tried to assist people, the UN finally obtained a cease-fire in 1992.

During 1991, the Somalia Salvation Democratic Front achieved political order in northeastern Somalia near Boosaaso, and the Issaq's SNM formed an independent Somalia Republic at Hargeysa. However, fierce combat erupted in southern and central Somalia, where competing clans used scorched-earth policies to destroy crops, homes and cattle. As Barre's forces retreated toward Kenya or Ethiopia in January 1991, they devastated the country's best agricultural land as well as roads, bridges and hospitals. The most intense fighting was at Mogadishu, where two generals involved in defeating Barre now led competing factions—Mohamed Farah Aideed and Mohamed Ali Mahdi.

The carnage following Barre's overthrow stimulated UN cease-fire efforts and additional humanitarian aid by the International Red Cross, Médecins Sans Frontières and other nongovernmental groups (NGOs). Finally, in December 1991, UN Secretary-General Javier Perez de Cuellar recommended that the UN Security Council (UNSC) sponsor a peacemaking venture if the two warlords would agree to a cease-fire. Together with Boutros Boutros-Ghali, who succeeded him on January 1, 1992, Perez asked the UNSC to assist in the search for Somalia's peace and security, and UN officers negotiated a cease-fire on March 3 with Aideed and Ali Mahdi. Although fighting continued in parts of Somalia, a UN technical team in Mogadishu prepared for UN monitors to ensure UN aid.

After the warlords agreed, UNSC Resolution 751 of April 24, 1992, established the United Nations Operation in Somalia (UNOSOM I). The UNSC combined the UN missions of humanitarian aid, peacemaking, peacekeeping and state building. It appealed for humanitarian assistance to be sent to Somalia, approved fifty unarmed UN officers to monitor the cease-fire and instructed the secretary-general to reconcile the combatants and enforce an arms embargo.

Between April and November 1992, UNOSOM I activity was handicapped by disagreement between UN bureaucrats in New York and Mohamed Sahnoun's UN staff in Mogadishu. Sahnoun was appointed by Boutros-Ghali, but the former OAU diplomat soon found that diverse UN relief groups failed to coordinate activities and delayed operations by bickering over distribution areas. Groups such as UNICEF did fairly well, he reported, but the UN High Commission on Refugees, the UN World Food Program, and the UN Department of Humanitarian Affairs worked at cross-purposes and refused to consult with Sahnoun. Moreover, UN humanitarian officers worked from comfortable lodgings in Nairobi, Djibouti and Mogadishu, avoiding contact with Somalis in the countryside. In contrast to UN bureaucrats, most NGO personnel worked effectively under dangerous circumstances to distribute relief among the people. The NGOs had meager resources but quickly provided relief to the people, while in eight months, the UN had distributed one-third of its relief supplies.

Equally seriously, Sahnoun disagreed with UN officials about negotiations with Somali leaders. While UN officers paid attention only to Aideed and Ali Mahdi, Sahnoun met many clan and subclan elders around the country, seeking their cooperation in the peace process. Sahnoun wanted the UN to involve clan leaders other than Aideed and Ali Mahdi in the forming of a government.

By October 1992, Sahnoun believed relief operations and peace talks were going well, and he arranged meetings between Sweden's Peace Institute and Somali intellectuals to discuss forming a government. Also, many clan leaders accepted his invitation to meet in January 1993 with representatives of Ethiopia, Eritrea, Djibouti and Kenya for a "Horn of Africa" peace conference. Sahnoun believed the airlift of supplies that President Bush and various Europeans began in August had increased relief aid. Moreover, fighting had decreased in Somalia except for problems between Aideed and Ali Mahdi. Sahnoun's evaluations were confirmed by experts on Somalia from Africa Watch.

Late in October, however, Boutros-Ghali dismissed Sahnoun because he had bypassed the hierarchic channels of the UN bureaucracy. The breaking point between Sahnoun and Boutros-Ghali came after the secretary-general's New York office announced an additional 3,000 UNOSOM I troops would be sent to Somalia, a decision made without consulting Sahnoun or Somali leaders.

Both Sahnoun and the leaders in Somalia protested because UN officials tended to support Ali Mahdi, who wanted more UN soldiers, against Aideed, who had the strongest following and did not want more UN troops. When the UN had sent five hundred Pakistani soldiers to Somalia in September, Sahnoun had difficulty in persuading Aideed to accept them. Thus, Boutros-Ghali's October decision to deploy another 3,000 soldiers enraged Aideed and alarmed Sahnoun.

Prompted by the troop announcement, Sahnoun criticized the UN bureaucrats to reporters and on the CBS network's popular *60 Minutes* program. For going public, Boutros-Ghali castigated Sahnoun, replacing him with a loyal bureaucrat, Ismat Kittani. Subsequently, Sahnoun's achievements broke down and turned many Somalis against Boutros-Ghali and the UN. Indeed, Aideed's followers charged that the UN was Somalia's real enemy—a claim that endangered all relief groups in Somalia.

Aideed's accusations against the UN prompted intense fighting in Mogadishu as he refused to deal with Kittani. On November 12, his forces shelled a Pakistani encampment at the airport, and armed gangs looted warehouses containing relief supplies and obstructed relief convoys distributing food and medicine. On November 23, Mahdi's clan joined the action against the UN by shelling a UN ship unloading at Mogadishu's port.

The UN's New York organization never admitted its shortcomings, of course, and the reasons for UNOSOM I's failures were not apparent to persons unfamiliar with past events in Somalia. More evident to Americans were the reports of warlord attacks on food supplies and the scenes of starving Somalis that followed Boutros-Ghali's ill-fated decision to send more UN troops to Somalia. UNOSOM I's intervention had failed, but President Bush apparently believed he could rescue it.[15]

BUSH'S INTERVENTION, 1992

Until more archival documentation is available, President Bush's decision to intervene in Somalia will be clouded by controversy. Either he lacked satisfactory information about Sahnoun's endeavors and the UN's policies, or he ignored those data because he desired to show that his new world order could be implemented by U.S. forces, perhaps before Bill Clinton took office on January 20, 1993. In August 1992 Bush, and especially General Colin Powell, had been reluctant to act militarily in Bosnia when reports of ethnic cleansing appeared, and in Somalia, they had opted for only an airlift of relief supplies. In November, however, Bush adopted the risky option of sending 28,000 U.S. troops to Somalia on a humanitarian mission because, as Powell wrote in his memoirs, Somalia "wrenched our hearts." Bush indicated it would be a "difficult and dangerous job," and Powell's "best guess" was that it would take "two to three months." Neither man, however, appeared to understand the true nature of UNOSOM, its troubles nor the vital connection between Somalia's political anarchy and the attainment of success for their humanitarian mission.

Perhaps like the American public, Bush, Powell and Secretary of Defense Richard Cheney simply judged Somalia by the television pictures reaching their homes. These instant photographs depicted the horrendous suffering of starving women and children but never captured the savage reality of the young gangs. These thugs were riding about in Land Cruisers equipped with heavy machine guns and grenade or rocket launchers and killing or threatening the humanitarian workers and Somali people. The gangs had robbed relief agencies and terrorized the population since the breakdown of government in 1991 and remained active in 1993. The full range of Somalia's political, social and economic anarchy and UNOSOM I's inability to deliver relief supplies was not adequately conveyed by the brief television clips shown the American public.[16]

Television supplied a moral imperative and public support for Bush's decision to intervene, but U.S. national interest was not directly involved because stabilizing Somalia's political order was not critical to U.S. economic or political well-being. Lacking a commitment to repair Somalia's political order, Bush proposed to open the food supply routes and quickly withdraw the U.S. military, a concept that seriously qualified the chances for the UN to succeed in restraining Somalia's warlords and achieving a peace settlement.

More is known about how than about why President Bush's national security team believed a quick military fix was possible in Somalia. Soon after losing the 1992 election to Bill Clinton, Bush ordered a study about Somalia's relief requirements and the options for U.S. intervention. Apparently, Bush believed that Somalia's humanitarian relief had failed because UN experts alleged that 50 to 80 percent of Somalia's relief supplies were stolen or extorted from relief groups by armed gangs. Moreover, because it could not be distributed to the needy, as much as 12,000 metric tons of food rotted in Mogadishu's warehouses. The airlift Bush adopted in August achieved some benefits in bringing food, medicine and supplies, but conditions in Somalia had become less secure in November. Notably, the U.S. airlift commander, Brigadier General Frank Libutti, warned Secretary of Defense Richard Cheney and General Powell that, "If the United States [was] not careful, it could be in Somalia for ten or fifteen years."

Although Libutti's cautionary words may have influenced Powell's demand for a quick U.S. exit from Somalia, the Joint Chiefs' reasons for discarding their previous reluctance to become involved in Somalia are unknown. On November 21, Admiral David Jeremiah, the vice-chairman of the Joint Chiefs, reported that the Pentagon's analysis of the situation indicated U.S. troops could deploy in Somalia, end the violence and make certain that "the people were fed *within a short period*" (italics added). Journalist Don Oberdorfer believes Jeremiah's report marked a sea change in the Joint Chiefs' thinking because Colin Powell accepted its conclusions provided an overwhelming U.S. force was deployed to secure the relief supply routes and quickly withdrawn.

Bush met with the Joint Chiefs on November 25, where he found that Secretary of State Lawrence Eagleburger and National Security Adviser Brent Scowcroft also favored aid for Somalia. Oberdorfer does not explain whether these officials considered the national interest or the chances for a peace settlement between Somalia's warlords. The Joint Chiefs gave Bush three options. Bush refused the first, to augment UN funds, and the second, to simply provide U.S. air and sea power—offshore—to support UN-OSOM I relief operations. Bush chose to have a U.S.-led multinational force intervene in Somalia, secure the area for relief distributions, withdraw in a short time and give responsibility back to the UN. Bush instructed Eagleburger to discuss this offer with Secretary-General Boutros-Ghali and prepare a UNSC resolution requesting the U.S.-led mission.

The UNSC passed the appropriate resolution on December 3, and the next day Bush announced that the United States would command a multinational United Task Force (UNITAF) led by U.S. General Joseph P. Hoar to establish protective conditions for humanitarian aid to reach Somalia's starving people. Bush did not refer to any U.S. national interest in Somalia but said the U.S. role was "humanitarian" and that he expected other nations would add to the 28,000-strong U.S. contingent. The final UNITAF force consisted of 37,000 military personnel, including 8,000 logistical troops.[17]

Immediately after the November 25 meeting, when Bush had chosen his option, journalists raised important questions about the objectives of the so-called humanitarian mission. They were joined by Secretary-General Boutros-Ghali in asking the Bush team what "a secure environment for humanitarian relief" required and what connection there was between the U.S. operation and a political settlement among Somalia's warring groups. The journalists accepted the Pentagon's explanation that, unlike Bosnia, the Somali intervention was doable because the northeast African terrain was neither mountainous nor tree covered and the disorganized warlords could not seriously threaten U.S. forces. But they did question the "quick exit" strategy under which the overwhelming U.S. force withdrew and left a much weaker UN force to sustain those routes against hostile warlords who had not accepted an effective political agreement. Generally, these reporters asked: What would happen after UNITAF ended? Former Secretary of State Henry Kissinger commented that if the warlords listened to the explanations of Bush and Powell, they would lay low and cooperate until the U.S. forces withdrew before renewing their struggle for power.

Among other critical reports, *U.S. News and World Report* disclosed doubts about the mission expressed in a note to the State Department by Ambassador to Kenya Smith Hempstone. Indicating that Somalia's difficulties involved the strife of militant factions as well as food relief, Hempstone referred to the 241 U.S. Marines killed in Lebanon in 1983 on

President Ronald Reagan's uncertain mission and commented that if you liked Beirut, you will "love Mogadishu."[18]

Secretary-General Boutros-Ghali addressed these concerns in a letter to President Bush after UNSC Resolution 794 was approved. On December 8, Boutros-Ghali informed Bush that his talks with U.S. representatives had continuously raised questions about the security standards necessary to provide safety for humanitarian aid after UNITAF's mission ended. Boutros-Ghali's three points of "cardinal importance" in order to maintain aid distribution were (1) UNITAF should place Somalia's heavy weapons under international control and disarm the irregular forces and gangs threatening the aid organizations, (2) UNITAF should establish a secure environment throughout Somalia, not only in UNITAF's designated supply route near Mogadishu and (3) there should be assurances of close cooperation between the UN and UNITAF commands to retain compatible political and humanitarian conditions *before* the United States transferred responsibility to UN peacekeepers. The Secretary-General said UNSC 794 stated "a secure environment" should mean peaceful conditions for future aid as well as temporary protection.

In December 1992, the Bush administration and Boutros-Ghali obviously held quite different interpretations of "a secure environment" and the meaning of Resolution 794. Former Bush official John R. Bolton indicates Bush's reply to the secretary-general stated ". . . the mission of the coalition is limited and specific: to create security conditions which will permit the feeding of starving Somali people and the transfer of this security function to the U.N. peacekeeping force." Bolton's words fall short of clarity about security and seem to contrast with Bush's December 4 speech that said he opposed Somalia's "armed gangs ripping off their own people, condemning them to death by starvation."

Whatever Bush intended, the divergent views reappeared in Boutros-Ghali's December 19 report to the UNSC. Except for the probable close cooperation between the United States and the UN, Boutros-Ghali indicated the Bush team rejected the important task of disarming Somalia's warring groups, which had been the major obstacle to UNOSOM I's success. The United States also refused to extend protection to all parts of Somalia, limiting UNITAF work to Mogadishu's central aid distribution region. In contrast to Bush's December 4 rhetoric, the actual U.S. mission was best represented by General Powell's comment when the first U.S. Marines landed near Mogadishu: "It's sort of like the cavalry coming to the rescue, straightening things out for a while and then letting the marshals come back to keep things under control." The problem with Powell's analogy was that Somalia had no marshals to "come back" and control Somalia's warlords. Bush's refusal to disarm the warring factions and make all of Somalia safe meant UNITAF was a quick police raid that provided no effective aid after the police left.[19]

UNITAF'S LIMITED SECURITY

By May 1993, UNITAF's limited military mission had created security areas around Mogadishu's airport and seaport and along convoy routes linking eight cities in central and southern Somalia. The awesome display of U.S. military power provided temporary safety for aid workers to distribute food, which saved the lives of about 100,000 starving Somalis. But UNITAF also created an illusion of security from the warlords, which evaporated when the weaker UNOSOM II force took over in May 1993. The Somalis who were rescued for five months in 1993 again experienced a precarious existence after May 1993.

President Bush seemed to recognize there was a connection between controlling Somalia's militant groups and having a successful military venture because in December he sent Robert B. Oakley to Somalia to obtain the cooperation of Somalia's warlords before Lieutenant General Robert B. Johnston's UNITAF forces landed. In retrospect, Oakley's political tactics as head of the U.S. Liaison Office in Mogadishu probably handicapped the UNSC Resolution 794's long-term peacemaking objectives in Somalia. Oakley arrived two days before the first 1,800 U.S. Marines landed on December 9. Outside the glare of television cameras, Oakley easily convinced Aideed and Ali Mahdi to restrain their guerrilla forces because the U.S. forces would destroy them if necessary, and both warlords knew the power of the U.S. forces, which had swept away Iraq's army in 1991. Oakley's initial goal was simple—he did not have to make strong demands on the warlords such as requiring them to disarm or to sign a peace agreement recognizing one government for the country. Thus, he secured the warlords' temporary cooperation. When the U.S. Marines landed on December 9, their only challenge was a beach full of rabid reporters and brightly lit television cameras.

Oakley's cease-fire agreement, finalized on December 11, was generally, but not completely, effective until May 4. During the next four months UNITAF confiscated some of the militants' arms and ordered the heavy weapons of Aideed and Ali Mahdi to be stored in areas outside the UNITAF "security zones." However, this disarming was coincidental to protecting the humanitarian convoy routes.

More serious, perhaps, Oakley's dealings with Aideed and Ali Mahdi gave them the appearance of being Somalia's legitimate rulers because he concentrated on the domains of these two Mogadishu leaders. UNITAF seldom moved into the rural areas of central and northern Somalia where gangs operated or local clans had some control despite frequent fighting. UNITAF authority extended from Mogadishu along convoy routes to the cities of Kismaayo, Baioda, Bardera and Beletweyne. UNITAF also took over the Soviet-built airport at Baledogle, located 160 kilometers from Mogadishu, but paid little or no attention to the northern regions of Somalia.

UNITAF's worst problems were at the southern port of Kismaayo, where extensive conflict revived. In December, fighting had taken place at Kismaayo between one group, allied with Aideed, led by Ahmad Omar Jess and comprising refugee Ogaden clans, and a second faction led by General Mohamed Slad Hersi (known as General Morgan), which included members of Siad Barre's national army and the Marehan clan that ruled Somalia before 1991. The fighting at Kismaayo stopped in mid-December but was renewed again in February and spread toward Mogadishu in March 1993.

In February, Belgian troops repelled Jess's men, who fled Kismaayo after looting the warehouses of the International Red Cross and other humanitarian relief groups. The fighting continued, however, and spread toward Mogadishu in violation of Oakley's cease-fire. To end the uprising, an American quick reaction force of 500 soldiers and helicopters reinforced the Belgians and restored order. As a result, Jess's men remained at a village near Kismaayo while U.S. soldiers moved Morgan's warriors to a village near the Kenyan border.

Because Jess's forces suffered the greatest losses, Aideed complained that UNITAF had interfered against Jess rather than Morgan. Consequently, his followers staged demonstrations that avoided U.S. forces but sacked the Egyptian embassy and attacked Nigerian troops. There were six days of disorder before U.S. Marines assisted the Nigerians and restored order in Mogadishu.

During January and February, Oakley and General Johnston took several ineffective measures to provide order in Somalia. They held a few meetings with regional and district clans and inaugurated a local police and judicial system in UNITAF's security zones. But as Oakley's deputy, Walter R. Clarke, concludes, these attempts were ineffective because Aideed and Mahdi appointed the judges and police officials, none of whom were properly supervised. UNITAF expected the Somalis to convict and punish gang violations, which they never did. UNITAF officers asked the remnants of UNOSOM I troops to control the militants; however, the UN troops lacked sufficient military power to carry out these requests. Under UNITAF, Aideed, Ali Mahdi and other warlords retained local authority and military capabilities which neither UNOSOM I, nor UNOSOM II, were strong enough to challenge. For the UN, the hopeful signs for future peace were two meetings at Addis Ababa that various Somali leaders attended.[20]

UN CONFERENCES AT ADDIS ABABA

The United Nations sponsored two conferences designed to establish political order before UNITAF withdrew. While as many as fifteen Somali groups were represented at these conferences, the UN experienced two major problems. First, UN and UNITAF officials disagreed over whether to deal solely with Aideed, Ali Mahdi and other militant leaders or to encourage Somali civilian elders to replace the military warlords. Second, many Somali warlords resented previous UNOSOM I interference and, in particular, Aideed disagreed with Secretary-General Boutros-Ghali, who wanted UNITAF to disarm all existing militias. Justified or not, Aideed, who personally disliked Boutros-Ghali, believed the UN favored Ali Mahdi because the Organization of African Unity had recognized him as Somalia's ruler.

At Addis Ababa I, from January 4 to 15, 1993, the UN hoped to begin Somalia's process of reconciliation, but General Aideed sabotaged these sessions by rejecting the UN agenda for a reconciliation conference. Later, at Addis Ababa II, from March 13 to 26, there were two separate meetings: the Humanitarian Conference of delegates from public and private relief agencies and representatives of nonmilitary Somali groups; and the National Reconciliation Conference of fifteen military factions. The humanitarian meetings were led by UN Undersecretary-General Jan Eliasson and the UN coordinator of humanitarian aid, Philip Johnston. The reconciliation meeting was supervised by retired U.S. Admiral Jonathan Howe, a former Bush administration official who replaced Kittani as Boutros-Ghali's special representative to Somalia, and Lansana Kouyate of Guinea, who, as Howe's deputy, chaired the conference.

The Humanitarian Conference brought donor representatives together with Somali civilian groups with which the UN wanted to replace the militant groups in reconstructing Somalia's political and economic society. These civilian delegates included signatories of the 1990 manifesto, traditional clan elders, Somali women's groups, and Islamic religious leaders. The UN hoped these groups would revive Somalia's traditional clan customs and prepare for a peaceful society by trying to restore regional councils and organize national political groups, education, job opportunities and the agricultural and medical rehabilitation of the country. At the end of the humanitarian sessions, donor groups pledged $130 million in aid, although the amount fell short of Eliasson's plans for $160 million. However, these pledges became irrelevant after UNITAF forces withdrew because the breakdown of Somalia's internal security repelled the donors.

The critical sessions at Addis Ababa II were primarily talks between the fifteen military groups, which had to be reconciled and disarmed to bring peace to Somalia. The reconciliation meetings began on a sour note because secessionists, who wanted a decentralized Somali government, filibustered against most resolutions and because Aideed delayed sessions to protest UNITAF's favorable attitude toward General Morgan after fighting broke out again in Kismaayo on March 16. Once Aideed came to the reconciliation table, the UN achieved a political agreement on March 27. The military leaders reaffirmed their January cease-fire and approved a Transitional National Council (TNC) for Somalia. The TNC was a fifty-seven-member council with representation for each of the fifteen warlords, plus other nonmilitary groups attending the humanitarian sessions, such as the women's group, which gained one-third of the TNC representation. Unfortunately, the documents did not spell out the details for selecting regional councils, for drawing boundaries and for enforcing the promises made by the signatories. After UNITAF forces withdrew on May 4, the Addis Ababa II promises were quickly forgotten by the warlords.[21]

TRANSITION FROM UNITAF TO UNOSOM II

By early March 1993, Robert Oakley and other UNITAF officials claimed "a secure environment" existed for humanitarian relief distributions. With great exaggeration, Oakley supported a quick U.S. withdrawal by asserting that "the problem of clan warfare which has taken Somalian lives is virtually gone," and urged a hasty transition from UNITAF to the UN. Before UNITAF withdrew, Boutros-Ghali wanted assurances about the Somali warlords' cease-fire and a new UNSC mandate. To satisfy the secretary-general, the Clinton administration delayed UNITAF's final withdrawal until May 4.

The first steps toward UNOSOM II began in March with a change in

U.S. and UN officials in Somalia. Robert Gosende replaced Oakley, and Boutros-Ghali appointed Admiral Howe to replace Kittani and Turkish General Cevik Bir to become the UN military commander when UNITAF forces withdrew. On March 3, Boutros-Ghali reported on conditions in Somalia and requested a mandate for UNOSOM II. His report contained the warlords' January promises to disarm and indicated that the turning over of heavy weapons had barely begun and the UN would require constant support to complete the task. UNITAF had disarmed few warring factions and accepted responsibility for only 40 percent of Somalia's territory; moreover, it had cleared few land mines outside its security routes. The UN had just started to form an independent police constabulary. Boutros-Ghali called UNITAF's military response a "police action" that separated the essential political-military mission from the "purely humanitarian" one and gave security to limited areas. UNOSOM II would require at least the 37,000 troops used by UNITAF, and the United States had agreed to provide a tactical quick reaction force to supplement the U.S. task force staying in Somalia. Boutros-Ghali's report asked the UNSC to expand UNOSOM I's mission to meet the unexpected dimensions of peacemaking and monitoring as well as peacekeeping and protecting humanitarian supplies.

Before UNITAF left, the Security Council's Resolution 814 established the UNOSOM II mission by adding peacemaking and nation-building missions to that of humanitarian assistance and "peacekeeping" after the parties agreed to a political settlement.[22]

UNOSOM II'S FAULTS—WARLORDS' CHALLENGE

Following UNITAF's withdrawal on May 4, UNOSOM II officials faced two major difficulties: first, they lacked specific plans to change Somalia's transitional government into a permanent regime; second, UNOSOM II's much less powerful military capability made it difficult to coerce the Somali warlords to accept peace. Consequently, within a month after UNITAF's withdrawal, UNOSOM II's peacemaking mission became a warlord hunting venture.

Although UNITAF's General Johnston had discussed a possible warlord challenge with Admiral Howe and General Bir in April, they developed no plans to deal with a military threat or to negotiate with the warlords. The lack of UNOSOM II's preparations resulted from many errors of judgment, such as Boutros-Ghali's depending on the cease-fire to hold, the U.S. and

UN officials underestimating the will and fighting ability of Somalia's clans, and disagreement about dealing with warlords or civilian clan leaders.

After UNITAF withdrew on May 4, UNOSOM II faced its new challenges with reduced military personnel and less heavy equipment. From UNITAF's total of 37,000 troops, mostly American, covering 40 percent of Somalia, UNOSOM II now had 14,000 troops for all of Somalia. New contingents raised the UN total to 28,000 in August, but these included many inexperienced and poorly equipped troops from small nations such as Botswana and Bangladesh. The new personnel also included "nation-building" units such as 1,500 German engineers and technicians who were not trained for combat. The Canadians withdrew their troops when UNITAF ended, but France, Italy and Pakistan kept most of their forces in Somalia. The United States retained a task force of about 4,000 members under Major General Thomas Montgomery, including 1,167 members of an elite Quick Response Force (QRF) stationed on U.S. navy ships offshore and under the independent command of U.S. Major General William Garrison. The QRF would respond to emergency threats to UNOSOM II provided the U.S. Central Command in Florida approved. Since the United States withdrew most of its heavy equipment and helicopters, except for those in Garrison's QRF, UNOSOM II forces had few armored vehicles and helicopters as well as fewer army personnel trained for combat.[23]

General Bir was also troubled by the breakdown of his central command authority that UNITAF forces had under U.S. General Johnston. This collapse began in June, when French officers learned that Garrison's Quick Reaction Force took orders from General Bir only after first checking with Washington via Florida. France was always contentious about the Americans' peculiar unwillingness to operate under allied commanders, and on learning about the U.S. command structure, the French and Italians reported the situation to their home governments. Thereafter, French officers accepted orders for their 1,130 forces only if Paris approved and, after July, the Italians' 2,538 soldiers sought Rome's approval before taking directions from General Bir. When difficulties began in Mogadishu, the French rejected Bir's orders to stay in their assigned locations and moved to safer and more comfortable quarters in Baidoa to protect relief supply lines. Following Rome's instructions, the Italians initially accepted Bir's orders to search for Aideed, but in July their officers refused to continue that mission.

The confrontation of UNOSOM II with the warlords began soon after UNITAF's departure. On May 4, UNOSOM II commander Admiral Howe started a process to empower Somalia's transitional government by declaring that the penal law code for Somalia would be the code devised by Somalia's democratic assembly in 1960, abolishing the 1969 code of Siad Barre's authoritarian regime. Howe intended to promote Somalia's police and judicial system, initiated by the UN in March 1993, and to allow UNOSOM II to enforce the cease-fire provisions of Addis Ababa II. The new law code favored a civil government of local councils under the TNC.

Initially, Aideed cooperated by asking Admiral Howe's support for a reconciliation conference between southern Somalia and the nearby province of Galcayo, which had not been under UNITAF control. Howe approved the meeting but insisted the UN, not Aideed, must sponsor it. Believing Howe's decision was evidence that the UN subverted his leadership, Aideed rejected the UN sponsorship and renewed his verbal attacks against the UN. Using Radio Mogadishu to broadcast charges that UN officials were asserting colonial authority, Aideed urged Somalis to boycott the UN conference on Galcayo by attending his alterative meeting.

Under these circumstances, Howe's conference on Galcayo reached no agreements, and after the conference, UNOSOM II officials decided to challenge Aideed by using coercive methods to assert UN strength. When U.S. intelligence reports indicated hostile forces were preparing attacks on UNOSOM II, Howe ordered troops to inspect the warlords' depots for heavy military equipment that UNITAF had ordered kept outside its security zones.

The clash with Aideed began on June 4 after Admiral Howe announced that UNOSOM II would enforce the March 26 Addis Ababa disarmament agreement and close down Radio Mogadishu because of its UN criticism. UN troops would inspect and inventory the weapons storage facilities in southern Mogadishu, an area dominated by Aideed. Although an official in Aideed's group warned UNOSOM II not to launch the inspection without consulting Aideed, Howe and Bir ignored the warning.

According to a UN investigation of the June 5 incident, Admiral Howe had sent Pakistani forces in armored personnel carriers on loan from the United States to carry out the UN weapons inspection. When the Pakistanis arrived at the buildings where the weapons and Radio Mogadishu were located, they faced protesters angered by UN policies. As the Pakistanis later left the buildings, Aideed's militia ambushed them and, simultaneously, his forces attacked a UN food distribution center elsewhere in the city. When Aideed's militia pinned down Pakistani troops, General Montgomery called in the U.S. Quick Reaction force to join Italian armored vehicles in dispersing Aideed's men. The firefight killed twenty-four Pakistanis and wounded fifty-six other UNOSOM troops. Aideed's followers celebrated by mutilating the Pakistanis' dead bodies and displaying them in public.

Because of attacks in two parts of Mogadishu, UN officials concluded the attacks were planned and strongly condemned Aideed. In New York, UNSC Resolution 837 of June 6 identified the attacks as "calculated and premeditated" and authorized all necessary measures against those responsible plus the disarmament of all Somali parties as agreed at Addis Ababa. Admiral Howe and Boutros-Ghali perceived Aideed as the number one enemy and demonized him as the obstacle preventing peace. Although some investigators said the UNOSOM II inspection provoked the June 5 incident, the UN insisted the Addis Ababa agreements permitted such inspections to control the warring factions' armaments.

UN peacemaking efforts now focused on the hunt for Aideed to punish the most powerful group in Mogadishu. Initially, Admiral Howe and General Montgomery minimized American participation in the hunt by using Pakistani, Nigerian, Moroccan, Italian and Malaysian units. These UNOSOM II units employed air attacks, ground sweeps, and arms searches in Aideed's enclaves. On June 17, after Moroccan forces suffered heavy casualties during their search, Howe offered a $25,000 reward for information leading to Aideed's arrest but found no informants. Many Somalis, however, accepted Radio Mogadishu's complaints about the UN and sympathized with Aideed. As a result, neither Howe's reward for Aideed's capture, coercion by UNSOM II forces nor a four-month search by an additional four hundred U.S. Army Rangers and Delta Force commandos revealed Aideed's hiding place.

In Washington, Clinton became more closely involved in Somalia policy, stating at a press conference that Aideed's forces were responsible "for the worst attack on UN peacekeepers in three decades. We could not let it go unpunished." A 1994 U.S. Senate Armed Forces Committee investigation indicated the president began a series of actions which he later admitted made the United States responsible for the October 3 disaster that ended U.S. intervention. In June, Clinton's advisers were divided about the proper policy to adopt. Admiral Howe wanted Aideed punished, but General Powell and Defense Secretary Les Aspin favored negotiating with Aideed. Talks with Aideed never occurred, but the White House sent CIA agents to Somalia to track down Aideed.

The CIA never found Aideed, but an unsuccessful raid to find him in

July and two incidents in August led to Joint CIA-Delta Force efforts to capture Aideed. A July 12 raid on "Aideed's headquarters" by the U.S. Quick Reaction Force seized documents, communications equipment, and armaments but not Aideed or his military officers. The QRF helicopter gunships killed fifty-four Somalis and wounded many more, although the UN claimed only twenty-four Somalis died. Most of the Somali casualties were not Aideed militants but clan leaders meeting in the building. There were no U.S. casualties, but angry Somali mobs attacked and killed four Western journalists, whose bodies were displayed before international television cameras. The journalists were Hansi Krauss of the Associated Press and Dan Eldon, Hos Maina and Anthony Macharia of Reuters.

Following the July raid, Aideed told his men to "kill all Americans," and General Montgomery asked President Clinton to dispatch additional special forces and heavy military equipment to Somalia. The State Department favored the additional U.S. firepower, but members of the U.S. Congress objected. Secretary of Defense Les Aspin and General Powell also opposed additional U.S. forces, but after a remote-control device exploded under a U.S. vehicle and killed four American soldiers on August 21, General Powell obtained Aspin's consent to send four hundred U.S. Ranger and Delta forces, a proposal Clinton approved. Nevertheless, Aspin refused to deploy the heavy tanks, Bradley Fighting Vehicles and additional AC-130 Specter gunships that Generals Montgomery and Garrison had requested.

As these additional troops left, Aspin voiced his fears that even greater military efforts would be needed to secure Somalia and urged the UN to undertake a more realistic program to create political groups that could bring peace to the region. Former President Jimmy Carter and many congressional critics urged a reevaluation of U.S. policy, while the Italians and French opposed the search for Aideed. UN Secretary-General Boutros-Ghali resisted changes in UN policy because he claimed all future UN peacekeeping efforts would be endangered if Aideed were not arrested.

The arrival of four hundred Delta and Ranger forces increased UNOSOM II military raids between September 5 and 15, and casualties escalated in Mogadishu, including the killing of Somali women and children. Although four Americans were killed in an August ambush, Aideed usually attacked Nigerian, Moroccan, Pakistani and Italian forces, which suffered twenty-one killed and forty-six wounded before October 3. And although the U.S. Delta-Army Ranger forces arrested many Somalis and rounded up a few of Aideed's officers, innocent Somalis and some relief workers, they never captured Aideed.

On September 25 after the downing of a U.S. helicopter killed three Americans, Congress quickly passed a nonbinding resolution asking the president to obtain congressional approval if U.S. forces remained in Somalia after November 15, 1993. Clinton wavered, however, until October 3, when U.S. Rangers experienced a disastrous episode, immortalized in the movie *Black Hawk Down*, based on the highly acclaimed account, *Black Hawk Down*, by investigative reporter Mark Bowden. The Rangers raided the Olympic Hotel in Mogadishu, where they captured twenty-four Aideed militants. On leaving the hotel with their prisoners, the Rangers were confronted by a contingent of Aideed's militia, who shot down two U.S. Black Hawk helicopters and surrounded the Rangers. For four hours, the U.S. Quick Reaction Force and UNOSOM II units engaged Aideed's troops in battle. UNSOM II suffered its worst casualties in a single battle, including the death of eighteen Americans and one Malaysian and the wounding of seventy-eight Americans, nine Malaysians and three Pakistanis. Somalis also captured U.S. Chief Warrant Officer Michael Durant and dragged his injured body through Mogadishu's streets while television cameras relayed the event to worldwide audiences. Durant survived, but the television reporters seldom noted the Somalis had sustained an estimated 312 deaths and 814 wounded.

Aideed's tactic of "killing Americans" achieved its goal. A previously apathetic U.S. public focused its anger on American policy in Somalia. Under severe pressure, Clinton reviewed his options in Somalia and consulted with congressional leaders. On October 7, he announced U.S. withdrawal plans. He ordered U.S. commanders to stop hunting Aideed and said all U.S. troops would withdraw by March 31, 1994. Clinton admitted the UN erred in seeking Aideed's capture, but the United States would try to negotiate Somalia's political reconciliation. Until the United States withdrew in 1994, Clinton helped UNOSOM II peace efforts in Somalia, appointing Robert Oakley to begin conciliation talks with the factions.[24]

Following the tragedy of October 3, Oakley returned to Somalia but could not persuade the warlords to end Somalia's political disorder. He did convince the militants to avoid interference with the U.S. troop departures, and on March 3, 1994, the last American soldiers left Somalia, leaving the U.S. public with the question, how did America go from feeding Somalis to fighting them?[25]

Boutros-Ghali asked the UNSC to reduce its Somalia mission in order to facilitate political reconciliation. On March 25, UNOSOM II forces were reduced to 1,900 troops and ordered to avoid conflict. The smaller UNO-

SOM II troops were units from nations such as Pakistan, Egypt, Zimbabwe and Morocco. But UN peacemaking efforts failed, and on November 4, the UNSC voted unanimously to withdraw entirely from Somalia. In March 1995, U.S. ships off the coast of Somalia assisted UNOSOM II's safe departure that ended UNOSOM II's mandate.[26]

The UN failed to achieve peace, but humanitarian agencies continued to provide relief and rehabilitation assistance to the clans while civil strife continued throughout 1996 and 1997 as new contenders competed for power. Aideed's claim to be president of Somalia was contested by Ali Mahdi and by Osman Hassan Ali (Atto), who led five Mogadishu subclans to attack Aideed in July 1996. Atto failed to capture Mogadishu's airport, but Aideed was wounded and died during surgery.

Aideed's death intensified the fighting after his son Hussein Mohamed Aideed was chosen SNA president. Hussein's mother had taken him to the United States during the 1980s, where he became a U.S. citizen and served with the U.S. Marines during Operation Restore Hope in 1993. In 1996, he returned to Somalia to replace his father as president of the SNA and continue the fight against Atto and Ali Mahdi. Hussein Aideed also had to contend with Islamic fundamentalist radicals who organized projects to "clean up" Mogadishu while converting Somalis to the Shiite Islamic concepts advanced by Iran's government since 1979 and by their disciples in Sudan and Egypt.[27] A ray of hope came from Cairo in December 1997 when, after four months of talks, Hussein Aideed and Ali Mahdi signed a "Declaration of Principles." They promised to launch reconciliation conferences beginning in February 1998 and to prepare a transitional government charter. Nonetheless, Somalia remained a dangerous place for years to come, the memory and lesson of which cast a haunting shadow over future international peacekeeping missions. And, for the United States especially, "Mogadishu" and "Somalia" were no longer place names but rather cautionary shorthand for political disasters to be avoided at all costs. The lesson was plain for all to see.

CHAPTER 4

A GLOBAL WEB OF RISK: COMPLEX CRISES IN A GLOBALLY NETWORKED WORLD

Yes, we all live in a house on fire, no fire department to call; no way out, just the upstairs window to look out of while the fire burns the house down with us trapped, locked in it.

—Tennessee Williams

The U.S. experience in Somalia demonstrated the costs and limits of humanitarian intervention. Intervening powers must be skilled in dealing with the complexities of the situations into which they send their armed forces. Publics must also be prepared to accept the potential cost in military casualties. Somalia was but one example of how a complex crisis can contain dynamics that will mutate swiftly, unpredictably and catastrophically. Recognition of the limits to intervention has not, however, been accompanied by recognition of the limits of intervention per se as a means to halt or prevent conflict. The obvious lesson of U.S. interventions in Afghanistan and Iraq in the first decade of the twenty-first century is that Cold War strategic paradigms are of limited use both for analyzing and responding to the challenge of Islamist terrorism. Likewise, strategies to promote human security that are uninformed by local circumstance and broader societal dynamics are doomed to the same fate. Complex crises thus require a framework of analysis that can accommodate complexity and permit the formulation of a global outlook on interconnected human security issues.[1]

In many parts of the world, globalization is not so much leading to the demise of the state as exacerbating conflicts over the very legitimacy of states that have smoldered for decades. Many of the world's states are nations in name only with political elites exercising little or no direct control over every part of their assigned territory. Contemporary conflicts in North Africa, the Middle East and South and Southeast Asia need to be analyzed against a backdrop of decolonization and persistent disputes over the legitimacy of states in which the institutional furnishings of independence—bureaucracy, parliament, legal system and territory—were not accompanied by popular acceptance of their legislative reach.

THE "IDEA OF THE STATE" IN SUDAN

The 2005 Nairobi Comprehensive Peace Agreement brought an end to the twenty-year conflict (1983–2004) between Khartoum and the Sudan Peoples' Liberation Army (SPLA). The conflict claimed an estimated 1.9 million lives caused by the lethal "dynamic" of combat, famine and disease. A parallel peace process covering warring factions in the western Sudanese region of Darfur was underway following the 2004 UN-brokered Ndjeema cease-fire, but in Darfur the killing continued. U.S. State Department estimates placed Darfur's death toll at between 63,000 and 146,000 people by late 2005—most killed as a result of fighting between the government-backed nomadic Arab militia and the *Janjaweed* (a Fur word meaning "hordes") on the one hand and the multi-ethnic Sudanese Liberation Army and the Justice and Equality Movement (JEM) on the other. UK and INGO calculations cite 300,000–400,000 dead by early 2007.[2] For every death, thousands were displaced, generating localized and transborder humanitarian crises. From the 1980s to 2007 at least 9.5 million people were displaced by conflict in Sudan. Sudanese refugees are scattered across the globe, but three-quarters remain crowded into camps in their own country,

3.5 million of these clinging precariously to life in Darfur. Their plight is further complicated by protracted civil war in neighboring Chad, which in turn generates flows of refugees into Darfur.

According to Alex de Waal, the UN, U.S. and European nations struggled to find a mechanism to fulfill their responsibility to protect African Muslim and non-Muslim Sudanese, who were alike the victims of government-sponsored violence in Darfur. Intervention with an "African" face came via the African Union, but AU peace monitors and, subsequently, AU peacekeepers were hobbled by Khartoum's resistance to UN "interference" and the inability of the UN Security Council to agree upon a formula to deal with the humanitarian crisis. Not least, there was understandable reluctance from Washington for U.S. forces to become embroiled in a situation similar to that of Somalia circa 1993.[3] China too was reluctant to support UN intervention—because of extensive Chinese investment in Sudanese oil infrastructure and China's leaping energy demands. Also, peace was clearly still to be accepted by all sides in Sudan. Yet from advocates on the floor of the U.S. Congress to human rights campaigners on the ground in Sudan, agreement was universal that Darfur was Africa's next Rwanda.

POLITICAL TRAJECTORIES

As with many colonial inventions, Sudan was a state in name only, with Khartoum barely in control of its assigned sovereign territory. A patchwork of different tribal groups divided by ethnicity and by the currents of Islamic and Christian conversion were incorporated into a single political entity by Britain and Egypt at the end of the nineteenth century. The trajectory of state formation (table 4.1, T1) reflected the consequences of unresolved tensions surrounding tribal, religious, and state identity. Because of its proximity to Egypt and the Middle East, northern Sudan was drawn into the Islamic and Arab orbit by Egypt in the early nineteenth century with Islamization and Arabization proceeding in tandem (table 4.1, T4). British-Egyptian collaboration in creating a new state on the Upper Nile to protect British interests in the Middle East further strengthened the position of the Islamized north vis-à-vis the underdeveloped south. Applying the traditional colonialist "divide and rule" principle to governing Sudan as a British protectorate, Britain treated the south as a separate entity to the economically more advanced north, thus creating and perpetuating a trajectory of regional rivalry (table 4.1, T3).

State formation inevitably perpetuated resentment of the northern-

Table 4.1. Political Trajectories in Sudan

	Early Nineteenth Century	1898–1955	1956	1964–1972	1972	1983–2001/2005	2001 (2005)	2004
T1	Egyptian hegemony	British-Egyptian "condominium" superceded by British protectorate	Independence: "Equatorial Corps" mutiny (1955)	CW1	Addis Ababa Agreement: SSLM	CW2	PA1: SPLM (Comp. Peace Ag.)	Ndjaema Cease-fire, SPLM, Darfur
			Sudan's Coups: 1958, 1969, 1985, 1989 (1999)					
T2			1958–1969: Sudan's first military ruler, President General Ibrahim Abboud, takes first steps to Islamize the south	1969–1985: President Colonel Jafar Muhammad Numayri declares Sudan secular state under 1973 constitution; ten years later reverses policy but fails to save his presidency 1985–1989: Elected president Al-Saddiq al-Mahdi resumes aggressive Islamization of southern Sudan 1989: Coup installs President General Omar Hassan al-Bashir. Hassan al-Turabi (leader of Sudan's National Islamic Front and Muslim Brotherhood); extreme Islamist "right" increases influence in Khartoum				

T3	Classic imperial "divide and rule" policy applied to north and south "Arabized" north governed separately from "African" south	North-south division becomes political inheritance of newly independent Sudan Southern officers rebel against northern dominance in the military	Southern rebellion culminates in Addis Ababa Agreement granting limited southern autonomy President Numayri makes and then breaks Addis Ababa peace agreement after oil is discovered in Upper Nile	1989–1999: Apex of National Islamic Front (NIF) and Hassan al-Turabi SPLM agrees to peace in return for assurance of future autonomy SSLM breaks away to negotiate separate treaty 1999: Al-Turabi and NIF pushed aside by President al-Bashir. Policy of Islamization continues in Sudan.
T4	Egyptian influence spreads south to Fur sultanate Fur sultanate incorporated into British protectorate of Sudan in 1916	Impact of southward migrations of nomadic Arab peoples from Saharan regions of Sudan Economic competition, "War of the Tribes" in 1980s; sporadic fighting continues between ethnic Fur and Arab tribes over access to land and water Climate change promotes desertification in northern Sudan; water and pasture become increasingly scarce 1978: Oil discovered south of Nuba Mountains; international oil interests drawn into Sudan's civil war		

Sources: Daly, *Darfur's Sorrow*; Meredith, *State of Africa*; Coll, *Ghost Wars*; and De Waal, "Darfur and the Failure of the Responsibility to Protect."

Notes: T1: colonialism and conflict in Sudan; T2: the military and political Islam; T3: north-south tensions; T4: resource competition in Darfur.

dominated government among geographically and culturally distant and marginalized rural peoples. Northern Sudanese was Muslim, better educated and enjoyed better economic opportunities. Resentment between "Arab" and "African" Sudanese were thus well entrenched before independence in 1956. The western area of Darfur was integrated into the larger entity of Sudan through a combination of Mamluk Egyptian and British imperial expansion. The sultanate was, according to M. W. Daly, a premodern African Muslim polity in which African Muslim rulers presided over a multi-ethnic and multireligious population.[4] Under British tutelage, Darfur suffered from the same neglect accorded to southern Sudan, adding a second layer of resentment toward Khartoum that compounded long-standing objection to northern political influence and the increasing inward migrations of nomads from northern Sudan and Chad seeking new pastureland. Independence brought no tangible benefits to the peoples of Darfur.

Divisions within the state were manifest immediately in the brief "Equatorial Corps" mutiny of August 1955. A reaction by junior officers of the Southern Corps against northern dominance in the military, the mutineers met with swift and brutal force. As M. W. Daly writes, the episode prefigured later, more protracted armed struggles between Khartoum and a coalition of southern insurgent forces, the Southern Sudan Liberation Movement (SSLM).[5] Division was also evident within the northern ruling elite (table 4.1, T2). As in Nigeria, the Congo, neighboring Chad and indeed across northern and much of sub-Saharan Africa, in Sudan, parliamentary rule by fractious coalitions proved unworkable. In its place came a succession of ruthless military rulers who used parliamentary machinery merely to endorse their political decisions. Civil war broke out in the south in 1964 and endured until the 1972 Addis Ababa Peace Agreement between Khartoum and the SSLM. Criticized by Daly as "vague in detail," the agreement was, according to Meredith, "a rare example in Africa of a negotiated settlement to a civil war."[6] The Addis Ababa compromise allowed the formation of a distinct Southern Region with its own political institutions and the right to raise taxation sufficient to fund regional autonomy, but, decisively, Khartoum retained its sovereign right to garrison the south.[7]

International developments worked against a durable resolution to the civil war. Economic grievances rather than a shared sense of regional or cultural identity maintained unity among the disparate multireligious and multi-ethnic SSLM.[8] Hence the southern rebels were viewed in Washington as Soviet sympathizers. U.S. economic and military assistance inevitably flowed toward the anti-Soviet Khartoum government while Washington turned a blind eye to the brutality of the Sudanese state toward southern rebels and their supporters. From independence until the late 1970s the Sudanese state was secular. President Colonel Muhammad Numayri (1969–1985) enshrined secularism in the 1973 constitution that confirmed a major condition of the peace between north and south. However, a reinvigorated and radicalized form of Islam, manifest in the Muslim Brotherhood, changed the complexion of Sudan's government.

The growing electoral appeal of Sudan's religious right gradually translated into political influence. To better navigate factional politics in Khartoum, Numayri admitted Muslim Brothers into senior government posts—a move that opened the way for Islamists to press for the alignment of Sudanese and Shari'a or Islamic law. Before his removal in 1985, Numayri abandoned secularism, declared his intention to convert all of Sudan and tore up the 1972 peace agreement, plunging the country back into civil war. Islamization was vigorously pursued by President Al-Saddiq al-Mahdi, leader of Sudan's largest Islamic political organization, the Umma Party. Al-Mahdi was the first to arm local Arab militias and use them against rebel forces, in this instance the *murahaleen*, presaging the tactics later used by his successors in Darfur.[9]

Precipitated by the military's disapproval at the prospect of a new peace agreement between the government and southern insurgents, yet another coup in 1989 installed General Omar Hassan al-Bashir as president, and he, in return for electoral support, granted substantial governmental authority to Hassan al-Turabi, a Muslim Brother, and his National Islamic Front (NIF). That the NIF did not command majority support among Sudan's Muslim population did not dissuade al-Turabi from pursuing an even more extreme vision of an orthodox Islamic state. Al-Turabi maneuvered the government to the far right of political Islam, negating the possibility of compromise with southern rebels and drawing the country into a dangerous if loose liaison with Islamist terror groups.

THE COMPLEXITIES OF DARFUR

Religion and identity do not map out precisely the lines of division in Darfur. Distinct tribal identities, religious beliefs, languages and competing economic interests between sedentary and nomadic peoples cut across issues of land ownership and support for or opposition to the central government. The Arabic or Arabized nomadic camel-herding tribes, *Abbala*, are constantly in search of adequate grazing lands in a region where decades of desertification have taken their toll. African tribes, including the Fur, Masalit and Zaghawa, are predominantly farmers and form the majority of Darfur's population. Tribal skirmishes became commonplace during the 1980s in what is known collectively as the "War of the Tribes." Into this mix poured armaments and an increasing array of armed militia from neighboring Chad. Darfur became a safe haven for Chadian militia and the Libyan-backed Islamic Legion fighting against the non-Muslim African government in Ndjaema. In political science terms, these "factors" created an environment conducive to the escalation of violence.

Resource conflicts are endemic in Sudan and are exacerbated by the country's steadily degrading natural environment. Successive major climate change–related droughts have hastened desertification, placing additional pressure on land and food resources. Poor resource and infrastructure planning over the years led to extensive deforestation and consequent soil erosion. These factors, combined with rapid population growth, created a level of social and environmental stress that contributed directly to the humanitarian tragedy unfolding in Darfur.[10]

By the time fighting in Darfur intensified, the _Janjaweed_ had been active there for the best part of six years.[11] Endemic poverty compounded crosscutting religious and tribal rivalries over land and political influence. This latter point is, according to Daly, crucial to understanding the vectors of conflict in Darfur and Sudan. Western analysis, he argues, has too easily succumbed to the simplifications of Huntington's clash of civilizations thesis, leading to erroneous conclusions of religious war between Muslim and non-Muslim, Arab and African. Rather, the demonstration effect of peace negotiations between Khartoum and the SPLA encouraged SPLM and JEM leaders to also press the central government for regional autonomy. Thus the violence in Darfur has the characteristics of both an intercommunal conflict and civil war inflamed by Khartoum's support for progovernment Arab Muslim militia.[12]

IDEOLOGY AND CONFLICT

In contrast to the first period of civil conflict (1964–1972), the second Sudanese civil war evidenced a distinct ideological dimension. The Sudan Peoples' Liberation Movement adopted an explicit socialist message to counter the Islamic reformism of Khartoum and as a consequence was treated by the U.S and the West as pro-Soviet. Political Islam in the NIF-dominated government was shaped by the teachings of the Muslim Brotherhood, of which al-Turabi was leader in Sudan. An anti-imperialist protest movement originating in Egypt in the 1920s, the Brotherhood advocated a return to "pure Islam" drawn from a literal translation of the Qur'an. Jessica Stern writes that the Islamist message of its founder, Hassan al-Banna, was inspired by extreme ideologies at both ends of the political spectrum. The methods employed by European fascist and Communist movements excited him, as did their particular "fascination with violence."[13] The Brotherhood's appeal was broadened in the 1950s by the viscerally anti-Western Sayyid Qutb, whose militant rhetoric garnered support among the millions of Muslims left behind by the postwar global economic boom. Driven out of Egypt, the movement spawned offshoots across the Middle East (Hamas being the most notable), also reaching into North Africa and South Asia.

With the Muslim Brothers ensconced in Khartoum, Sudan became a haven for Islamic militants from the Middle East. Osama Bin Laden famously found refuge there after expulsion from his native Saudi Arabia. A latecomer to the Afghan war against the Soviets, Bin Laden was, writes Steve Coll, a fringe fighter who rarely experienced close combat, yet he was able to cultivate an image of a "veteran" soldier of Islam. Deeply disturbed at the stationing of Western troops on Arabian soil after the 1991 Gulf War, Bin Laden incurred the suspicion of a Saudi government increasingly sensitive to the activities and popular appeal of Islamist militants and their financial backers. Bin Laden fit both descriptions. In Sudan, Bin Laden established a construction company, poured money into infrastructure development projects and secured import and export "incentives" from a grateful government. It was from his base in Sudan that Bin Laden allegedly forward-planned the 1998 attacks on U.S. embassies in Tanzania and Kenya. Sudan had helped incubate Bin Laden's Al Qaeda network. Though Bin Laden relocated to Afghanistan after his expulsion by al-Turabi in 1996, establishing new training camps under the protection of a triumphant Pakistan-backed Taliban government, his terror cells and plans in Africa remained intact.[14]

U.S. interest in Sudan derived from Cold War strategic concerns. In the late 1970s and early 1980s, socialism appeared to be gaining ground in the Horn of Africa and across North Africa and the Middle East. After the discovery of oil south of Sudan's Nuba Mountains on the Upper Nile, the American oil major Chevron secured concessions from Khartoum, which hoped oil would be eventually piped to a government refinery on the Red Sea. Strategic and economic self-interest meant that the United States provided support to Khartoum against the SPLM which, as said, Washington thought pro-Soviet. Reflecting the official thinking that influenced Washington's relations with the entire Islamic world, U.S. strategists believed Islam presented an impenetrable shield to Communist ideology. In winding back aid to Sudan after 1989, U.S. influence waned, but Washington was still able to exert sufficient pressure to force Bin Laden's expulsion.

Given this diplomatic success, U.S. power was, one might think, significant enough to also exert pressure over Darfur. However, Washington's influence was eroded by the expansion of Chinese mining capital into Africa. With civil war raging across its oil concessions, Chevron pulled out of the Sudan in the early 1990s, after which al-Bashir developed the country's oil infrastructure, including the Red Sea pipeline, with investment from Chinese and Malaysian oil interests. With China's diplomatic support at the UN and substantial investment from the China National Offshore Oil Company (CNOOC), Khartoum was in a stronger position to resist international calls for large-scale intervention in Darfur. Still, al-Bashir ejected al-Turabi and the NIF from his government in 1999 and since September 11 has rebranded his government as a U.S. ally against Islamic extremism—a much higher strategic priority for U.S. policymakers. Washington is also concerned that any visible increase in the U.S. military presence in North Africa could likely backfire by radicalizing Muslim opinion and enhancing the appeal of the Islamists. In prosecuting its global war on terror, the U.S. military quietly expanded its operations in East Africa, working with governments rather than against them to suppress Islamist activities in the Horn of Africa.[15]

Self-determination for the southern Sudan is broadly supported by the international community, but Khartoum is unlikely to concede the region's lucrative oil resources.[16] For its part, the United States prefers not to antagonize or bring about the balkanization of Sudan or East Africa. With U.S. military resources stretched by interventions in Afghanistan and Iraq, humanitarian intervention is left to a hybrid UN-African Union presence. The International Crisis Group declared the 2006 Darfur Peace Agreement "a failure." The United Nations Mission in Darfur (UNAMID) has proved ineffectual, with reports of serious divisions between UN and AU staff and complaints of underresourcing.[17] Intervention, if it is to work, has to be supported by the world's most powerful states, but as already mentioned, the international community is divided, and the priorities of the United States and its allies lie elsewhere.

HEGEMONIC INTERVENTIONS

With regard to military interventions in Afghanistan and Iraq, the United States abandoned the cautious approach to humanitarian crises in the 1990s—from Rwanda to Bosnia. Despite repeated attempts by the Bush administration to justify continued military involvement in Iraq as a humanitarian imperative, U.S. interventions in both countries satisfied perceived strategic priorities justified by an ill-conceived "global war on terror." While the U.S. mission in Afghanistan received UN blessing, both Afghanistan and Iraq were cases of hegemonic intervention in defense of U.S. strategic self-interest—namely, to eradicate the threat of further terrorist attacks on U.S. soil and on overseas assets. In the case of Iraq, subsequent events have proven the strategic doctrine upon which military action was based to be seriously flawed.

SOUTH ASIA AND THE MIDDLE EAST

Multiple layers of complexity between local and global politics expose the superficiality of Huntington's civilizational logic and the ill-conceived paradigm of the "Global War on Terror." Ethnic diversity rather than religion is at the center of subnational politics in the disputed Indian province of Jammu and Kashmir (hereafter Kashmir). As Navnita Chadha Behera writes in *Demystifying Kashmir* (2006), the lines of political division within Indian-controlled Kashmir are not congruous with religious belief, and hence the "Hindu-Muslim paradigm" does not explain the roots of conflict and confrontation there. Kashmir is a multi-ethnic region where the aspirations of different Muslim ethnic groups range between support for integration into Pakistan or accommodation with India, which is also home to a large Muslim minority.[18] Yet Kashmir has been a flash point in relations between India and Pakistan since partition and independence in 1947, and the standoff between two nuclear powers frequently invites international speculation about the prospect of nuclear war on the subcontinent.

Competing Indian and Pakistani claims derive from the confusing array of expedient compromises made at the time of Indian and Pakistani independence (table 4.2, T3). The partition of Hindu-majority India and Muslim-majority Pakistan was marked and marred by a violent upsurge in sectarian violence and in a communal violence "bloodbath" in which Hindu and Muslim turned against each other. Kashmir, a princely state within the British Raj, was predominantly Muslim but ruled by a Hindu

Table 4.2. Trajectories of Risk in South Asia

	Eighteenth Century	Nineteenth Century	1907–1922	1922–1979	1979–1989	1989	1996	2001	2002
T1	Afghan protostate emerges	Afghanistan: A buffer state between Russian and British empires	British Afghan protectorate	Independent statehood for Afghanistan	Soviet invasion	"Civil" war between mujahideen factions and Afghan state	Kabul falls to Taliban	September 11	Northern Alliance and U.S.-led coalition defeat Taliban
T2				Afghan state increasingly dependent upon Soviet support. 1970s attempts to secularize Afghan society	Afghan opposition coalesces around Islam and the defense of Islamic values	Pakistan backs Islamist Taliban in preference to other opposition groups (United States endorses Pakistani policy and supplies cash and armaments)	Pakistani Islamist groups relocate from Afghanistan to Kashmir after Soviet withdrawal in 1989	Parliamentary government restored in Kabul but heavily dependent upon foreign aid and foreign military forces	
								Taliban seeks refuge and regroups inside Pakistan's Northwest Frontier	

	British Indian empire emerges, spanning modern-day Pakistan, India and Sri Lanka	1947: Partition of India and Pakistan followed by independence for both	Pakistan seeks to extend influence into Central Asia
T3		1948: India and Pakistan go to war over Kashmir 1949: Kashmir partitioned along line of control 1965: Pakistan initiates conflict with India over Kashmir 1971: Pakistan and India fight war over status of East Pakistan, which becomes Bangladesh 1984: India seizes Pakistan-controlled Siachin glacier 1988: Pakistan adopts strategy to acquire Indian-controlled Kashmir by subterfuge using Islamist militants	1999: Kargil War initiated by Pakistan's occupation of Indian-controlled Kargil in Kashmir
T4	1945: World's first and only nuclear attack by United States on Hiroshima and Nagasaki	1974: India tests first nuclear device and becomes world's seventh nuclear power	1998–1999: India and Pakistan conduct nuclear tests in contravention of NTB Pakistan now world's eighth nuclear power

Notes: T1: cycles of invasion, occupation, and resistance in Afghanistan; T2: Islamism, Pakistan, and Afghan politics; T3: Pakistani-Indian rivalry in Kashmir; T4: Pakistani-Indian nuclear rivalry.

maharajah, Hari Singh, who exercised his prerogative and chose integration with India. While the majority sentiment favored Kashmiri independence, Kashmiri Muslims accepted the decision in the belief that the region would be granted a greater measure of autonomy than if it were incorporated into Pakistan. Islamabad's attempt to reverse the decision by force merely increased Kashmiri opposition to integration with Pakistan, but the 1947–1949 conflict led to the partitioning of Kashmir, and since this time Kashmir has come to symbolize the rivalry between the two countries.

Indian and Pakistani forces face each other down across the icy Line of Control that reaches high into the Himalayan foothills to the Siachen Glacier. To this day, it is part of Pakistan's official worldview that Muslim-majority Kashmir is naturally and rightfully part of Pakistan, and it is Pakistan's pursuit of this objective by subterfuge that paved the way for Islamist radicalism to take hold in South Asia. Pakistan's Inter-Services Intelligence (ISI) trained and deployed Islamist militia against Soviet forces in Afghanistan after the Soviet invasion of 1979. Following the Soviet withdrawal in 1989, these Islamist militias were set loose in Kashmir to wage a guerrilla campaign against Indian forces—a campaign that endured until the U.S.-led intervention in Afghanistan in 2001.

Islam, or more precisely the Muslim Brotherhood, connected Sudanese, Afghan and Pakistani politics. The Pakistan-based offshoot, Jamaat-e-Islami, was instrumental in assisting Pakistani intelligence and the CIA to create an Islamic front to hobble the Soviet war machine in Afghanistan during the 1980s. The Afghan civil war, which began before the Soviet invasion, is yet another example of how U.S.-Soviet strategic rivalry exacerbated human suffering in the developing world. The conflict and the external interests clandestinely deployed to prolong the fighting exemplify the failures of old-world realpolitik and illustrate how new conflicts often have their origins in failed solutions to old wars. The old Great Game of nation-state rivalry opened the door to a new form of asymmetrical warfare led by a transnational Islamist movement, motivated less by territorial ambition than by antipathy to Soviet socialism and American capitalism. A paradox of the war on terror, this movement profited from Western oil dependence as Saudi petrodollars rolled in to finance "jihadi" campaigners.

AFGHANISTAN

A Pashtun-dominated Afghanistan emerged in South Asia toward the end of the eighteenth century and survived as a buffer state between British

India and the Russian empire, becoming a British protectorate in 1907 (table 4.2, T1). From the time of gaining its political independence little over a decade later until the Soviet invasion of 1979, the country's ethnic divisions and tribal loyalties were subordinated to the idea of the Afghan state.

Afghanistan was all but a Soviet satellite state in 1979 when Soviet troops moved in to prop up the country's increasingly unpopular Communist government. Muslim resistance to secular socialism escalated into all-out civil war, driving millions to seek refuge in neighboring Pakistan, where Islamabad nurtured the Taliban and then turned it against Soviet troops. Covert U.S. assistance for the Taliban and Muslim mujahideen fighting the Soviet invasion was predicated on the same thinking applied in Sudan: that Islam could be mobilized to counter Marxist ideology and arrest Communist expansion. Washington determined to turn Afghanistan into a quagmire, a Soviet Vietnam that would further degrade Moscow's capability to challenge U.S. interests elsewhere.

Determined to break the Soviets, the CIA failed to recognize the dangers of sponsoring radical Islamic forces that were as much anti-West as they were anticommunist.[19] American arms and combat expertise materially assisted the ISI to build up its Islamic front in Afghanistan. Pursuing a short-term Cold War objective, the authors of U.S. policy in Central and South Asia, from CIA station chiefs up to the State Department and the White House, did not or could not foresee the consequences of their strategy for strategic security in South Asia or the global heroin trade. In the wake of the Soviet withdrawal in 1989 and the consequent suspension of U.S. assistance to the *mujahideen*, Afghan factions turned to the illegal opium trade to fund their internecine struggle for control of the state, feeding a cycle of violence and corruption that engulfed neighboring Pakistan.[20] Still backed by Pakistan, the Taliban succeeded in imposing a harsh Islamic regime over much of the country, including the capital, Kabul, which fell in 1996. But the harshness of the regime and the ongoing armed struggle between the Taliban and forces loyal to mujahideen commander Ahmad Shah Massoud and grouped under the banner of the Northern Alliance fueled the production of and trade in opium.

Sponsorship of Islamic militancy in Afghanistan enabled Pakistan to marshal Islamist groups in support of its ambitions in Kashmir. With the Soviets out of Afghanistan and the Taliban in the ascendancy, the ISI turned its attention back to Kashmir. Having failed to secure control over the disputed state in open warfare with India, Pakistan turned to the armed wing of Jamaat e-Islami, the Lashkar e-Toiba, to carry out guerrilla attacks against Indian forces and foment civil unrest in Indian-held Kashmir. To Pakistan's dismay, Kashmiris resented their intervention and did not rise up against India as the ISI had hoped. President Pervez Musharraf's ill-fated and ill-conceived occupation of Kargil in Indian-controlled Kashmir was a reckless strategy against a nuclear-armed state that viewed Pakistan's nuclear program with equal suspicion (table 4.2, T3 and T4). Effectively, two nuclear-armed powers were fighting a guerrilla war in Indian-held Kashmir that inflamed nationalist sentiment on both sides.

Dependent upon U.S. military aid, Pakistan was forced to support U.S. intervention in Afghanistan. The history of Afghanistan post–September 11 need not be rehearsed here, but despite ending Taliban rule in 2001, the U.S.-led coalition and an elected Afghan government grapple with persisting ideological, factional and economic divisions that suggest the reconstruction of Afghanistan is a substantial and long-term challenge. The future for Afghanistan without long-term international assistance is bleak. The government of President Hamid Karzai has yet to establish popular legitimacy among the country's multi-ethnic population, is unable to control all parts of the country and is hence powerless to prevent the movement of civilians and Taliban combatants across the frontier between Afghanistan and Pakistan.

Cross-cutting strategic objectives of the U.S. and Pakistan governments exacerbated the refugee crisis along Pakistan's Northwest Frontier, which remains a seedbed of Islamic radicalism and, at the time of writing, a safe haven for Osama Bin Laden's Al Qaeda movement (and, allegedly, Bin Laden himself). The Pakistan military has long coveted a submissive or at least pro-Pakistan government in Kabul, while Pakistani politicians see Afghanistan as a gateway to Central Asia, in particular a passageway for Central Asian oil to reach the Indian Ocean through Pakistan.

It is a double irony that Pakistan's entry into the geopolitics of oil should rebound on it to the extent that the Islamist militants still defying central authority along the Northwest Frontier should be so well endowed with Saudi finances. The jihad against the Soviets and, at the time of writing, U.S.-led international forces in Afghanistan, has created a terror industry in which the children of poor tribespeople are drawn into radical madrassas and inculcated with the Islamist mission to drive the United States from the Arabian peninsula and rescue Islam from the corrupting influences of secular Western culture. The mission and the message resonate throughout the Middle East to South and Southeast Asia. It appeals to the poor and undereducated, who resent Western affluence and for whom jihad is as much an economic as a religious calling. It also appeals to the educated middle classes who, like those who flew jets into the Twin Towers and the Pentagon, despise Western values, societies and cultures.

RECONSTRUCTING IRAQ

The U.S.-led invasion of Iraq was a case of strategic preemption, not an instance of humanitarian intervention. Predicated on false intelligence, the invasion precipitated a counterinsurgency that transformed Iraq into a magnet for Islamist militants connected to Al Qaeda. U.S. forces were confronted with a three-dimensional conflict: Ba'athist resistance fighters against the United States and coalition partners, Shi'ite militia loyal to Islamic cleric Moktada al-Sadr against Sunni Ba'athists and periodically against the United States, and Islamist "foreign fighters" against the United States and its coalition partners. From the U.S. invasion and occupation of Iraq in 2003 to October 2008, a total of 4,124 U.S. service personnel died, with another 30,000 injured.[21] The dryly named Iraq Body Count Project estimates Iraqi civilian violent deaths as of December 31, 2007, to range from 78,280 to 85,289 people.[22]

The human impact of the invasion and occupation extends beyond combat to rising infection rates and poor health care, sanitation and nutrition. Taking these factors into account, the British medical journal *The Lancet* estimated that some 654,965 more Iraqis had died from 2003 to 2006 than would have died had there been no invasion and occupation.[23] Insurgent casualties are "unknowable."

Cast retrospectively as a humanitarian intervention to rid Iraq of an evil dictator, the U.S.-led invasion in 2003 was based upon flawed or massaged intelligence. The greatest failure of judgment stemmed from Washington's hubris over the presumed universal appeal of American ideals and a naive belief in the transferability of liberal democracy.[24]

Iraq, formerly Mesopotamia, is one of Britain's more enduring colonial legacies. Split into three distinct regions, dominated by Kurds to the north, Sunni Muslims in the center around Baghdad and Shi'ite Muslims to the south, the former British protectorate was predominantly tribal. It is a country born out of and into violence. The rationale for creating an Iraqi state was undoubtedly influenced by the presence of substantial oil reserves discovered in the 1920s, which Britain hoped to secure for British

---

THE RATIONALE FOR INVADING IRAQ

- Iraq either possessed or was well advanced in the development of weapons of mass destruction (WMD). This contravened UN Security Council resolutions and posed a threat to regional order.
- Saddam Hussein's Ba'ath regime sponsored terrorism in the Middle East and had links with Al Qaeda. His removal would thus deny resources to terrorists.
- The removal of Saddam would be popular with Iraqi people and would engender an upsurge in popular democratic sentiment.
- Democratic politics would take root once the Ba'ath regime's apparatus of control was dismantled, and Iraq would become a beacon of secular modernism in the Islamic world.

---

oil interests. Britain used military force to compel warring factions to accept their incorporation into the Iraqi state in 1920.[25] Cold War rivalry between Washington and Moscow in the 1980s and 1990s exacerbated regional tensions. The 1979 Islamic revolution in Iran elevated Iraq's strategic value. The Ba'ath Party regime of Saddam Hussein proved to be particularly brutal, but it was courted by both the United States and the Soviets. Iraq made extensive use of chemical weapons against Iranian forces during the Iran-Iraq war (1980–1988) with full knowledge of both the United States and Britain. Both subscribed to the Iraqi war effort in a vain attempt to provoke counterrevolution in Iran and bring down the Islamic theocracy of the Ayatollah Khomeini.[26]

The saga of Iraq from 1990 to 2007 offers a perspective on how the optimism of the immediate post–Cold War era was misplaced. The 1990s were a unique era in international cooperation at the UN—a result of Soviet collapse and Russia's domestic difficulties, which made it necessary for Moscow to be more accommodating toward the United States and the West. This Iran-Iraq war, writes Dilip Hiro, turned Iraq into a heavily militarized country, which both enabled and emboldened Hussein to invade neighboring Kuwait in 1990 to expropriate additional oil revenues with which to settle war debts and maintain a large standing army. UNSC Resolution 660, which called upon Iraq to withdraw from Kuwait after Iraq occupied the tiny Gulf state on August 2, 1990, was followed by the imposition of UN sanctions, which failed to dislodge Hussein and his family from power. Military intervention, when it came on January 15, 1991, was authorized by the Security Council but clearly served the foreign policy aims of the United States, which devised and led the international intervention in Kuwait. These aims were the eviction of Iraq from Kuwait and the restoration of the regional status quo, the protection of Saudi oil fields and the preservation of Saudi royal power. Despite the transparency of U.S. policy, the UN Security Council vote on Resolution 678 went 12–2 with no permanent members exercising their right of veto. China abstained.[27]

A brief First Gulf War ended with Iraq's expulsion from Kuwait. Conscious of regional sensitivities, the United States allowed surviving Iraqi units back into Iraq and opted not to remove Saddam Hussein by force. Instead, the international community, led by the United States acting through the UN, sought to bring about Hussein's downfall and that of his Ba'athist regime by maintaining sanctions. The Iraqi economy depended upon oil, which constituted nearly two-thirds of all exports. Following a public outcry in the West about the plight of ordinary Iraqis dying for lack of medical treatment, medicines and food, Resolution 986 allowed limited sales of Iraqi oil, the proceeds of which could be used to purchase food and essential medical supplies from 1995 onward.

The UN Oil-for-Food Programme and thus the entire set of Iraq sanctions was subverted by collusion between Baghdad and many reputable businesses, including the Australian wheat marketer AWB Ltd., carmakers DaimlerChrysler and Volvo, and Siemens and ChevronTexaco, to name but a few.[28] For geostrategic reasons, the United States tolerated sanctions busting by Iraq's neighbors, and much illegally purchased Iraqi oil found its way into the West. Sanctions were designed to bring down Hussein without recourse to armed intervention. Companies profited from the abuse of human rights in Iraq and undermined a UN regime designed to avoid a war which, when it eventuated, cost hundreds of thousands of lives.

Post-Hussein Iraq struggled to become the exemplary Islamic democracy idealized by U.S. planners. Instead, historic internal fissures came to the fore as Shi'ite and Sunni insurgents fought each other and the U.S.-led coalition, with Al Qaeda–linked Arab volunteers joining the fray to prevent any prospect of peaceful accommodation. The financial cost of the ongoing military occupation of Iraq, by early 2008 an estimated US\$3 trillion, eroded the U.S. economy's capacity to absorb the costs of sustaining military hegemony and to combat economic crises at home. In terms of U.S. international credibility, as in Vietnam, U.S. military pride was dented by the ability of ill-equipped militia to inflict heavy casualties upon U.S. forces. National support for the war fell away dramatically after the initial swift removal of Hussein, raising questions about the preparedness of the U.S. voting public to support future military interventions of any kind.

A GLOBAL SECURITY DEFICIT

At the international level, the degree of major-power consensus evident in the 1990s is rapidly evaporating as China becomes more economically assertive in defense of its development imperatives and as Russia scrapes the rust from its superpower image. In a multipolar world, the United States, despite its military advantages, cannot exert the same degree of influence over its competitors as it did a decade ago. The era of U.S. hegemony is long past, but the sharp decline in credibility for the international order that the United States largely constructed, occasioned by the travesty of the Iraqi intervention, leaves a substantial deficit in global security. The reputation of the United Nations was shredded by the Oil-for-Food scandal. International support for future interventions in potentially more threatening strategic crises or in Darfur will be more difficult because of mistrust over U.S. intentions and UN complicity with U.S. foreign policy goals—reinforced by the UN's global security rhetoric. This is perhaps the greatest long-term, we might say intergenerational, cost of U.S. hegemonic interventions in the Islamic world.

REFUGEES AND ASYLUM SEEKERS

Refugee flows are indexes of the uneven geographic distribution of human insecurity. From nineteen million "persons of concern" counted at the end of 2004, the United Nations High Commission for Refugees (UNHCR) was by the end of 2006 responsible for nearly thirty-three million such persons, the vast majority of whom were internally displaced persons (IDPs) (see table 4.3). A refugee recorded as such in official statistics is a person accorded official refugee status by UNHCR and entitled to join the commission's resettlement program. Asylum seekers are people seeking sanctuary in another country but who have yet to be assessed as genuine refugees. IDPs are persons fleeing conflict or environmental stress who remain resident in their own country, not all of whom become the responsibility of UNHCR. As such, they are located on the fringes of the world's major conflict zones, are the least accessible to humanitarian aid and are the largest

Table 4.3. Regional and Global Refugee Flows: UNHCR Persons of Concern, 2004–2006, Selected Data

	Year End (2004)				Year End (2006)			
	Refugees	Asylum Seekers	IDPs	Total	Refugees	Asylum Seekers	IDPs	Total
Chad	259,880	—	184	260,064	286,743	83	12,686	399,457
D.R. Congo	199,323	354	13,843	213,520	208,371	94	1,075,297	1,814,990
Sudan	141,588	4,271	662,302	845,867	196,200	4,460	1,325,235	1,622,222
Uganda	250,482	1,809	91	252,382	272,007	5,812	1,586,174	2,169,028
Tanzania	602,088	166	2	602,256	485,295	380	—	485,679
Africa	**3,022,606**	**206,931**	**1,199,762**	**4,859,135**	**2,607,600**	**244,100**	**5,373,000**	**9,752,600**
Afghanistan	30	29	159,549	1,127,468*	35	5	129,310	527,710***
China	299,375	44	—	299,419	301,027	83	—	301,130
Iraq	46,053	1,353	—	241,403**	44,406	2,180	1,834,368	2,181,189
Islamic Rep. Iran	1,045,976	48	698	1,046,722	968,370	1,019	—	969,492
Pakistan	960,617	8,157	—	968,774	1,044,462	2,677	—	1,047,141
Asia	**3,471,342**	**56,157**	**1,327,537**	**6,899,589**	**4,537,800**	**90,100**	**3,879,100**	**14,910,900**

Continued

Table 4.3. (Continued)

	Year End (2004)				Year End (2006)			
	Refugees	Asylum Seekers	IDPs	Total	Refugees	Asylum Seekers	IDPs	Total
France	139,852	86,151	—	152,160	145,996	39,571	—	186,471
Germany	876,622	86,151	—	973,392	605,406	52,801	—	668,226
Netherlands	126,805	28,452		155,257	—			
Serbia (and Montenegro)	276,683	40	248,154	627,476	98,997	6,074	227,590	419,099
UK	289,054	9,800		298,854	301,556	12,400		314,161
Europe	**2,067,920**	**269,763**	**899,730**	**4,430,012**	**1,612,400**	**244,000**	**542,200**	**3,430,000**
Australia	63,476	5,022	—	68,498	68,948	1,420	—	70,368
Canada	141,398	27,290	—	168,688	151,827	23,593	—	175,420
United States	420,854	263,710		684,564	843,498	124,223	—	967,721
Global Total	**9,236,763**	**837,926**	**5,427,029**	**19,195,383**	**9,877,700**	**743,900**	**12,794,300**	**32,865,300**

Source: UNHCR, State of the World's Refugees 2006, 2004
Note: 2006 refugee data for Serbia only
*Includes 940,469 returned refugees
**Includes 193,997 returned refugees
***Includes 387,917 returned refugees

and least globally visible refugee group. Between 2003 and 2007 at least 1.2 million Iraqis were displaced into neighboring countries, with a further 700,000 displaced internally by rising sectarian violence.[29] By the end of 2006, there were 1,834,368 Iraqi IDPs recorded by UNHCR (see table 4.3). Clearly, the use of force and the clandestine pursuit of national strategic interest has not fashioned a solution to endemic instability in the Middle East or South Asia.

Globally, as many as six million refugees returned home during 2002–2005, 4.6 million of which returned to Afghanistan to confront escalating conflict between a resurgent Taliban, the Afghan army and international coalition forces. Unresolved and resurgent societal conflicts have added further to the list of displaced peoples. The refugee exodus from Darfur into Chad and Uganda rapidly increased UNHCR responsibilities in each country during 2004–2006, but as stated earlier, the vast majority stayed behind to face the daily threat of violence and disease—and the vast majority of these are women and children. Dealing with this escalation in human misery is doubly problematic because, as with Sudan, many governments resist UN involvement in their domestic affairs for fear of the political consequences arising from increased exposure to international scrutiny. Compounding this tragedy, in the developed world, governments are reluctant to accept increased numbers of refugees for fear of a domestic political backlash from right-wing nationalist groups eager to whip up racial anxieties.

IDENTITY CRISES

The mass movement of people is a globalizing phenomenon to which governments in the developed world have responded defensively with tightened border controls and selective immigration. Many people in Western societies, affected by the rapid internationalization of national economies and exposed to the vicissitudes of unpredictable and volatile global markets, sense globalization as an assault on their national identity.[30] Refugee flows frequently reflect the hydraulics of economic exchange and wealth concentration in the global economy. The promise of better living standards draws thousands of illegal migrants from North Africa into Spain, from where they disperse throughout Europe. This clandestine migration creates friction at the interstate level between Spain and Morocco, especially given the latter's proximity to the Iberian Peninsula.[31] But a fraction of the world's vulnerable or at-risk persons arrive as asylum seekers in

Western countries and present at worst a negligible economic burden to the receiver.[32]

The 1951 Refugee Convention and the UNHCR were created to protect refugees, but the realization of a genuinely humanitarian refugee regime remains subordinated to the pursuit of narrow state interests. According to Michael Barnett and Martha Finnemore, the global policy balance has over the course of the past sixty years tilted against resettlement toward "voluntary" repatriation or refugees. Indeed, repatriation is celebrated by the UNHCR as a "durable solution" to refugee crises. This shift in emphasis, they argue, followed the mass exodus from Indochina in the 1970s and 1980s. Immigration is bound tightly to concerns about national identity.[33] All states bear the imprint of human migrations, forced and free, making cultural diversity the international norm rather than the exception. Yet today, the prevailing cultural reflex is to assert singular and exclusive identities.

In the West, public perceptions of risk associated with refugee and minority migrant groups are easily manipulated by extremists in receiving states who imply that each new arrival poses a threat to "national cohesion." Anticosmopolitans, from white supremacists to Al Qaeda, welcome any hardening of identities wrought by fear and revulsion of cultural or religious difference in a world of seeming chaos and deepening insecurity. Gaining in political popularity, extreme nationalist movements in Europe propagandize refugees as threats to national cohesion and incite systematic racist attacks on minority neighborhoods. Both refugee groups and culturally diverse migrant populations are singled out for their alleged unwillingness or inability to shed their cultural ways and assimilate. Linked to globalizing pressures generated by inequities and human rights abuses at the global periphery and to popular fears in the West about the implications of economic globalization for living standards and national identities, this hardening of nationalist views is yet one more political undercurrent that threatens to reverse progressive global trends.

Both the policies and the rhetoric deployed by Western governments against asylum seekers are designed to dampen public sympathy for genuine and extreme human suffering. The chaotic nature of refugee dispersal and the geographical location of refugee camps mean that the resettlement process does not function according to developed countries' notions of efficient social service, thus rendering as absurd the notion of an orderly "queue" of refugees waiting patiently to be called forward. Frontline camps bordering on "hot" combat zones in countries can be extremely unsanitary and dangerous, doubly so if the receiving country adopts a hostile attitude and uses force to expel or deter refugees, as often happens in the early stages of a refugee crisis.

The chaotic nature of refugee crises and the geographical location of refugee camps mean that resettlement processes do not run in a prompt and orderly manner, according to developed countries' notions of efficient social service. More than half of all refugees are women who, along with children, bear the greatest burden of forced migration. Violence against women, including rape, is commonplace in Central African refugee camps and those in Central and West Asia, rendering women more at risk of severe physical harm and of contracting sexually transmitted diseases.[34] Regarded as collateral damage in the traditional security paradigm, such individualized suffering must be recognized and factored into any security calculus.

GLOBAL TRAFFIC

More subtle forms of displacement render people vulnerable to kidnapping and trafficking. Searching for higher wages to supplement meager agricultural earnings or compensate for the lack of economic opportunity at home, seasonal urban workers are vulnerable to exploitation. In Indonesia, the Philippines and Thailand, the capital cities have attracted masses of rural people who congregate around the city centers and on the city outskirts in slum areas—living in appalling squalor. Young girls are sold by their parents, coerced or otherwise volunteered to work in the global commercial sex industry, where they swell the ranks of the estimated 700,000 to two million persons trafficked internationally each year.[35] Similar scenarios are played out across Eastern Europe, where the opportunities presented by the global market for drugs, commercial sex and illegal access to a better life spice the region's transition from Communism to capitalism.

Immigration controls can be circumvented by sophisticated smugglers and traffickers—usually one and the same. Elaborate global people-smuggling routes take people into the United States across the U.S.-Mexico border. Integrated services networks of forgers, money launderers, carriers and government officials responsible for localized border control are integral to the process. A salient feature of global criminal activity in the past decade is the transformation of criminal organizations parallel to the changing structure of business organizations in the legitimate economy. Criminals have diversified their business activities to incorporate, for example, drug and people trafficking, to take advantage of "upstream" and "downstream" or "vertical" business "synergies."[36] As legitimate transnational corporations have diversified their staff to cope with increasingly diverse markets and have developed more flexible business strategies including an emphasis upon flexible partnerships and networks in preference to rigid hierarchical structures, so criminal organizations have downsized into flexible, multicultural "brokerages."[37]

An invisible form of globalization, narcotics trafficking is a major transnational industry. As the International Crisis Group reported on the growth of trafficking networks out of Latin America,

> Well-armed, well-financed transnational trafficking and criminal networks are flourishing on both sides of the Atlantic and extending their tentacles into West Africa, now an important way station on the cocaine route to Europe. They undermine state institutions, threaten democratic processes, fuel armed and social conflicts in the countryside and foment insecurity and violence in the large cities across the Americas and Europe. In Colombia, armed groups derive large incomes from drug trafficking, enabling them to keep up the decades-long civil conflict. Across South and Central America, Mexico and the Caribbean, traffickers partner with political instability.[38]

Such criminal activity must be interpreted through a security framework that recognizes them as symptoms of deeper human insecurities arising from underdevelopment and lack of economic opportunity rather than as destabilizing security challenges that can be thwarted only through intergovernmental cooperation. Contrary to the new war thesis, the protracted conflicts that sustain the global narcotics industry have their origins in disputes over the idea of the state dating again from post-1945 decolonization in Burma and the unresolved and violent political rivalry between left and right in Colombia.

A Brief History of Narcotics Control

As obvious as it might seem, criminals thrive on illegality. The modern system of sovereign nation-states, to which codified law is central, defines the boundaries of what is legal and illegal and perversely influences the market price of contraband. Demand drives one side of the market for these goods and services, but the risks of detection and imprisonment set the premiums. Without national legislation to outlaw certain drugs— heroin, cannabis, cocaine and a suite of amphetamine and methamphetamines—there could be no illegal global drug trade. Although opium has been around for centuries, only in the twentieth century was opium and its derivative, heroin, outlawed. Poppies decorated the countryside of Bengal and what are now northern Burma, Thailand and Laos (the Golden Triangle), and the opium extracted from these poppies was historically traded largely for its medicinal qualities. The Dutch, Portuguese and British sought a share in this regional opium trade, over which Britain established a virtual monopoly by the mid-nineteenth century.

In British Burma colonial officials collected opium in lieu of taxes from northern hill tribes where opium cultivation flourished. Opium production in other British colonies likewise grew rapidly to service the China market forced open by the Opium Wars (1839–1842). In this way Britain maintained a favorable trade balance with China and ensured the viability of its Asian empire. Western opinion, however, began to equate opium consumption with moral iniquity in the late nineteenth century, as reflected in the rise of temperance movements in Britain, the United States and Australia.[39] Temperance fused with racism to cast Chinese immigrant minorities as morally degenerate, thus handing political and business leaders the ammunition to curtail Chinese opium trading. U.S. anti-opium legislation, write John Braithwaite and Peter Drahos, also protected pharmaceutical companies from European, principally German, drug manufacturers. Indeed, it was the German pharmaceutical giant, Bayer, which invented heroin in 1898 and marketed the drug as a nonaddictive cure for respiratory illness. As Braithwaite and Drahos point out, the international moral crusade against opium by the United States also had the geopolitical consequence of undermining British commercial power in Asia.[40] The upshot, however, was to create a black market for opiates.

Higher profits increased incentives to circumvent national legislation, and as Britain still permitted opium cultivation in India, opium and opium-derived narcotics remained legally available in many parts of the world. The League of Nations Convention for the Restriction of the Production and Sale of Opium (1931) was designed to restrict the use of opium to medicinal purposes only, and there is evidence that opium cultivation and illicit sales of opium declined in the interwar years—although this merely raised the stakes of illegal production and trade. The Indochina wars gave impetus to production and trafficking of heroin, which, contrary to Bayer's pronouncements, proved highly addictive and highly popular in the West. Since the UN Convention against Illicit Traffic in Narcotic Drugs and Psychotropic Substances (1988), opium eradication programs and drug seizures have slowed growth in the supply of heroin from northern Thailand and Laos. Still, UN drug control statistics indicate that Golden Triangle opium production doubled between 1986 and 2000, with Burma accounting for the increase.

Poppy eradication remains hindered by the twin dynamics of narcotics demand and intrasocietal conflict. It is no coincidence that opium cultivation is most prevalent in countries affected by prolonged civil war. Afghanistan accounted for 82 percent of global opium production in 2007, with Burma falling a long way behind with 11 percent, down from 28 percent in 2006. For the Burmese government, poppy eradication complements the strategic imperative to deny economic resources to insurgents. For remote rural communities, economic uncertainty coupled with economic hardship strengthens the appeal of insurgents offering protection in return for support. Locked in combat with better-equipped government forces, anti-state forces sustain their struggle through a narcotics-based "war economy" in which the distinction between legitimate and illicit commodities is blurred.

BURMA'S INSURGENCY

The legitimacy of the Union of Burma was challenged from its inception in 1947, in no small part due to the Panglong Agreement, an agreement, writes Martin Smith, "riddled with inconsistencies" but which laid the constitutional foundation for independence. Burma's largest ethnic minorities, the Shan, Karenni, Karen, Mon and Chin, were granted individual states within the Union, but only two, the Shan and Karenni, won the right to secede. Independence demands from the remainder went unheeded by Burmese and British constitutional negotiators. Karen, Mon and Arakhanese preparations for armed struggle were already well advanced before formal independence was received. Once British troops withdrew, fighting erupted between the state and ethnic separatists, initiating five decades of secessionist war that widened into an ideological struggle with the entry of the Burmese Communist Party (BCP) into the fray. Even constitutionally agreed rights to secede were never recognized by the central government, which, despite being civilian and democratic, was dominated by the military upon which it relied to govern the country. Unlike India, where mass political parties emerged under British rule, Burmese politics was shaped by ethnic rivalries and the power of the military. After fifteen years of parliamentary rule, military control was entrenched when General Ne Win

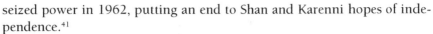

seized power in 1962, putting an end to Shan and Karenni hopes of independence.[41]

Formed in the late 1930s, the Burmese Communist Party was largely ineffectual as a political force. From the 1960s until its disbandment in 1989, the BCP funded its guerrilla activities by monopolizing the production and trafficking of heroin out of northern Burma.[42] Kachin, Shan and Wa separatist movements replaced the BCP and used income from narcotics to supplement dwindling external military assistance. For Khun Sa, the most notorious opium trader in the Shan state in the 1980s and early 1990s, Burma's internal conflicts provided lucrative business opportunities.

Ethnic independence movements occupying territories along Burma's frontiers with China and Thailand likewise created virtual autonomous states.[43] For decades, both China and Thailand derived strategic advantage from the weakness of the Burmese army in adjacent border regions. However, Chinese and Thai attitudes toward Burma changed again as the Cold War came to an end. Seeking to open an alternative trading route to the Indian Ocean, China pressed Burma's State Law and Order Council (SLORC) to negotiate cease-fires with ethnic separatists. Faced with the withdrawal of Chinese military aid, one of the largest of these, the Kachin Independence Organization (KIO), had no alternative other than to accept accommodation with Rangoon.[44] Similar developments soon followed along the border with Thailand. In mid-1995, a cease-fire was negotiated between SLORC and the New Mon State Party (NMSP).

The surrender of Khun Sa in January 1996 eliminated the well-equipped Tailand Revolutionary Council (TRC) and brought Khun Sa's liberated area on the border between Thailand and the Shan State under Burmese control. Opium cultivation continued in upland areas of northern, eastern and southern Shan State, but the trajectory of drug control in the 1990s favored the center. Pressed hard against the Thai border, the Karen National Union (KNU) remained in open conflict with the Burmese state. Kachin and Wa separatists and some units of Shan continued to skirmish with Burmese forces, and the KNU remained the most potent source of military opposition to the Burmese government throughout the 1990s. But the Karen are not a homogeneous or united ethno-nation. As with Burma's other ethnic minorities, there are many expressions of Karen ethnicity and many different ethnic subgroups. Exposing religious cleavages, Buddhist Karens of the Democratic Karen Buddhist Army (DKBA) allied with the SLORC (rebadged as the State Peace and Development Council, or SPDC)

Table 4.4. Opium Cultivation and Trade in Burma and Afghanistan

	Production (hectares)		Farm Gate Price* 2007 (US$)	Export Value* 2007 (US$)	Main Centers of Production
	1996	2006			
Burma	163,000	21,500	72 million	N/A	Shan, Kachin and Wa states
Afghanistan	56,824	165,000	0.76 billion	3.1 billion	Hilmand, Uruzgan and Badakhshan provinces

Source: UNODC, World Drug Report 2007
*Aggregate values

in its campaigns to push the predominantly Christian-led KNU toward the Thai border.[45] While the KNU is not reported to engage in drug trafficking, its campaign for an independent homeland is subject to the same regional and global dynamics that give advantage to the Burmese government and military.

LATIN AMERICA

The U.S. government is at the forefront of international efforts to suppress drug production and trafficking, but it is most heavily involved in Latin America. Washington has long treated the region not only as its strategic preserve but also as a region in which it has a special responsibility. The Monroe Doctrine enunciated in 1823 by President James Monroe warned European colonial powers against pursuing imperial aggrandizement in the Western Hemisphere. At the time, the Spanish and Portuguese empires were in retreat as Latin American independence movements gathered momentum. Within two decades the region was virtually decolonized, save for vestiges of British, Dutch and French power in the Caribbean and along the northeastern coast of South America. The Spanish-American War of 1898 left the United States with, in President William McKinley's eyes, a moral obligation toward Cuba's political and economic development.[46] President Theodore Roosevelt gave substance to the doctrine and set out the grounds for U.S. intervention in Latin America. In terms that resonate with the responsibility to protect (R2P) ideal, Roosevelt argued that should any country collapse into internal chaos, the United States had the moral obligation to exercise "international police power."[47] In application, the doctrine focused on small Caribbean and Central American states where the United States intervened frequently in the twentieth century. However, as Ward writes, "Such direct action was not feasible elsewhere."[48]

According to World Bank researchers, "The only region that would have inequality levels above those found in Latin America is Sub-Saharan Africa."[49] Neo-Marxists of the *dependencia* school emphasize the role of neocolonial forces: former colonial powers and an overbearing United States, which, so they allege, acts historically to suppress the popular political will in favor of conservative military and economic elites.[50] But support for governments deemed favorable to U.S. interests or the dealings of U.S. banks and transnational corporations cannot alone account for the political and economic turmoil of the region's larger states. Indeed, much of the region's difficulties are self-inflicted.

COLOMBIAN DRUG WARS

Colombia's drug wars stunt broad-based economic development and deliver lucrative returns to a powerful few. Although UNODC statistics indicate an overall decline in the area of land under coca cultivation along the Andean ridge, cocaine trafficking out of Colombia, Peru and Bolivia to the United States and Europe was rising as of 2006 (table 4.5). As in Burma, cocaine production in Colombia is driven by complex demand-supply dynamics. There are four principal societal conflict dimensions that allow the cocaine trade to survive: between the Revolutionary Armed Forces of Colombia (FARC) and the Colombian state, the Colombian state and drug trafficking networks that replaced the larger cartels such as the Medellin in the latter 1990s, the Colombian state and the National Liberation Army (ELN) and right-wing paramilitaries and FARC/ELN revolutionaries. For these reasons Colombia is the principal target of Washington's "war on drugs" and the main Latin American recipient of U.S. military assistance and aid funding.

Of all Latin American countries, Colombia experienced the most violent and protracted internal political struggles after independence in 1819. Two elite factions, the "Liberals" and "Conservatives," fought periodic but costly civil wars that prevented the development of political institutions with broad-based legitimacy. The rise of revolutionary movements in the 1960s was preceded by twenty years of political violence between right and left, the "*La Violencia*," unmatched for its brutality in the country's short history.[51] The absence of durable political order limited the capacity of the Colombian state to suppress new vectors of political violence as the Liberal front splintered, with its dissidents joining Marxist revolutionaries to form FARC and ELN. Left-wing insurgents in their early days funded their campaigns through the sale of coffee beans, but coca production and trafficking became the economic staple of conflict by the 1980s.[52] Political authority was further compromised by the reality that drug syndicates had infiltrated the government through the electoral system and the bureaucracy. As in Afghanistan, the state in Colombia concedes substantial territory to non-state groups engaged in guerrilla war and drug trafficking.[53]

U.S. military and law enforcement assistance to Colombia has succeeded in weakening the FARC and undermining larger players in the drug trade, but the socioeconomic drivers of the Colombian trafficking have yet to be removed—even as Colombia enjoys an economic boom in the early twenty-first century. An enduring cause of social inequality, concentrated

Table 4.5. Coca Production in Andean Ridge Countries

	Production (Ha)		Avg. Farm Gate Price* (US$)	Main Centers of Production
	1996	2006		
Bolivia	48,100	27,500	180 million	Chapare, Yungas of La Paz
Colombia	67,200	78,000	1 billion +**	Meta-Guavire, Pacific, Putumayo-Caqueta, Central
Peru	94,400	51,400	285 million	Alto Huallaga, Apurimac, La Convencion-Lares

Source: UNODC, *World Drug Report 2007*
Note: Export prices not stated
*Aggregate potential value of coca leaf
**Coca paste

land ownership, is a feature of former Spanish colonies in the Americas and Asia. Colombian right-wing paramilitaries were formed initially to protect the property and interests of wealthy landowners, who were the insurgents' prime targets. As with the FARC/ELN, however, these paramilitaries moved into drug trafficking and used extortion to fund their expansion, bringing them into conflict with FARC/ELN forces for commercial rather than ideological reasons. As Michael Kenney writes, the Colombian trade was never dominated by cartels but rather consisted of flexible social networks that are much harder to suppress.[54]

Colombian President Alvaro Uribe succeeded in negotiating peace with the United Self-Defense Force of Colombia (AUC) in 2003 and the demobilization of some 31,000 AUC personnel. While peace negotiations between the state and the ELN stalled in 2007, developments in Colombia parallel those in Burma in the mid-1990s.[55] As of 2008, the FARC appeared on the verge of disintegration. One of globalization's many paradoxes, the globalization of crime creates a dynamic that can enhance the territorial reach of central governments and consolidate rather than dissolve nation-states—but not to the extent that trafficking networks are eliminated.

THE BURDEN OF INFECTIOUS DISEASE

Setting aside heart disease and cancer, the burden of disease is heaviest among the poorest sections of societies in the developing world. Unlike war, however, disease is a silent killer, invisible to the naked eye until the symptoms are well advanced. While the victims of war or genocide lie heaped within a limited geographical area, victims of disease are, with the exception of plagues, geographically dispersed. But conflict and disease are closely linked. Infectious disease prevalence rates are an indicator of human quality of life, and in countries where the burden of disease is greatest there is a statistically high incidence of political violence. Data for HIV indicate that the virus thrives in social environments characterized by an accumulation of risk factors, principally extreme poverty and illiteracy, economic underdevelopment and civil conflict. These correlations translate into HIV prevalence rates in sub-Saharan Africa that are more than six times the global average. An estimated 22.5 million African adults and children are infected with HIV out of a global total of 33.2 million known cases (table 4.6).

Though numerically much smaller, a sharp upward trajectory of HIV infections and deaths is also evident in Oceania. Dire predictions of a pub-

Table 4.6.   The Global HIV/AIDS Pandemic, 2007

		Adults and Children with HIV	Newly Infected Adults and Children	Adult and Child Deaths	Adult Prevalence (%)
Global Total	2007	33.2 million	2.5 million	2.1 million	0.8
	2001	29 million	2.2 million	1.7 million	0.8
Caribbean	2007	230,000	17,000	11,000	1.0
	2001	190,000	20,000	14,000	1.0
East Asia	2007	800,000	92,000	32,000	0.1
	2001	420,000	77,000	12,000	<1.0
Eastern Europe and Central Asia	2007	1.6 million	150,000	55,000	0.9
	2001	630,000	230,000	8,000	0.4
Europe (Western and Central)	2007	760,000	31,000	12,000	0.3
	2001	620,000	32,000	10,000	0.2
Latin America	2007	1.6 million	100,000	58,000	0.5
	2001	1.3 million	130,000	51,000	0.4
Middle East and North Africa	2007	380,000	35,000	25,000	0.3
	2001	300,000	41,000	22,000	0.3
North America	2007	1.3 million	46,000	21,000	0.6
	2001	1.1 million	44,000	21,000	0.6
Oceania	2007	75,000	14,000	1,400	0.4
	2001	26,000	3,800	<500	0.2
South and Southeast Asia	2007	4 million	340,000	270,000	0.3
	2001	3.5 million	450,000	170,000	0.3
Sub-Saharan Africa	2007	22.5 million	1.7 million	1.6 million	5.0
	2001	20.9 million	2.2 million	1.4 million	5.8

Source: Joint United Nations Programme on HIV/AIDS (UNAIDS), *AIDS Epidemic Update 07* (Geneva: UNAIDS and WHO, December 2007), 7.

lic health crisis in Papua New Guinea raise security concerns for neighboring Australia should the former Australian-governed territory sink into social chaos. HIV prevalence was 2.4 percent and rising in 2006, with higher rates recorded in the countryside.[56] Sudden explosions of infectious disease can destabilize entire societies and cause serious security crises for neighboring countries. Were such a pandemic to erupt in one or more of the world's most populous and militarily significant states, the consequences could be catastrophic and potentially global in scope. The UN Commission on Human Security painted a worst-case scenario of new HIV infections in China and India rising sharply.[57] From this followed concerns of destabilization in two nuclear-armed states, the risk of internal stresses generating conflict that would spread quickly and uncontrollably.

Proof of the perils of prediction, however, UNAIDS data (table 4.6) indicate that the worst-case scenario of infections reaching fifteen and twenty-five million in India and China, respectively, by 2010 is unlikely to be realized. Total HIV infections for East, Southeast and South Asia combined reached "only" five million in 2006. This does not, however, mean that HIV/AIDS is lessened as a global security challenge.

CONTAGION

With the exception of respiratory illness, HIV/AIDS is the most significant cause of death from communicable infectious disease, according to the World Health Organization. HIV and AIDS are causally related viral infections. The deadly HIV pathogen first evolved in African primates and, according to Alan Whiteside, is thought to have crossed to humans as early as the 1930s. HIV attacks the human immune system, depleting vital CD4 T-cells and leaving the victim defenseless against infection. As the virus advances, a victim's CD4 count drops to a level where the immune system simply breaks down—hence the term *acquired immunodeficiency syndrome*, or AIDS for short. At this point even the most innocuous of illnesses, a common cold, for example, will have devastating effects. Viral and bacterial infections multiply, causing death that can be delayed but only by a prohibitively expensive and rigorous regimen of antiretroviral drug treatments unsuited to the vicissitudes and rhythms of life in rural environments across the developing world.[58]

HIV is transmitted through unprotected sexual intercourse, through needle sharing between intravenous drug users and from infected mother to child. Across the Asian Pacific but mostly in Africa, it is the young working-age population who is most at risk of contracting HIV. The impact of the virus registers in declining average life expectancies and declining workforce productivity in the more seriously affected countries. Effective countermeasures require substantial government investments, but once a society admits to the presence of the pandemic, the spread of HIV can be arrested. HIV prevention programs have impacted the spread of the virus in sub-Saharan Africa, as evidenced by declining infection rates. In new regions of extreme instability, however, primarily Eastern Europe and Central Asia, infections have doubled in the past decade, while mortality has jumped by 600 percent (table 4.6).

Prevalence and incidence rates respectively measure the total number of known cases relative to a country's population and the number of new infections over a given period of time, permitting some future projections. In Thailand HIV/AIDS cases were first reported in the mid-1980s. Within a decade the spread of the virus reached crisis proportions. Human mobility was closely linked with the contagion—and truck drivers identified as a high-risk group of carriers. As mainland Southeast Asia opened up to intraregional trade following the end of Cold War tensions, border checkpoints and border markets became major sites of transmission where prevalence rates exceeded those of the major cities. One mid-1990s estimate envisaged as many as 1.8 million Thais with HIV by the year 2005. The demographic impact of this was predicted to be catastrophic, with Thailand's population declining by nearly three-quarters of a percent in the first decade of the twenty-first century.[59] That these predictions have not yet become a reality suggests that corrective measures adopted by Thailand's government and international aid agencies were successful in at least arresting the spread of the disease. Beyond Thailand's borders, Cambodia's prevalence rate reached 2 percent in 1998 before falling back to less than 1 percent in 2006. The sharp rise was due allegedly to increased risks of infection with the presence of UN peacekeepers in the country following the end to Cambodia's thirty-year civil war. Also a contributor to the higher prevalence rate was the ease of transmission in bordellos ranged along the Thai-Cambodian border.

Importantly, the risk of infection is not gender neutral, and women tend to be the most at risk in developing countries where entrenched sexual mores subordinate the rights of women to control their bodies. Even in countries with more liberal attitudes toward women's rights, women are becoming a high-risk group, with women in Thailand accounting for 43 percent of new infections in 2005.[60] Female labor is relatively cheap and relentlessly exploited throughout Asia. Female guest workers employed as home help from Hong Kong to Singapore, writes Nedra Wirakoon, are extremely vulnerable to sexual exploitation, either casually by those for whom they work or by organized commercial sex and trafficking syndicates. At the heart of this vulnerability sit entrenched perceptions of gender roles.[61] Economic circumstances and a gendered division of labor leave many women and girls with few options to earn income. The death of a husband or parent is financially catastrophic in societies where there are no social support networks beyond immediate family. Indebtedness exposes women and young girls to the risk of being drawn into commercial sex work.

SOUTH AND SUB-SAHARAN AFRICA

Although HIV cases were first detected in South Africa and Thailand at roughly the same time, the South African state responded much more slowly. Thus, while in Thailand HIV prevalence barely exceeded 2 percent, in South Africa prevalence leapt from 0.7 percent in 1990 to 14.2 percent in 1996 and 26.5 percent in 2002.[62] The delay is in part explained by the fact that HIV/AIDS was a disease of South Africa's black population and hence of limited significance to the white minority apartheid governments that ruled South Africa until 1993. There has, however, been a pattern of denial among South Africa's post-apartheid leaders. President Thabo Mbeki was forced to acknowledge the seriousness of HIV after previously questioning the worth of antiretroviral drugs. Responding to economic models that warned of a significant impact upon economic growth, the Mbeki government drastically increased HIV/AIDS-related spending. Even then, South Africa's prevalence rate reached a staggering 30.2 percent with an estimated 5.54 million people infected out of a total population of forty-three million.[63] In stark contrast, Thailand at the height of its epidemic had an estimated 800,000 HIV positive cases out of a population of nearly sixty million.

Those who are unable to comprehend the seriousness of the disease are more susceptible to HIV infection. While both Thailand and South Africa register high levels of adult literacy, low levels of educational attainment work against public recognition of the biomedical facts of HIV. In both countries, "natural" medicines are freely available, which their makers allege can flush the HIV virus out of one's system. In South Africa, the Mbeki government controversially allowed the trial and sale of uBhejane as an anti-HIV treatment. In a serious breach of international HIV funding conditions, the Mbeki government granted an export license for the unregistered and unproven product to German doctor and businessman Matthias Rath. Not until 2008 was Rath banned from selling any clinically unproven HIV remedies by the Cape High Court after a sustained campaign from the South African medical community and health NGOs.[64]

The effectiveness of HIV/AIDS prevention programs is limited by discriminatory practices that are in some cases imposed by international donors. The United States, as do most other aid donors, attaches conditions to its development funds that reflect the values and priorities of the donor country. The adoption of an abstinence-only approach to HIV/AIDS prevention by the Ugandan government came, writes Joseph Tumushabe, in response to a sizable financial carrot offered by George W. Bush. The incentive complemented the conservative thrust of U.S. domestic social policy and the political interests of Uganda's president Yoweri Museveni. An attempt to evangelize rather than accommodate social policy to the biological realities of sexual maturity, male promiscuity and sexual exploitation, the approach exuded the conservative American values of the country's religious right and President Bush.[65] Buttressed by the threat of funding withdrawal, the program was heavily criticized by Human Rights Watch for denying the many risk factors that contribute to infection and transmission and for increasing the risk of infection for Ugandan women in particular. In its 2005 report on Ugandan HIV prevention strategy, Human Rights Watch asserted that

> Abstinence-only programs also fail to recognize that, as in all countries, AIDS in Uganda is a disease of poverty. Many Ugandans live on less than U.S. $1 per day, a situation that has been exacerbated by decades of political violence and civil war. New HIV cases occur among girls trading sex for school fees, women enduring violent marriages because they lack economic independence, and orphans being pushed out into the street and sexually exploited.[66]

This abstinence-only approach was also criticized for promoting a heterosexual worldview and for compounding official hostility toward homosexuals in Uganda, where President Museveni is notorious for his homophobic diatribes.[67] The popular association of HIV infection with sexual promiscuity and homosexuality attaches stigma to HIV sufferers, which leads to ostracism from society and often familial estrangement. In Islamic societies where homosexuality is illegal, the social cost to victims of the virus far exceeds the high price of antiretroviral drugs. Even in more tolerant societies such as Thailand and Russia, treatment is often denied to social groups that arouse the moral indignation of policy elites. While lauding Thailand's efforts to provide extensive drug coverage, Human Rights Watch accuses the Thai government of deliberately excluding intravenous drug users from prevention programs, even though these addicts are the most at risk of contracting HIV from contaminated needles.[68] Alarmingly, in many countries women are frequently denied treatment because they are women.[69]

The level of funding for international HIV/AIDS prevention makes both the issue and the policy machinery within states with high levels of infection a lucrative source of political patronage. Political leaders such as Uganda's Museveni have explicitly tied their electoral fortunes to the disbursement of HIV prevention funds. The Ugandan president's wife has aggressively pursued U.S. Republicans for financial support and personally manages U.S.-funded AIDS education programs.[70] The connections between HIV funding and national politics are also explicit in South Africa. Corruption is difficult to quantify and prove in a court of law, but South Africa sits well down the Transparency International rankings for corruption perceptions.[71] Lack of public oversight for public monies spent directly through the health ministry and indirectly through some nongovernmental agencies ensures that misappropriations occur along the funding "food chain." At the end of this chain is an illegal market for ARV drugs among HIV sufferers unable to access treatment legally through the health system.[72]

THE DYNAMICS OF UNDERDEVELOPMENT

It is difficult to overstate the centrality of extreme global inequalities to contemporary humanitarian crises. Bombed out buildings, fractured streetscapes and the despairing faces of civilians dominate the imagery of humanitarian disasters. The dynamics of human despair are, however, less visible to the naked eye. The invisible risks of illiteracy, discrimination and denial of economic opportunity gather unseen until they manifest in mass protest or political violence. Failures of governance compound human suffering. The risks of official corruption are greatest in countries with limited scrutiny of political and administrative affairs or where illiteracy is so high that the majority do not respond to media revelations of high-level malfeasance.[73] As the anticorruption watchdog Transparency International reported in 2005, rebuilding efforts in countries devastated by war is

THE IMPACT OF HIV/AIDS

Individual

- Declining physical and mental capacity
- Emotional trauma
- Loss of family and social networks
- Death

Family

- Declining level of nutrition for spouse and children
- Likely infection of spouse and children
- Loss of income
- Stigmatization
- Breakdown in family unit

Community

- Declining skills and knowledge base
- Declining economic productivity
- Increased prevalence of and susceptibility to HIV

Government

- Increased costs of health care
- Increased absenteeism in government agencies
- Impaired organizational performance
- Below-optimum economic growth
- Population decline
- Social and political instability—in worst cases

Source: Tony Barnett and Alan Whiteside, *AIDS in the Twenty-first Century: Disease and Globalization*, 2002.

seriously compromised by corruption, no more so than in Iraq. As Peter Eigen summarized,

> Corruption doesn't just line the pockets of political and business elites; it leaves ordinary people without essential services, such as life-saving medicines, and deprives them of access to sanitation and housing. In short, corruption costs lives.[74]

As mentioned, corruption distorts allocation of development funding and acts as a disincentive to international aid donors, but this is not the principal reason for decline in developed country assistance as a proportion of GDP. The UN estimates that UN member states should allocate 0.7 percent of their annual GDP to overseas development assistance (ODA). Globally, however, developed country ODA as measured by the OECD fell in the 1990s, from an average of 0.3 percent in 1990 to 0.22 percent in 2001 before rising slightly after the interventions in Afghanistan and Iraq. Economic transfers from developed to developing countries through foreign direct investment, tourism and the consumption of low-cost manufactures in part counteract this decline in aggregate terms. Guest-worker remittances too, rising from a little over US$100 billion in 2001 to US$233 billion in 2005, of which 71 percent was transferred to developing countries, highlight further compensatory income flows. While World Bank economists advocate the virtues of global free trade, the reality is that global trade is demonstrably "unfree" and that market returns are unevenly distributed across the developing world, creating pockets of prosperity while leaving vast areas in absolute or near-absolute poverty.

The end of the Cold War brought with it the comfortable assumption that liberal capitalism would naturally "correct" remaining economic imbalances in the international system. For three decades after the end of the Second World War in 1945, the international community recognized an explicit connection between poverty and international security. For the Western powers, aid and development assistance served the dual purpose of improving the quality of economic opportunity and dampening the fires of Communist insurgency at the contested global periphery. Declines in ODA are a larger reflection of the same priorities that led to the drawdown of covert U.S. assistance to Afghan rebel forces. Ideological confrontation so dominated strategic perspectives that developed countries ignored the deep societal roots of insecurity.

With 75 percent of the world's wealth concentrated in a handful of rich countries and the majority of the world's Muslims living in developing or underdeveloped countries, it is relatively easy for extremists to portray themselves as the defenders of the poor and the marginalized. Likewise, with so many millions living in near or absolute poverty, Islamists find willing recruits from among the despairing, the disillusioned and the politically ambitious.

World Bank statistics point annually to declining rates of poverty measured as US$1.07 per day in purchasing power parity (PPP). But this does

Table 4.7. Cascading Trajectories of Human Security Risks

| | Risk Factors | Local | Trajectories of Risk | |
			Regional	Global
Sudan	Absence of universal state legitimacy; government discrimination against African minority; North-South economic divide	Political extremism, splintering rebel front, resource competition and human rights abuse	Unregulated population movements (UPMs) Destabilization of Sudan's neighbors, Chad and Uganda Rising tide of Islamic militancy	UPMs Spreading humanitarian crisis in North Africa Islamist terror mission against the West Geoeconomic competition between United States and China
Afghanistan	Absence of universal state legitimacy; extreme poverty; low industrial base; tradition of factional and regional rivalry	Political extremism, "warlordism," drug production and trafficking, human rights abuse	Drug and human trafficking UPMs Political crises and destabilization	Drug and human trafficking UPMs Islamist terror mission against the West
Iraq	Absence of universal state legitimacy; history of political violence between religious and ethnic communities	Political extremism, "warlordism," drug production and trafficking, human rights abuse	UPMs Strategic rivalry Destabilization	UPMs Nuclear proliferation Islamist terror mission against the West Erosion of UN legitimacy in Islamic world and U.S. "loss of face"

Continued

Table 4.7. (Continued)

	Risk Factors	Local	Trajectories of Risk Regional	Global
Burma	Absence of universal state legitimacy; extreme poverty and inequality; history of state violence against minorities	Opium cultivation, secessionism, human rights abuse	Drug trafficking Human trafficking Rising intravenous drug use (IDU) Rising HIV infections	Drug trafficking Human trafficking IDU increases Rising HIV infections
Colombia	Endemic political conflict; extremes of poverty and inequality	Increasing coca production and trafficking, political violence, human rights abuse	All of the above Rising influence of sophisticated organized crime networks	All of the above Rising influence of transcontinental organized crime networks
South Africa	History of racial segregation; extreme inequality and poverty	High rates of urban crime, drug use and sexual abuse of women, rising HIV infection rates and mortality, economic decline	Rising HIV infections Economic crises and political destabilization	Rising HIV infections Escalating humanitarian crises across Africa

not mean that those earning the equivalent of US$1.08 per day and above are not poor. Poverty is multidimensional and hence cannot be gauged by income measures alone. Reflecting the influence of Indian development economist Amartya Sen on development thinking, the World Bank's 2000 *World Development Report* paid particular attention to the nature of poverty and its risks. The report's authors asserted:

> Poor people live without fundamental freedoms of action and choice that the better-off take for granted. They often lack adequate food and shelter, education and health, deprivations that keep them from leading the kind of life that everyone values. They also face extreme vulnerability to ill health, economic dislocation, and natural disasters. And they are often exposed to ill treatment by institutions of the state and society and are powerless to influence key decisions affecting their lives. These are all dimensions of poverty.[75]

Sen's most recognizable contribution to development economics was the concept of human development. Poverty alleviation is fundamental to the achievement of sustainable human development but, writes Sen, this requires not only increases in income but also better state expenditure on health, education and other enabling social goods. Referring to life expectancy in poor countries, he asserted, "The impact of economic growth depends much on how the *fruits* of economic growth are used."[76] Improvements in literacy, nutrition, public health and economic opportunities impact human well-being measured in life expectancy and national economic growth. Without these basic freedoms, he argues, sustainable development is impossible.[77]

Sen lauded the success of East Asian states in achieving high rates of growth and for lifting millions out of poverty. While the East Asian experience indicated that developing countries could, through the adoption of appropriate industrial policies, reduce poverty and increase life expectancies, there are question marks over the possibility of African states following suit. Sight must not be lost of the strategic role of the United States in opening its markets to manufactured goods from Japan and East Asia's rapid industrializers. Unlike Africa, there are few landlocked states in East and Southeast Asia. Thus while colonial governments laid down economic infrastructure, roads, rail and ports that segmented both Africa and Asia according to colonial interests and colonial boundaries, Asian industrializers were able to overcome this disadvantage. Although many newly independent African states entered the world at a time of booming commodity prices, poor infrastructure hindered the passage of goods from rugged interiors to emerging markets in Asia.[78]

The fundamental political consensus upon which human development depends is absent in many parts of the world. The UN Office of the High Representative for the Least Developed Countries, Landlocked Developing Countries and Small Island Developing Countries (UN-OHRLLS) registered fifty least-developed countries at the beginning of 2008.[79] Since the early 1990s, around fifteen LDCs annually experienced serious political violence. Correlating infectious disease, conflict and economic development, Ted Gurr, the United Nations Conference on Trade and Development (UNCTAD) and others detail high rates of violence-related and disease-related deaths in low- to middle-income countries relative to the affluent industrialized world.[80] Two-thirds of the world's population lives outside the industrialized world in countries where political, social, economic and environmental stresses are becoming more acute. As this proportion rises over the next half century, so the frequency and scale of humanitarian crises can be expected to rise.

In Colombia, Sudan, Afghanistan and Burma, long-standing economic disparities compound political rivalries and render current political accommodations fragile at best. Disease, population displacement and crime travel in the wake of instability. Connections between all these dimensions of human security can easily be detected, but durable solutions remain elusive. The view of the international community as encapsulated in UN policy and the development agendas of the European Union and United States are that democratic development is fundamental to sustainable economic and social development. As noted in chapter 2, the risk of conflict is not confined to the developing world. Industrially advanced states in Europe, North America and Asia have fought costly wars in the twentieth century against each other and in defense of colonial empires. In many parts of the developing world, however, conflicts are long running, and while the ideological or religious motives of combatants in Afghanistan or Sudan might appear intractable, the susceptibility of these societies to political violence is increased by the prevalence of poverty, disease and weak or illegitimate governments. Europe was at war with itself for a total of nine years, whereas in Afghanistan, for example, conflict has raged for three decades. In countries torn apart by civil conflict, questions of market openness or export-oriented industrialization are subordinate to the more fundamental issues of political order and basic subsistence. This grim reality has implications for another pillar of human security—human rights.

CHAPTER 5

HUMAN RIGHTS AND HUMAN SECURITY: PRAGMATIC PERSPECTIVES ON HUMAN RIGHTS

Whereas recognition of the inherent dignity and of the equal and inalienable rights of all members of the human family is the foundation of freedom, justice and peace in the world,

Whereas disregard and contempt for human rights have resulted in barbarous acts which have outraged the conscience of mankind, and the advent of a world in which human beings shall enjoy freedom of speech and belief and freedom from fear and want has been proclaimed as the highest aspiration of the common people.

Whereas it is essential, if man is not to be compelled to have recourse, as a last resort, to rebellion against tyranny and oppression, that human rights should be protected by the rule of law.

—Universal Declaration of Human Rights, 1948

Perpetrators of the grossest human rights abuses take extreme steps to hide the evidence of their inhumanity. The mass murder of unarmed men, women and children is a recurring reality despite the evolution of a global human rights regime designed to uphold the value of human life and dignity. Viewed through the crude lens of political realism, human rights do not exist because international human rights law carries no legal force. Yet the idea endures that there are acts that affront human decency and which should be prevented or punished. There are strong pragmatic grounds for asserting the value of and encouraging respect for international human rights. Even allowing for variations in cultural values, there is fundamental agreement around certain basic humanitarian principles—"natural" principles—including the acknowledgment of humanity as the basis of durable political order. In a world of increasing economic complexity, transnational business actors also confront human rights issues affecting investment or supply management decisions. Human rights issues are frequently at the center of contemporary human security crises, from struggles for self-determination to conflicts over natural resources or access to medical care. The practicalities of rights extend to contemporary business practice. As stated in the Universal Declaration of Human Rights, human rights are a pillar of international peace and hence can be conceived as fundamental human security "goods."

SOURCES OF INTERNATIONAL HUMAN RIGHTS

Human rights at the international level depend upon a broad acceptance that there is a higher moral authority to the state. Today's key human rights instruments are clearly the outgrowth of inquiry into natural law in the Western tradition. Natural rights thinking is traced to ancient Greece, where Cynic and Stoic philosophers each in their own way argued that there was a higher law to which they and all citizens of a state were subject and which ought to be mirrored in the laws of the state. Roman jurists recognized a form of universal custom, the *ius gentium*, or laws found to be common to human societies. This empirical basis for natural rights carried through to Christian theologians like St. Thomas Aquinas, who argued that there were fundamental human requirements common to all societies. Thus there had to be common universally binding natural laws deducible through reason.

The notion of subjective rights, rights held by individuals, took hold in the seventeenth century as ideas about sovereignty were recast. Sovereignty derived from the divine right of kings was displaced by the idea that political sovereignty resided in the populace who, by virtue of a contract with their ruler, agree to entrust their safety to the state while retaining the right to withdraw from that "social contract" should any ruler act contrary to the public will. This displacement of religion as the source of political legitimacy was as intellectually liberating as it was politically explosive. Subjective rights justified first regicide, then peaceful revolution in Britain and a little over a century later formed the keystone of the Declaration of Independence and Constitution of the United States of America. The science of observation conferred legitimacy on the right to "life, liberty, and the pursuit of happiness," which the U.S. Declaration of Independence claimed were "self-evident truths." Reason rather than dogma was thus used to define and justify rights "designed to protect morally valid and fundamental human interests, in particular against the abuse of political power."[1] In the seventeenth century, the language of natural rights changed again to accommodate Immanuel Kant's argument that people possessed rights because of their innate moral worth as people. Kantian philosophy is integrated into the wording of the Universal Declaration of Human Rights (1948) and associated covenants which declare that "rights derive from the inherent dignity of the human person."[2]

The idea of a universal moral order is not peculiar or specific to the Western Judeo-Christian tradition. Each of the world's major universal religions, Islam, Hinduism, Buddhism, Taoism and the philosophical teachings of Confucius, assumes a higher authority to the state. Empirical observation supports the contention that Eastern and Western religious traditions accord a high priority to human life and dignity, leading to the conclusion that the right to life is a natural right. However, much of this right might be qualified in different social contexts. While the language of rights evolved in the West, the principles upon which Western rights thinking evolved can be traced through the Qur'an, the *Bhagavad Gita*, and the teachings of Confucius. The Analects contain many specific recommendations against the arbitrary exercise of power, and Confucius enjoins those in authority to cultivate their humanity which, it is asserted, is the source of durable political legitimacy.[3] Such concerns have a contemporary and cosmopolitan ring.

Universalists such as Robert E. Goodin claim an objective "universal morality"—arising from a "convergence" of solutions to common human problems. Arguing from a natural law as custom perspective, Goodin asserts that all societies confront similar moral challenges; from distributive justice to the rights of people against the state, for which they formulate roughly similar solutions based upon roughly similar rules—with some cultural variations in emphasis.[4] Strengthening the claim that there are grounds for agreement between culturally distinct societies, Sumner B. Twiss points out that Chinese delegates were present at the drafting of the Universal Declaration of Human Rights at San Francisco in 1945 where they influenced the wording of the Declaration's preamble to balance the emphasis on Western individualism with acknowledgment of the social orientation of the individual self common to Asian societies.[5] Thus international law could truly be said to be more international than Western and the result of cultural accommodation rather than cultural imperialism.

The Universal Declaration is the fundamental legal instrument underpinning all post-1945 human rights law. The declaration set out minimum expectations for the recognition of fundamental rights defined positively as freedom of speech, association, religion, and movement; and negatively as the freedom from political oppression, from exploitation and from discrimination. The document establishes equality of rights as a benchmark, from the equal right to a fair trial, to the right to a reasonable standard of living, to education and health care irrespective of social class, ethnicity, language or religion and to engage in representative politics. Two attached covenants introduced in 1966 spelled out what are categorized as first- and second-generation rights: the International Covenant of Civil and Political Rights (ICCPR), stating the rights of individuals to free speech, trial by jury, freedom from torture—termed first-generation rights because their recognition is seen as essential for the enjoyment of all other rights; and the International Covenant on Economic and Social Rights (ICESR), setting forth second-generation rights, including the right to fair wages, the right to work and the right to food and shelter, enjoyed free of any discrimination based on gender, ethnicity or religion. Indeed, there has been a significant enumeration of human rights since the declaration came into force, which highlights the complexity of this area of international politics. These key rights documents are: the Genocide Convention (1948), the Refugee Convention (1951), the International Convention for the Elimination of All Forms of Racial Discrimination (1969), the International Convention on the Rights of the Child, the International Labor Organization Convention, the Convention on the Elimination of All Forms of Discrimination against Women (CEDAW) (1979), and conventions addressing torture (1987), migrants (2003) and the treatment of people with disabilities (2006).[6]

What are called third-generation rights, the rights of peoples, emerged in recognition of the special collective rights of minorities and indigenous peoples. The principal instruments asserting this category of rights are the African Charter on Human and Peoples' Rights (1981) and the Declaration on the Rights of Indigenous Peoples (2007). Indigenous rights also come within the purview of conventions addressing biological diversity and intellectual property. While genetic research delivers medical benefits, biotechnologies have allowed food and drug companies to distill and manipulate the genetic structure of plants known to local communities for their medicinal qualities. Thus conventions protecting traditional intellectual property rights to natural medicines from patent laws, falling within the scope of a new category of fourth-generation rights, give added weight to the emerging indigenous rights regime.

"NONSENSE ON STILTS"

The body of international law limiting state behavior in wartime acts as a corrective to the realist position on international human rights. Even though natural rights theory fell out of favor with utilitarian philosophers in the nineteenth century, European governments accepted the principle that there were moral constraints on the use of military force. The Geneva Conventions are an example of international humanitarian law emerging out of a sense of common humanity and moral revulsion at the human consequences of war. Inspired by Swiss businessman Henri Dunant, founder of the International Committee of the Red Cross (ICRC), the First Geneva Convention came into existence in 1864. The convention's focus upon the welfare of wounded soldiers is directly attributed to Dunant's reflections on the cruelties he witnessed in the aftermath of the Battle of Solferino in 1859. Dunant's *A Memory of Solferino* (1862) and his personal fortune were catalysts for the 1864 Diplomatic Conference in Geneva from which the Geneva Conventions draw their name. The sixteen European states in attendance, including France, Italy and Spain, ratified the convention, which accorded certain rights to combatants from opposing armies who were wounded or sick, including the right to medical care.[7] The convention established that that International Red Cross (IRC) should be granted access to war zones, where IRC staff could provide medical aid to wounded soldiers on all sides—in effect codifying the principle of neutrality to the benefit of future generations of aid workers. Three more conventions followed: the second in 1906 codified rights of shipwrecked and wounded sailors; the third in 1929 established the rights of prisoners of war and a fourth in 1949 gave protection to civilians in combat zones. In spite of the brutality of war, the fact that states entered into agreement to limit the effects of war represents more than naive idealism.

A second complementary body of war law, the Hague Conventions of 1899 and 1907, went further than the Geneva Conventions by setting limits on the prosecution of war. The 1899 convention offered a framework for conflict prevention through negotiation or mediation, protocols for declarations of war and rules for the humane treatment of prisoners.[8] Reflecting concern at the impacts of new military technologies, the 1907 convention specifically outlawed the use of poison gas as a weapon of war and aerial bombing—albeit from fixed balloons—but did not ban the weaponization of deadly chemicals. None of the signatories could foresee the carnage of World War One or the extensive use of new chemical weapons by all sides on the western front.[9] While cynically it could be argued that signatories sought to curtail any strategic advantage that potential enemies might otherwise enjoy by the tactical deployment of poisonous substances, the fact is that a significant body of war law persisted beyond the carnage of 1914–1918 and on into the twenty-first century, reflected the potency of humanitarian principles that survive in spite of the repeated horrors of war.

WAR CRIMES

In World War One, moral revulsion at the effects of gas warfare quickly succumbed to the imperative of tactical advantage. In the Pacific War, the bitter fighting between Japanese soldiers and U.S. marines allegedly degenerated into a race war in which combatants regarded each other as less than human and in which no quarter was given and few prisoners taken. On the Russian front, fighting between Russian and German forces was also relentless and merciless. The nuclear bombings of Hiroshima and Nagasaki in 1945 arguably ended what would have been a long and costly war of attrition as the Allies invaded Japan, but the killing of tens of thousands of Japanese civilians ran contrary to the spirit of the Geneva and Hague conventions.

Fundamental differences between Japan and the Western powers were evident in attitudes toward war. War crimes were perpetrated on all sides during World War Two, but the treatment of prisoners of war once removed from the battlefield was a point of difference. Japanese atrocities in

China from 1931 to 1945 and throughout Southeast Asia during the Pacific War were extensive. Contravening the Hague Conventions, to which Japan was a signatory, the right of prisoners of war to humane treatment was ignored. Allied POWs were subjected to torture and summary execution and were used as slave labor on the notorious Thai-Burma railway, where thousands died from malnutrition, beatings and disease.

Differences in martial tradition discussed briefly in chapter 2 in part explain Japan's treatment of POWs. *Bushido*—the Japanese way of the warrior—stressed the virtues of honesty, valor and sacrifice and is said to have encouraged an ethic of fighting to the death.[10] However, Yuki Tanaka argues that Japanese officers inherited a corrupted version of the code, bereft of humanity and overburdened by an ideology of total submission to the emperor.[11] Surrender was thus equated with dishonor, hence Japanese officers, if not the ranks, viewed enemy prisoners in a vastly different light from that intended in international law. Of course, the Nazi dream of an Aryan super-race embodied a perversion of European philosophical ideas and points to equally violent and destructive tendencies in the Western tradition—as did earlier European colonial expeditions into Africa and Asia.

War crimes trials at Nuremberg in Germany and Tokyo in Japan found that individual officers of the state could be held morally and legally accountable for actions taken while acting under orders. That is, German and Japanese soldiers were complicit in the crimes of the states they served and in violation of the higher moral principle to disobey orders that conflicted with international law.[12] The trials demonstrated that with sufficient political will, governments could prosecute war criminals, albeit from the losing side only. However, the prospect of prosecution for breaching international humanitarian law in wartime has resulted in the use of legal advisers in operational deployments. The 1949 Geneva Convention reaffirmed the illegality of attacking civilians in war, even though during World War Two the United States and Britain, both signatories, targeted civilian population centers during bombing raids against Nazi Germany. This marked a trend in military thinking away from the belief that attacks on civilians were a necessary and acceptable strategy to weaken enemy morale and degrade a country's capacity to wage war, although the "accidental killing" of civilians in the course of combat operations remained a gray area. Legal advisers were not employed in battle zones until the Second Gulf War (1990–1991) when the United States and its coalition partners recognized the potential ramifications arising from the unintentional killing of civilians. Military lawyers have since become a fixture in tactical planning for international peacekeeping and peace enforcement operations.[13]

NEW WARS AND INTERNATIONAL LAW

Victors in war have the luxury of determining which higher moral authority holds sway. Thus the appearance of arbitrariness in the enforcement of international laws weakens the foundations of the global human rights regime. This is nowhere more aptly demonstrated than in U.S. treatment of captured Taliban and Al Qaeda cadres in its campaign against Islamists in the Middle East and South Asia. Further evidence of the vulnerability of rights to shifts in strategic doctrine and battlefield tactics, asymmetrical warfare between national and insurgent armies poses new challenges for war law and international humanitarian law. Insurgents using terror tactics discount any notion of moral or legal obligation to international law by appealing to a higher authority—in the case of Islamists, an extreme interpretation of the Qur'an. The nature of terrorist and insurgent activity in Iraq and Afghanistan, where Islamist fighters use civilians as camouflage, has prompted U.S. rethinking of commitments to civilians under the Fourth Geneva Convention. Speaking to the World Economic Forum in Davos in 2006, Secretary of State Condoleezza Rice attempted to reconcile these new realities with a U.S. commitment to the greater global good:

> We do not accept a firm distinction between our national interests and our universal ideals, and we seek to marry our power and our principles together to achieve great and enduring progress. . . .
>
> Though we realize that our ideals and interests may be in tension in the short term, and they are surely tested by the complexities of the real world, we know that they tend to be in harmony when we take the long view.[14]

At the beginning of its antiterror campaign the Bush administration made clear its belief that the United States and the West faced an implacable enemy in Al Qaeda and the global Islamist movement that presented a vast monolithic threat to civilization. Reasons of state were thus invoked to set aside U.S. obligations not just under the UN Charter, but under the Hague and Geneva conventions as well.[15] The "war on terror" is an undeclared war under the Hague Convention and thus a new kind of war, one in which "enemy" combatants are held to have surrendered their rights by engaging in acts of terror. "By literalizing its 'war on terror,'" argues Kenneth Roth, "the Bush administration has broken down the distinction between what is permissible in times of peace and what can be condoned during a war."[16] Hence the suspension of basic human rights for inmates at Guantanamo Bay and the ghosting away of captured suspected terrorists for interrogation in secret locations in contravention of international human rights law—the euphemistically termed practice of "rendering."

LAWS OF EVOLUTION

Humanitarian ideals and reasons of state are rarely in alignment. While legalists assert the inviolability of human rights, political conditions as much as the disposition of political leaders affect how rights are interpreted and respected in practice. For liberal modernizers, political and economic development in the long run leads to greater enjoyment of basic human rights. The world has acquired a growing corpus of international humanitarian law, and this, it can be argued, is a consequence of increasing sophistication and interdependence. At the national level it is possible to plot a trajectory of gradual recognition of rights: political, economic, social and cultural. The collapse of Communism in Eastern Europe was replicated in lesser ways by the demise of military-controlled regimes in Asia and Latin America. Military control gave way to popularly elected governments in Thailand, South Korea, Chile and Argentina. The rule of Chile's General Augusto Pinochet from 1973 to 1989 is characteristic of Latin America's era of military dictatorship from the 1960s to the 1980s. Pinochet came to power in a military coup in 1973 and immediately suspended parliamentary government and banned political parties. Opposition activists were imprisoned, and many were "disappeared"—a euphemism for political execution. But the Pinochet regime could not survive the changing international circumstances brought by the end of the Cold War, and Pinochet eventually succumbed to international pressure, including pressure from the United States, to restore democratic rule.[17] As in neighboring Argentina, parliamentary democracy resumed and with it greater recognition and respect for civil and political rights. As historian Marshall C. Eakin observed:

> Despite an enormously wide range of variations, the pattern in all of Latin America over the last century has been a move toward greater political participation by larger and larger numbers of people from all sectors of society. Although Latin America continues to be a society characterized by a deeply

rooted, hierarchical culture and the concentration of power in the hands of a relatively small sector of the population, these long-standing historical patterns have been substantially attenuated by the growing participation of the vast majority of Latin Americans in electoral politics over the last century.[18]

This turn toward democracy is attributed by Fukuyama to late-twentieth-century globalization of liberal capitalist values, in effect a reassertion of Rostow's liberal modernization thesis. In China, the world's largest totalitarian state, ordinary people are challenging the system. Since the late 1980s, China has pursued a strategy of economic modernization that entailed opening the economy to Western investment and to capitalist enterprise. The change was in part driven by demands from the country's urban middle classes for greater political freedom, which led to the Tiananmen Square protests and massacre in June 1989. Economic modernization offered a release valve for social pressure for political change, but the stresses created in Chinese society by rapid modernization have merely highlighted structural weaknesses within the state. In their controversial book, *Will the Boat Sink the Water?* (2007), Chen Guidi and Wu Chuntao open with the story of a villager from Lixin, one Ding Zuoming, who, in return for challenging the fairness of local government taxes imposed on his village in a time of economic hardship, was first detained by authorities on trumped-up charges and then beaten to death while in custody.[19] The perpetrators of Ding Zuoming's death were investigated and punished by a central government fearful of the potential for political destabilization to ensue from popular resentment toward corrupt party officials at all levels of government.

These events occurred in 1993, but the authors assert similar abuses of power are commonplace throughout China and threaten to undermine China's economic ambitions.[20] Ironically, the Chinese Communist Party has in many ways bettered the lives of peasant farmers, but the ideological commitment to peasant welfare is at odds with actual state practice. Sen recognizes that the reforms of the Mao era laid the foundations for social development, in particular the expansion of literacy and provision of public health care.[21] Economic development and democratization might well be complementary processes, but neither occurs automatically as a consequence of the other, and it is possible for countries, such as China, to maintain high rates of economic growth while severely restricting or even curtailing political participation. The question is how long authoritarian regimes can maintain a viselike grip on the reins of government.

The history of Asia's post–World War Two development demonstrated that authoritarian governments can monopolize political power in times of economic prosperity. Many states retain authoritarian systems of government where, despite formal democratic mechanisms—elections, political parties, parliamentary government—one party monopolizes political power. The ethnic Malay dominated Malaysian government for many decades after independence, maintaining a policy of discrimination against Malaysian Chinese, sectioning off senior government positions from persons of Chinese descent, restricting the number of university places open to Malaysian Chinese, and restricting access to government loans. In breach of the spirit of the Universal Declaration, discrimination was perpetuated to advance the economic and social status of the ethnic Malay population. Criticism of government policy was strangled by strict press censorship justified in the name of stability. According to Mahatir Mohamad, Malaysian prime minister from 1981 to 2005, press freedom was fine "so long as it is not used to rob others of their freedom, dignity, and well being." The argument here was that complete freedom of speech in Malaysia would allow extremists an opportunity to exploit interethnic resentment to challenge the state and thus threaten the stability upon which all other economic and social rights depend.[22]

Debate about human rights in Asia was dominated in the 1990s by the idea of Asian values. The "author" of the debate was Singapore's then-prime minister, Lee Kuan Yew, whose views were widely reported in the Western media and roundly condemned by Western and Asian intellectuals. Lee argued that in "Eastern societies" the rights of the community came before the rights of the individual. Asserting an organic view of society, he argued to the journal *Foreign Affairs*, "In the East the main object is to have a well-ordered society so that everybody can have maximum enjoyment of his freedoms. This freedom can only exist in an ordered state and not in a natural state of contention and anarchy."[23] Speaking in defense of the suppression of democracy protesters at Tiananmen Square, Lee Kuan Yew suggested that the alternative was cataclysmic political disorder in China. In times of rapid economic change, a firm hand was both a necessity and a moral good. To buttress his case, Lee contrasted the Asian experience with the apparent disorder, endemic immorality and rampant crime of Western societies:

> The liberal, intellectual tradition that developed after World War II claimed that human beings had arrived at this perfect state where everybody would

be better off if they were allowed to do their own thing and flourish. It has not worked out, and I doubt if it will.[24]

Perhaps the most potent rejoinder to the cultural relativist critique of human rights comes from Sen, who, like Fukuyama, stresses the diversity of intellectual traditions within "Western" and "Asian" cultures. Asian essentialism or "exceptionalism" stands on shaky historical and moral ground, not least because it is argued the denial of rights is an impediment to the development to which Asian modernizers aspire. Lee invokes Confucian ethics to distinguish between Western individualism and the allegedly Asian ethic of familial and social responsibility, yet as mentioned, Confucianism can be interpreted to support subjective rights. Human rights scholars emphasize the principle of reciprocal obligation on Confucian thought. Students of Chinese philosophy emphasize the humanism implicit in the writings of Confucius and the injunctions for superiors to remember their obligations to their subordinates.[25] The proliferation of Asian human rights NGOs is further evidence that humanitarian values are not "un-Asian."

Rights and the laws that enshrine and uphold them have increasing practical utility in an increasingly complex world. Denial of basic civil and political rights, argues Sen, inhibits the achievement of basic enabling economic and social rights and consequently could be perceived as a drain on a country's economic growth rather than a prerequisite for social stability.[26] Sen's pragmatism negates the arguments of leaders like Mahatir, Lee and Deng, who justify denial of individual rights by appealing to the imperatives of development. Asian countries confront a different array of challenges to those which confronted modern European states during their early stages of state formation. Still, there is an established tradition of cultural borrowing from the West in Asia. As Lawson points out, democracy is itself a word inherited from the West.[27] Asian democracies are not mirror images of Western democratic systems, but the durability of parliamentary regimes in Thailand, Malaysia, Indonesia, the Philippines, Japan and South Korea, despite imperfections, suggests a deep attachment to parliamentary rule as a source of political legitimacy.

To these cultural arguments must be added the political reality that Asian governments have endorsed international human rights law and hence enjoy the rights and privileges of members of the international community, which in turn incur obligations. As Sumner B. Twiss argued,

> The Universal Declaration of Human Rights (1948) was reached through a pragmatic process of negotiation between representatives of different na-

tions and cultural traditions. While it may be true that Western representatives had the upper hand in this process, the simple fact remains that pragmatic negotiation between differing views about the same subject matter was the process of choice, not theorizing about matters of moral knowledge, political philosophy, or even jurisprudence.[28]

There is a danger, however, in dismissing assertions of Asian-style democracy and Asian values as merely smokescreens behind which authoritarian regimes can work to entrench their political dominance. To dismiss the Asian values debate is to ignore lingering resentment over Western colonialism and the enduring presumption of Western cultural superiority and popular attachment to national identities. Advocates of Asian regionalism stress the increasing self-confidence of Asian politicians, business leaders and intellectuals who would not consistently seek to differentiate Asia from the West if it did not guarantee some political returns. As the noted Australian journalist, Greg Sheridan, argues, "The fact that governments are groping to give expression to what they regard as their national genius, their enduring, distinctive national culture . . . indicates a realization that there is something of value."[29] In evolutionary terms, human rights need not be converging upon some ideal point of common agreement.

ISLAM AND HUMAN RIGHTS

Efforts to integrate human rights into Islamic practice are further proof of the evolutionary nature of human rights and of the potential for constructive dialogue to overcome cultural differences. The Organization of the Islamic Conference, an intergovernmental organization of fifty-six Islamic countries from Africa, the Middle East and Asia, developed the Cairo Declaration on Human Rights in Islam in 1990. Premised upon natural rights as revealed in Islamic teaching, the declaration is in many ways complementary to international human rights law and the law of war. Article 1 of the declaration recognizes rights as derived from "basic human dignity" and proscribes "discrimination on the basis of race, color, language, belief, sex, religion, political affiliation, social status or other considerations."[30] The document includes sections specifying the crime of genocide, the rights of prisoners of war and the rights of civilians in conflict. However, women's rights are differentiated from the rights enjoyed by men. The Cairo Declaration assigns a specific gender-based role toward women, which for women's rights advocates is repugnant to CEDAW. Specifically,

CEDAW is premised on the idea that the gender-based differentiation of social roles encourages discrimination and violence against women.

As Michael Freeman points out in relation to the rights of women in Islamic societies, CEDAW calls for an end to the denial of basic rights and freedoms to half the world's population. Yet in many Islamic societies, women are subject to discrimination on the basis of their gender—from repressive dress codes to restrictions on freedom of movement and the denial of the right to tertiary education, or even the right to sign a bank check. Such discrimination constitutes a form of oppression that is not sanctioned by the Qur'an or the Cairo Declaration, which upholds the right to reject and to speak out against injustice.[31] Still, rights campaigners point to a difference in interpretations of justice for women between CEDAW and the Islamic Conference. On this issue, "pragmatic" compromise is unlikely to be acceptable to either side of the debate.

Feminist rights campaigners argue that the struggle for women's rights within Islam is as much a struggle against pre-Islamic tradition as it is against conservative interpretations of the Qur'an.[32] Thus the *purdah* (honor killings), the forced wearing of the *burqah* and female circumcision are not sanctioned by Islamic tradition but instead sustained by customary practice. With regard to modesty of attire, many Muslim women choose to wear the *hijab* and the *burqah* and do not feel their rights in any way compromised. This is a vexed question, for if we are to respect people's rights to their cultural traditions, agreement needs to be reached upon the meaning or boundaries of acceptable cultural tradition for each culture and each social group.

This is difficult when cultural traditions are contested and open to political manipulation. For the Minangkabau of western Sumatra and the Malay State of Negeri Sembilan on the Malay Peninsula, a tradition of matrilineal inheritance means that women rather than men control the inheritance of ancestral property and thus play a central role in local society. This accommodation between *adat* (local custom) and Islam is possible in part because the Indonesian state remains secular and thus tolerant of diverse cultural traditions and practices where these do not conflict with the prevailing state ideology. In Malaysia, family law, including divorce law, is the preserve of Shari'a courts, which entrench a male-dominated social structure for the majority Muslim Malay population. Malaysia responded positively to CEDAW and has taken firm steps to lift the status of women, but in the family sphere, Islamic law discriminates on the basis of gender.

DIVIDING PRINCIPLES

Cairo Declaration

ARTICLE 6:

(a) Woman is equal to man in human dignity, and has her own rights to enjoy as well as duties to perform, and has her own civil entity and financial independence, and the right to retain her name and lineage.

(b) The husband is responsible for the maintenance and welfare of the family.

CEDAW

Recalling that discrimination against women violates the principles of equality of rights and respect for human dignity, is an obstacle to the participation of women, on equal terms with men, in the political, social, economic and cultural life of their countries, hampers the growth of the prosperity of society and the family and makes more difficult the full development of the potentialities of women in the service of their countries and of humanity,

Concerned that in situations of poverty women have the least access to food, health, education, training and opportunities for employment and other needs, . . .

ARTICLE 5:

States Parties shall take all appropriate measures:

(a) To modify the social and cultural patterns of conduct of men and women, with a view to achieving the elimination of prejudices and customary and all other practices which are based on the idea of the inferiority or the superiority of either of the sexes or on stereotyped roles for men and women.

Even for the Minangkabau women of Malaysia, the Shari'a exerts downward pressure on social status. There is a diversity of tradition within Islam regarding the status of women, but it is evident that as globalization challenges established religious identities, women's rights campaigners face a significant anti-Western and conservative reaction to their calls for gender equity, which threatens to reverse the gains of the past two decades.[33]

WOMEN'S RIGHTS

Feminist rights advocates assert the direct correlation between social acceptance of gender discrimination and violence against women. In Burma as in Bosnia, women were sexually assaulted as part of ethnic cleansing campaigns designed to create a generation of mixed-race children. Their inheritance of "hegemonic genes" would dilute primordial attachment to their ethnic group. Rape is used consistently as a weapon of war, but not until the Rome Statute was rape specified as a war crime. Beyond the conflict zone, in refugee camps women do not enjoy the same rights as men because of their special vulnerabilities and entrenched attitudes toward women. Women do not enjoy the same level of safety as male refugees because they are targeted on account of their gender by men in the camps.[34]

Writing for Human Rights Watch, LaShawn Jefferson detailed the connections between a woman's sexuality and family or national pride:

> In far too many countries, the honor of a community or family is still closely tied to control of the sexual activity of women and girls. Male family members often put a premium on female virginity, "purity," or sexual inexperience. Consequently, combatants the world over know that targeting women and girls both inflicts grave harm on individuals *and* symbolically assaults the larger community (or ethnic group or nationality) to which the female victims belong. Until this fundamental fact changes, women and girls will always be at risk.[35]

Discrimination extends to the language of rights and more broadly the language of international relations. Feminist writers charge that human rights instruments are reductive in that they claim to accord equal rights to all irrespective of gender, religion, ethnicity or social class but fail to recognize that each influences how these rights are enjoyed. Human rights law is thus blind to the informal exclusion and victimization of women. As Eva Brems argued in relation to the Universal Declaration,

> We realize now that however well intentioned the drafters of the declaration, their attempt to assume a common human nature inevitably resulted in the projection of their own experiences, needs, and values onto the rest of humanity. Despite the participation of Eleanor Roosevelt, those were predominantly the experiences, needs, and values of well-off white Western Men. The same holds true for developments in human rights theory and practice since 1948.[36]

Official declarations and covenants confer formal rights, but specific societal circumstances shaped by religious, political or economic structures and pressures limit the enjoyment of these rights. The case for differential rights for women rests partly upon the fact that women are singled out for exploitation and abuse by men on the basis of gender. Economic factors heavily influence a woman's ability to enjoy the full range of rights to which she is entitled. In societies where there is a large gap between rich and poor and where people subsist within the cash economy, the poor are forced to sell their labor cheaply to survive. For a poor rural rice farming family in Asia, dependent upon fertilizer for a precarious annual crop, accustomed to the use of farming equipment such as motorized plows or iron implements and perhaps looking to purchase a motor vehicle, cash from the sale of rice would never be enough. Women and young girls are disadvantaged in these circumstances by virtue of their weak economic position and their gender. Alternative sources of family income are sought through seasonal work in major cities and towns. Daughters can earn more working in sweatshops or, worse, in the commercial sex industry. In desperate economic circumstances, parents are amenable to persuasion by labor agents and "pimps." Women's rights are thus breached on a daily basis by those who might be most expected to care about their welfare.

In seeking to advance the specific human rights of women, feminists have to battle entrenched perceptions of gender differences. The exploitation of women as low-wage workers in modern electronics factories and the consequent gendering of assembly work were discussed in chapter 2. Thus while a woman's right to work is in one sense valued because of perceived physiological and intellectual differences, that is, the perceived dexterity and malleability of the "Oriental female," her human rights are not. In workforces where only women are employed, the ILO Convention requirement that the equivalent male wage be paid is either sidestepped or simply blatantly ignored.

Tracing the interlinked chains of human rights abuses back to systemic failures of governance opens the way for a much broader search for the origins of human security crises. Citing abuses ranging from denial of health care, to economically and culturally marginalized peoples, to legal discrimination against women as causal factors in the spread of HIV/AIDS, Human Rights Watch highlights the human rights dimension of the pandemic. Health care is technically a second-generation human right but one that depends for its enjoyment upon the realization of fundamental rights to freedom and equality, in particular freedom from discrimination on the basis of social class, gender or ethnicity. HIV/AIDS and many other communicable diseases can be combated if the right to adequate health care is respected in sub-Saharan Africa, South Asia and the Pacific. Pointing to practical solutions, Joseph Amon argues that respect for human rights creates the social and legal conditions in which human health can be better protected, thereby obviating the need to deal with the longer-term economic and social consequences of galloping infection rates.[37]

RIGHTS AT RISK

The imperatives of economic development in a competitive self-help system mean that governments, in the developing world especially, are wont to ride roughshod over the interests and rights of communities.

Frequently, international nonstate actors, including TNCs and intergovernmental institutions, are complicit in these breaches. The activities of TNCs in conflict zones are fraught with human rights risk, but even in relatively peaceful countries, international interventions can have a deleterious impact upon human rights. While regulatory regimes exist to track and bring to account abuses perpetrated or tacitly condoned by international actors, these regimes are, because of their voluntary nature, weak and susceptible to behind-the-scenes influence through highly paid and well-connected lobbyists.[38]

MEGAPROJECTS AND COMMUNITY RIGHTS

Funding assistance from the World Bank aids developing countries in building essential roads, power stations and hydroelectric dams. Hydroelectric dams, the World Bank's panacea for rising water and energy consumption in rapidly industrializing states, are held as symbols of modernity by governments in developing countries.

In the case of the Pak Mun Dam, built by Thailand Electricity Generating Authority with the World Bank, dam construction proceeded in the face of massive opposition from villagers whose livelihoods were threatened by the project. Thailand's dam-building experience exemplifies the potential for such projects to generate unforeseen but nonetheless catastrophic consequences for those least able to influence global and national decision makers through democratic decision-making processes. The Pak Mun Hydroelectric Project, completed in 1994, was built to provide power for a booming national economy. Yet when finished, the dam swamped not only rice paddies, wetlands and other food-producing areas within the

Table 5.1. Dimensions of Human Rights Risk

	Drivers		Local	State	International
Politico-Military	Strategic competition	⟱	Violence between rival communities or armed gangs for control of resources	Violent conflict between state and minorities for control over resources and territory	Border incursions and general wars between neighboring states over resources and territory, affecting traditional land usage and causing widespread displacement
Political	Totalitarian government	⟱	State suppression of dissent and grassroots opposition	Assertion of total control over bureaucracy and political institutions, extending to the negation of civil society	Solidarity between totalitarian/authoritarian states to resist international pressure from UN, United States, EU, etc., thus perpetuating humanitarian disasters and abuse

Continued

Table 5.1. (Continued)

	Drivers		Local	State	International
Political	Religious and ideological competition	⇑	Conflicts between different religious groups and/or state suppression of local religious identity	Competition between religious groups for control of the state and/or between the state and ideological opponents	Ideological rivalry between states leading to proxy wars and direct armed confrontation compounded by the spread of religion-oriented terror networks
Economic	Resource competition	⇑	Between commercial interests and local communities over access to resources	Between the state and local communities in pursuit of development priorities	Between competing groupings of states over access to resources, leading to the bargaining down of human rights protections
Societal	Corruption	⇑	Impeding the provision of public services to communities, including health, education, environmental management and more	Impeding the effective setting of national priorities and the allocation of economic resources	Undermining international regimes designed to advance human rights and international security

sixty-square-kilometer reservoir area, it displaced the traditional riverbank cultures of villagers who were forced to relocate.

Traditional environmental rights were ignored, as were the project's environmental impacts. For more than a decade after the dam's completion, local villagers campaigned for a more sympathetic management of river flows to compensate for the destruction of fisheries and disruption of irrigation water.[39] The consequence of inadequate risk assessment, the Pak Mun Dam also spawned Thailand's most extensive counterhegemonic protest movement of the 1990s, the Assembly of the Poor, which enlarged its agenda to challenge state agricultural and development policies on behalf of Thailand's rural population.

Dams, because of their extensive human and environmental impacts, have generated strong public opposition. It is also the case that affected communities have acquired a greater degree of political consciousness due to the work of NGOs and the opportunity to bypass state information agencies and campaign directly through the Internet. Malaysia's indigenous people, the Orang Asli, confronted the ongoing destruction of their forest home to make way for dam projects to provide water and energy for Malaysia's industrial center in Selangor's Klang Valley. Environmental impacts extend to the destruction of rain forest habitat which, according to environmental and community rights campaigners, threaten the region's biodiversity.[40]

An extensive hydroelectric project on the Yangtze River, the Three Gorges Dam, inundated an area of some 632 square kilometers and is expected to have displaced in excess of five million villagers by 2020.[41] The World Bank elected not to provide financial support for the dam, citing its extensive human impacts and acknowledging the bank's inability to restrain the Chinese state by imposing environmental and human rights loan conditions. Canadian, French, German and Swiss investors, however, financed a substantial share of the dam's construction costs with minimal apparent concern for the project's potential impact on the human rights of millions. Allegations have regularly leaked about the failures of resettlement strategies deemed as woefully inadequate and leaving vast numbers of displaced villagers in greatly reduced circumstances.

Accusations of underpayment of compensation echo the excesses reported by Guidi and Chuntao, while reports of mass protests against corrupt government officials highlight a systemic weakness in the Chinese state that is directly attributable to the state's failure to respect the human rights of its citizens.[42]

THE RIGHT OF SELF-DETERMINATION

In Tibet and among the Tibetan diaspora, long-standing demands for China to uphold human rights and free Tibet erupted in March 2008 into anti-Chinese violence in Lhasa and worldwide protests against Beijing's occupation and incorporation of the former Himalayan theocracy. According to Chinese official statements, Tibet, prior to its "reintegration" in 1951, was a feudal theocracy where an allegedly "parasitical" religious caste exploited the Tibetan people to sustain their exclusive and nonproductive monastic lifestyle. Religion is anathema to committed Communists following Marx's dictum that "religion is the opium of the people," echoed in the rhetoric of Chinese policymakers. Tibet's historical position is ambiguous, hindering the legitimation of both Beijing's territorial claims and those of Tibetan nationalists. Any effective Chinese control or domination over the Tibetan region was weakened in the nineteenth century as China's imperial system of government was rendered impotent by Western colonial encroachment. The collapse of imperial authority in 1911 offered the opportunity for Tibetans to proclaim independence—which suggests that Tibetan nationalists acknowledged a measure of Chinese control prior to this date.

For post-1949 China, the reclamation of territories lost during the colonial era became a matter of national pride, although the Communist state was prepared to acknowledge the legality of treaties with both Britain and Portugal concerning their respective colonies, Hong Kong and Macau, subject to fixed leases and returned to China upon the expiration of these leases in 1997 and 1998, respectively.

In contrast, Taiwan, taken by General Chiang Kai-shek's retreating Nationalists in 1949, could not be reintegrated without provoking strong international opposition. With regard to Tibet, Beijing simply ignored the 1911 independence declaration and occupied the country in 1951. China has consistently ignored international condemnation of its actions, including several UN General Assembly resolutions, although the UN has not explicitly demanded that China withdraw. Under greater international scrutiny, China was, however, conscious of the need for a historical defense. Only then, writes Eliot Sperling, did China make any historical claim to Tibet as an "integral" part of China. Sperling's analysis of official British documents indicates that the British position in the early twentieth century was that China exercised little or no direct control over Tibet. Anglo-Russian competition in Central Asia, however, prompted the British to placate the Chinese court and to acknowledge Tibet as a Chinese protectorate.[43]

For Beijing and many Chinese, the establishment of a single Chinese state incorporating Tibet and Taiwan is a matter of national pride and proper atonement for the humiliations exacted upon the Chinese people by the Western powers.

For opponents and critics of Beijing, this "One-China policy" is merely a grab for resources and power by an expansionist Chinese state determined to assert regional hegemony in the twenty-first century. This is the view of a new generation of Tibetan nationalists protesting against Chinese human rights violations and campaigning for Tibetan independence. The conservative older generation of Tibetans, including the Dalai Lama and his followers who fled to India in 1951, however, is cautious not to issue any demands beyond calling for the human rights of all Tibetans to be respected by Beijing.[44]

Historical argument is important to understanding the respective Chinese and Tibetan positions, but legal settlement of the dispute in an international court of law is improbable. Politically, the international community—primarily the UN—is in no position to demand China's withdrawal from Tibet. Given China's size, its nuclear arsenal and substantial conventional forces, intervention is not an option for the international community. Should Tibetan nationalists turn to armed resistance, India would be forced to expel the Dalai Lama and his supporters or risk breaching its cease-fire agreement with China under which New Delhi agreed not to sponsor any Tibetan uprising. Tibet's strategic value to India was well appreciated during British imperial rule—a fact that makes Indian officials sensitive to the merest perception that India is harboring Tibetan insurgents.

We have already seen how in Burma, the state's refusal to acknowledge demands for democratization or accept demands for secession from the Shan, Karen and others has exacerbated political violence and created the conditions in which the narcotics trade thrives. Similarly, the failure to acknowledge popular demands for land redistribution in Latin American countries, Colombia, for instance, fuels the illicit production and trade in cocaine.

SOUTHERN THAI MUSLIMS

In southern Thailand, ethnic Malay resentment toward Bangkok dates back to the early nineteenth century, when much of the northern Malay

Peninsula was a peripheral part of the Thai kingdom. Attempts by the Thai state to extinguish Muslim Malay separatism have served only to deepen the sense of alienation felt by Muslims in the south, irrespective of whether they are directly involved in the insurgency or not.

The international watchdog organization Human Rights Watch alleges that a heavy-handed response by the military toward renewed separatist activity from 2001 onward is a major contributing factor to the escalation of this conflict into a major human security crisis.[45] Even if the Thai government is able to again stifle separatist activity as it did in the 1980s and 1990s, there are serious doubts about the capacity of the state to solve underlying economic and political problems that give the insurgents sufficient political traction to sustain their low-level campaign.

Economic, cultural and political marginalization exacerbates feelings of resentment among the Muslim population, but with government and the national and provincial levels compromised by powerful patronage networks that use high office to acquire resources and concessions, government-led development programs rarely achieve full efficiency. In the case of southern Thai Muslims, the denial of economic opportunity is as much attributable to the interests of entrenched local elites and failings in Thailand's system of government as it is to policy choices made in Bangkok. But this is a crisis with regionwide security implications, not least for its impact upon relations between ASEAN members Thailand and Malaysia, where the latter by virtue of a common border is used as a refuge by Thai Muslim insurgents.

INDIGENOUS RIGHTS

Indigenous rights became another fundamental part of the international human rights architecture with the Declaration of Indigenous Rights (2007). Although the rights of indigenous peoples are covered in the UNDHR and ICCPR, as with gender, experience teaches that these rights, if they are to be enjoyed fully by indigenous peoples, have to be stated separately to guard against the invisible workings of racial discrimination. As further evidence that absolutist notions of state sovereignty hinder creative responses to human rights deficits, central to the declaration is the principle of autonomy within the nation-state. Article 5 allows that "indigenous peoples have the right to maintain and strengthen their distinct political, legal, economic, social and cultural institutions, while retaining their right to participate fully, if they so choose, in the political, economic, social and cultural life of the State."[46] Such assertions, however commendable, do little to address the consequences of sustained discrimination over extended periods of time.

Indigenous rights bear significantly upon indigenous human security. Indigenous Australians register life expectancies well below the national norm. Communities experience a higher incidence of disease—from diseases of the eye to STDs—high unemployment, overrepresentation in the prison population, high youth suicide rates, alcohol and drug abuse, domestic violence and sexual abuse of minors, all of which stem from official neglect of the underlying causes of social disintegration. Indigenous people suffer discrimination because insufficient attention is given by the state to indigenous disadvantage, the source of which is their historical dispossession from their traditional lands. The impact of British colonization was catastrophic for indigenous Australians forced to live on the margins of European settlements and assimilate to an alien culture. The consequences of this are a collapse of crucial social structures, including traditional patterns of authority, and kinship groups—the latter a consequence of conscious policies to assimilate indigenous people to white Australian norms of social behavior.

The intrusions that destroyed indigenous Australian cultures took place in the nineteenth century, away from the critical scrutiny of international media. Yet the same processes and consequences are observable today throughout Africa and Latin America, where indigenous peoples inhabit territory rich in natural resources, timber and minerals, especially oil. Across the developing world, writes UN Special Rapporteur Rodolfo Stavenhagen, "indigenous peoples endure grave violations of their human rights, including threats, forced disappearances, the targeted assassination of their leaders, torture, massacres, forced recruitment for combat, forced displacement, the exile of entire communities, loss of internal autonomy and social control and lack of access to places where they can engage in traditional activities."[47]

Human Rights Watch reports extensive indigenous rights abuses in the Niger Delta where oil companies—Chevron and Mobil (U.S.), Shell (Anglo-Dutch), Elf (France) and Agip (Italy)—are allegedly complicit in the use of state-sanctioned force to suppress local protests to oil exploration and production. Indigenous communities effectively have no bargaining rights against foreign companies or the state because the legal system is corrupted, as is the country's political elite. Oil runs through the veins of Nigerian politics to the extent that any challenge to the oil industry is instantly a challenge to the political elite and hence meets with swift and brutal suppression. In return for access to oil deposits, foreign companies are obliged to form joint venture operations with the Nigerian government through the Nigerian National Petroleum Corporation—thus implicating them in Abuja's mining policies and practices. The arrangement establishes a commercial relationship between companies and the state, which uses access rights as a bargaining chip with foreigners but excludes indigenous communities from a share of the wealth extracted from their traditional lands.[48]

The evidence is overwhelming that where the rights of indigenous peoples and minorities are ignored, conflict is the outcome. The impacts of these failures of governance fall most heavily on the weakest members of society. UN Special Rapporteurs reported in 2004 and 2005 on the shortfall in indigenous rights recognition, even in developed countries such as Canada, while in Latin America especially, conflicts over access to natural resources have resulted in substantial and underreported human rights abuses. The expansion of capital-intensive mining into indigenous territories has in the past imposed enormous environmental and social costs on local populations—indigenous and settler communities alike. Throughout Latin America's mining districts, NGO groups and rights advocates detail how the investment brought by mining leads to the formation of "boomtowns" and attendant informal economies. Highly paid foreign mine workers support formal and informal industries centered on alcohol and prostitution, while local communities exposed to the brutal realities of the outside world verge on societal collapse. The Canadian company Greenstone is accused of generating such a boomtown at La Libertad, Nicaragua, in 1994, only to close four years later, leaving in its wake a serious unemployment problem, a degraded environment, and a community in severe distress.[49] No laws were broken, no violence perpetrated against indigenous peoples, but economic and social rights were undermined.

TOWARD A GLOBAL CRIMINAL CODE

It is more apt to conceive human rights theory as an evolving dialogue within and between cultural traditions. In practice, the realization of rights is constrained by the dominant logic of political self-interest, which frequently inhibits the altruistic pursuit of humanitarian goals. Taking a lateral approach to human security issues, human rights advocates stress the interconnectedness of rights and military security. Logically, if intrasocietal conflicts, for example, the long-running Muslim insurgencies in southern Thailand and the Philippines, are the result of official failure to recognize the economic, social and cultural rights of minority groups, then respect for such rights can be advanced as one more step toward avoiding or resolving conflict and its attendant human security risks. By moving human rights issues to center stage, it becomes easier to see the dynamics of human security risks and identify practical strategies to alleviate human suffering.

The International Criminal Court and its founding document, the Rome Statute, exists to try people for genocide, crimes against humanity and war crimes as defined in the statute. But the ICC is not universally recognized as the rightful court in which war criminals are to be tried. The United States famously refuses to ratify the Rome Statute for fear of the consequences for U.S. service personnel on active duty while the perpetrators of hideous crimes escape capture.

The statute defines what is claimed to be a universally applicable and universally acceptable codification of "inhuman" crimes. It is an advance upon individual documents seeking to establish principles of common humanity to be upheld even and especially during times of war. The preamble

---

A CRIME AGAINST HUMANITY

After all the men had been massacred, they ordered the truck driver to drive their heavy vehicles over the corpses. After many trips over the bodies, they had been pushed down until they were even with the surface of the earth. Jalil was riding in one of the trucks as it ground into the earth bodies of the men with whom he had been traveling only an hour before. Later, I heard from some of my friends who had returned to the airport a few days after the killings that the bodies of the dead men had all been devoured by wild dogs and vultures. The dogs had become mad because of all the human flesh they had consumed. The next time I was at the airport, there was no sign of the mass murder I had witnessed—somebody must have buried whatever was left of the victims.

Source: Alex Klaits and Gulchin Gulmamadova-Klaits, *Love and War in Afghanistan*, 2005.

makes explicit connection between the protection of human rights and global security. Genocide, crimes against humanity and war crimes so defined in the statute are regarded as crimes that "threaten the peace, security and well-being of the world."[50] However, with no provisions for enforcement without the authorization of sovereign governments, like all international legal instruments, the Rome Statute can be ignored by signatory states should they so choose.

But practicalities can work in the opposite direction. Should pragmatism enter into discussions, for instance, on the treatment of war criminals or the perpetrators of crimes against humanity and genocide? International law must contend with international political realities, and if political or strategic considerations are paramount, there are grounds for granting amnesties for persons suspected of crimes. While human rights NGOs balk at the practice of granting amnesties to former dictators and their military supporters from Argentina to Afghanistan, such amnesties can serve a pragmatic purpose—to end a civil war by giving all parties to the conflict a reason not to defect, or to reassure demobilized militias and prevent their remobilization.[51] Is there a point at which the interests of peace require that combatants on both side be given assurances of immunity from prosecution in return for laying down arms? This is an emerging and fractious area of international human rights and criminal law, compounded by U.S. determination to exempt its service personnel from ICC jurisdiction.

Crimes covered in the above legal instruments do not address all forms of international criminal activity, but only those relating to the exercise of political and military power to coerce or to kill. If we accept, however, that people trafficking, drug production and trafficking, expropriation of intellectual capital from tribal communities, child exploitation and the like are crimes that substantially diminish human rights, then international law enforcement should extend to international conventions and treaties covering these criminal actions. Taking the legalist position, all forms of human rights abuse should be integrated into the global corpus of criminal law, however unworkable the enlarged case load might become. Environmental codes too, especially those governing the use of natural resources, have a bearing upon the enjoyment of economic and social rights by those who depend upon waterways or the oceans, for example, for some or all of their food. Currently, the international preference for such international "crimes" is local legislation backed by self-regulation in the private sector.

Human rights have proliferated in law since 1945, but this does not mean that the significance of human rights is diluted as a consequence.

Where rights are perceived to clash, jurisprudence should prevail. The pragmatic logic of rights asserted by Sen in some part counters the pessimism of Morgenthau and Waltz. Respect for human rights facilitates greater social and political participation and enhances economic opportunity; all key ingredients for political stability or peace. Whether or not this translates into a more stable international order is a matter for conjecture. There is, however, a measure of persistence in the way that the international community, regionally and globally, has acknowledged the importance of human rights in international laws. Were respect for human rights at the local level to be a universal phenomenon, human well-being would be improved generally, which is surely in itself a desirable goal.

CHAPTER 6

AVERTING NUCLEAR ARMAGEDDON: REALITY CHECKS AND NUCLEAR BALANCES

> We can sum it up in one sentence: the civilization of the machine has just achieved its ultimate degree of savagery. A choice is going to have to be made in the fairly near future between collective suicide and the intelligent utilization of scientific discoveries. . . . In a world that has torn itself apart with every conceivable instrument of violence and shown itself incapable of exerting any control while remaining indifferent to justice or even mere human happiness, the fact that science has dedicated itself to organized murder will surprise no one, except perhaps an unrepentant idealist.
>
> —Albert Camus

We begin our analysis of nuclear weapons—the only weapon of mass destruction that really matters—with a deceptively simple question: Does the spread of nuclear weapons make the world safer or more dangerous? Most people usually have an instinctive reply to this question: Of course, it makes things more dangerous. How could it not? It might seem surprising, therefore, that not all nuclear analysts agree, and the debate remains unresolved. Like so many of the issues relating to nuclear weapons, the debate is built largely on speculation and ambiguous historical experience. Nuclear weapons remain attractive to insecure or ambitious states. In regional rivalries such as the Indian subcontinent, East Asia and the Middle East, the bomb still has influence. Whatever else one has to say—and presumably not much has been left unsaid about the nuclear strategy of the past six decades—nuclear status still imparts extraordinary prestige and power. The nine current members of the nuclear weapons club—the United States, Russia, Great Britain, France, China, Israel, India, Pakistan, and North Korea—still possess about 27,000 operational nuclear weapons of various types among them. At least another fifteen countries have on hand enough highly enriched uranium for a nuclear weapon.[1]

PROLIFERATION

Since 1945, many influential voices have expressed alarm that the spread of nuclear weapons will inevitably lead to world destruction. So far, that prediction has not been proved right. But is that because of effective efforts to stop the spread of nuclear weapons, or, to borrow a phrase from former Secretary of State Dean Acheson after the Cuban Missile Crisis, just plain dumb luck?

Nuclear proliferation remains urgent not just because of the risk of a terrorist organization getting its hands on nuclear weapons, but because the proliferation of weapons necessarily means a proliferation of nuclear deterrents. Nuclear weapons have long been a force multiplier, able to make up for imbalances in conventional military power. Paradoxically, then, the unassailable lead of the United States in military power and technology might actually invite other nations to acquire the bomb as a way to influence or even deter American foreign policy initiatives. The lesson of the first Gulf War, one Indian general was reported as saying, is that you do not go to war with the United States without the bomb, the 2003 invasion of Iraq serving as yet another glossy advertisement of the protective power of a nuclear arsenal. This is not a new development. It is, in fact, a lesson American policymakers have been concerned about for some time, and one for which no easy solution seems likely. Bill Clinton's secretary of defense, Les Aspin, outlined the problem in December 1993:

> During the Cold War, our principal adversary had conventional forces in Europe that were numerically superior. For us, nuclear weapons were the equalizer. The threat to use them was present and was used to compensate for our smaller numbers of conventional forces. Today, nuclear weapons can still be the equalizer against superior conventional forces. But today it is the United States that has unmatched conventional military power, and it is our potential adversaries who may attain nuclear weapons.

Accordingly, Aspin concluded, the United States could wind up being the equalized.[2] To take an earlier example, John F. Kennedy acknowledged in the wake of the Cuban Missile Crisis that even a small number of nuclear weapons could deter even the most powerful states.

A central element of the proliferation debate revolves around the perceived effectiveness of nuclear deterrence. If deterrence works reliably, as optimists argue, then there is presumably less to be feared in the spread of nuclear weapons. But if nuclear deterrence does not work reliably, pessimists maintain, more nuclear weapons states will presumably lead not just to a more complicated international arena, but a far more dangerous one.

Some analysts have made a compelling case that the fear of nuclear proliferation or the spread of nuclear weapons has been exaggerated. Some go even further and argue that proliferation may actually increase global stability. It is an argument peculiar to nuclear weaponry, as it does not apply and is not made with regard to other so-called weapons of mass destruction such as chemical and biological weapons. Nuclear weapons are simply so destructive, this school of thought argues, and using them is such a high bar that it would be madness itself to launch against a nuclear-armed foe. Put another way, nuclear states should know better than to fight wars with each other. The argument that proliferation is not necessarily a dire threat has been made in expansions both lateral—to other countries—and vertical—in the growth of nuclear stockpiles. "Since 1945," remarked Michael Mandelbaum twenty-five years ago, "the more nuclear weapons each has accumulated, the less likely, on the whole, it has seemed that either side would use them." Others have made similar arguments. Kenneth Waltz maintains, for example, that nuclear weapons preserve an "imperfect peace" on the subcontinent between India and Pakistan. Responding to reports that all Pentagon war games involving India and Pakistan always end in a nuclear exchange, Waltz argues, "Has everyone in that building forgotten that deterrence works precisely because nuclear states fear that conventional military engagements may escalate to the nuclear level, and therefore they draw back from the brink?"

It was an idea frequently debated during the Cold War. French military strategist General Pierre Gallois observed in 1960 that the path to greater stability lay in increased proliferation. "Few people are able to grasp that precisely because the new weapons have a destructive power out of all proportion to even the highest stakes, they impose a far more stable balance than the world has known in the past," he said. "Nor is it any easier to make people realize that the more numerous and terrible the retaliatory weapons possessed by both sides, the surer the peace . . . and that it is actually more dangerous to limit nuclear weapons than to let them proliferate." Gallois made this argument in the context of justifying the French bomb and increasing NATO nuclear capabilities. "These," Gallois concluded, "are the realities of our time, but no one is willing to accept them at first blush."[3]

Notwithstanding a few notable proponents of the "proliferation equals more security" argument, the weight of opinion is mainly on the other side of the ledger, especially since 9/11, that the spread of nuclear weapons is a bad thing—a very bad thing, in fact. The issues driving nuclear-armed states and even terrorist groups are no longer just political; we have also seen the obsessiveness of religious fundamentalism, which does not seem amenable to either diplomacy or humanitarian restraint. Indeed, since 9/11 the rules have changed, and experts suggest that there are at least some terrorists who do want to inflict mass casualties. In this context, nuclear terrorism not only represents an effort to intimidate and coerce, but also poses a critical threat to states and peoples around the world.

Political scientist Scott Sagan has also highlighted the ways in which organizations and communications can fail; for example, rather than being anomalies, accidents should be seen as an inherent part of organizations. When nuclear weapons are thrown into the mix, the risk of catastrophic accidents becomes inevitable. Moreover, Sagan holds the view that a fundamental level of risk is inherent in all nuclear weapons organizations regardless of nationality or region. Clearly, it is an element that compounds the problem of nuclear weapons in regions still embroiled by centuries-old religious, cultural and ethnic tensions. All of these elements combine in a barely controllable milieu of states' nuclear weapons policy, a disaster waiting to happen.

HALTING THE SPREAD OF NUCLEAR WEAPONS

This invariably leads us to our second, essential question: How can a nation—or a community of nations—prevent the spread of nuclear weapons? Since the question was first raised during the closing stages of World War Two, a wide range of answers has been given and tried, from the legislative, through international norms and treaties, and even to preventive military action. None has proved entirely satisfactory.

Whereas the Baruch Plan equated controlling the atom and disarmament, President Dwight D. Eisenhower managed to separate the two in his 1953 proposal known as "Atoms for Peace." The focus of the proposal was on stopping the spread of nuclear weapons, not on disarmament. In a speech to the United Nations on December 8, 1953, Eisenhower called for a renewed emphasis on peaceful uses of atomic energy and on providing commercial incentives for reaping the benefits of atomic energy. The price was that all fissile material would be placed under the custody of a UN agency. Again, the initiative met with mixed success. On the plus side, it contributed directly to the establishment of the International Atomic Energy Agency (IAEA) in July 1957, charged with monitoring and encouraging the safe use of nuclear technology for peaceful purposes while acting as an international, neutral watchdog of nuclear weapons transfers and developments. The Vienna-based IAEA, a United Nations–affiliated organization with 137 member countries, has played an important role in recent years, but its power depends heavily on international political tides. On the negative side, a few nations, including India, chose to use the Atoms for Peace project to establish their own nuclear weapons programs.

In the 1950s and 1960s, while the United States, the Soviet Union, Great Britain and France built their nuclear arsenals, frequent estimates of the future size of the nuclear-armed community centered on two dozen states. But with the People's Republic of China's initial nuclear test in October 1964, a worried White House and Kremlin hastily put forth proposals to restrict the spread of nuclear weapons. In the Eighteen Nation Disarmament Committee, which had been discussing this matter, nonaligned members argued that a nonproliferation treaty must not simply divide the world into nuclear "haves" and "have nots," but must balance obligations. The Nuclear Non-Proliferation Treaty (NPT) was signed in 1968 after the Americans and the Soviets reluctantly agreed "to pursue obligations in good faith" to halt the arms race "at the earliest possible date" (the fig leaf they hid behind) and to seek "a treaty on general and complete disarmament under strict effective international control." Questionable adherence to this pledge annoyed nonnuclear nations at subsequent NPT review conferences, only to draw renewed feeble pledges from the superpowers.

Nevertheless, the Non-Proliferation Treaty, with its 185 signatories—save India, Israel and Pakistan—became the cornerstone of a loosely structured nonproliferation regime. The IAEA established international inspections and safeguards aimed at preventing nuclear materials being diverted to military uses. During 1974 and 1975, a Nuclear Suppliers Group was established in London to further ensure that nuclear materials, equipment and technology would not be used in weapons production. Various Nuclear-Weapons Free Zones meanwhile extended the nonproliferation regime to Latin America (1967), the South Pacific (1996), Africa (1996), Southeast Asia (1997), and Central Asia (2002), while a Comprehensive Nuclear Test Ban Treaty, which the U.S. Senate has refused to ratify, rounded out the regime. For all its faults, the NPT stands out as the high-water mark of multilateral global efforts to establish an enforceable regime to curb the further spread of nuclear weapons.

By the time the NPT was signed, the nuclear club already had five members: the United States, the Soviet Union, the United Kingdom, France and China, who greeted each new addition with varying degrees of concern. American policymakers engaged in serious discussion against both the Soviet and Chinese nuclear programs before each successfully exploded its first atomic device in 1949 and 1964, respectively. The Indian government of Prime Minister Indira Gandhi seriously considered, but ultimately rejected, plans for preventive military attacks on Pakistan's nuclear facilities in the early 1980s. Israel, not a signatory to the treaty, actually carried out a military strike against an Iraqi nuclear power facility on June 7, 1981, at Osirak. Less-aggressive measures have also had a mixed record of success. American efforts to thwart the British nuclear program consisted mainly of cutting off the flow of information and materials to their erstwhile atomic partner. The French were in point of fact actively discouraged from developing an independent nuclear option, and offers were made for a European nuclear force instead. None of these efforts was decisive.

Not every nuclear and prospective nuclear power has regarded the NPT and its subsequent indefinite renewal in 1995 positively.[4] After all, the NPT is specifically designed to freeze the status quo. The leading nuclear states party to the treaty naturally regarded this as a positive arrangement because it preserved their status while retaining their freedom with respect to modernizing their own nuclear arsenals, which they have clearly done.

But other countries such as India, not a signatory to the treaty, saw it as exclusionary on the part of the established nuclear powers and bristled at what it perceived to be the nuclear double standards of the West, Russia and China. For, according to former Indian defense minister K. C. Pant, "We very seriously proposed a fifteen-year plan for the phased elimination of nuclear weapons. However, after the NPT was extended 'in perpetuity,' it was apparent the big powers had no intention of shedding their nuclear arsenal." India may well have gone nuclear because of double standards and the wish to be taken seriously.[5]

Disarmament critics also argue that under the NPT, the nuclear powers should not be expanding their nuclear arsenals but rather moving toward total nuclear disarmament. Article VI of the treaty is clear: "Each of the Parties to the Treaty undertakes to pursue negotiations in good faith on effective measures relating to cessation of the nuclear arms race at an early date and to nuclear disarmament, and on a treaty on general and complete disarmament under strict and effective international control." Moreover, continue critics, what possible purpose could nuclear weapons serve in the war on international terrorism? And could not the expense of modernizing nuclear forces be put to better use?

Typically, and in defense of his government's decision to update and replace the United Kingdom's Trident nuclear weapons system, former British Prime Minister Tony Blair responded to his opposition by pointing out that the NPT did not commit member states to total disarmament but rather to negotiations on effective measures and that his government had fulfilled this pledge. It had, in fact, cut its nuclear weapons explosive capacity by 70 percent since the end of the Cold War, given up bombs carried by strategic aircraft, and reduced the operational readiness of its four Vanguard submarines, each carrying sixteen U.S.-supplied Trident ballistic missiles equipped with up to three warheads. In any case, only one submarine was on patrol at any one time and would require several days' notice to fire. Nonetheless, there was considerable resistance. On February 24, 2007, the national "No Trident" demonstration brought up to 100,000 protesters to the streets of London to demand the government reverse its plans to build a new generation of nuclear weapons to replace Trident. There was also considerable resistance from Labour MPs, and enough of them voted against the Trident replacement proposal to force Blair to rely on support from the Conservatives. By the end of March, Blair got his way: a replacement submarine, including missiles and warheads, and even that would be no less than seventeen years in the making.

Clearly, nuclear proliferation is one of the key challenges to the stability of the contemporary international system, and the current nonproliferation regime seems increasingly unable and, perhaps, unwilling to meet the expectations of its designers. Since the signing of the NPT in 1968, nuclear powers have barely fulfilled their commitments to reduce their atomic arsenals, while the number of nonnuclear states that have crossed the threshold status and are now regarded as full-fledged atomic powers has increased and threatens to keep growing. What can be done about it?

In recent years, a team of leading nonproliferation experts, assembled by the Carnegie Endowment for International Peace, offered a sober blueprint for rethinking the international nuclear nonproliferation regime. They offered a fresh approach to deal with states and terrorists, nuclear weapons, and fissile materials alike. According to this plan, an effective strategy for nuclear security will require universal compliance with the norms and rules of a toughened nuclear nonproliferation policy, where *compliance* means more than declarations of good intent. In future, it will also mean performance. *Universal*, moreover, means that nonproliferation norms and rules must be extended not only to treaty members, but to all states and to individuals and corporations as well.

Six obligations form the core of the universal compliance strategy; together, they constitute a balance of obligations among the nuclear and nonnuclear states and erect a defense in depth against the spread of nuclear weapons. They are: making nonproliferation irreversible, devaluing the political and military currency of nuclear weapons, securing all nuclear materials, stopping illegal transfers, committing to conflict resolution and persuading Israel, India and Pakistan to accept the same treaty obligations accepted by the other NPT signatories. The alternative, with the human misery that would most likely occur, would be a deadly lesson in consequence management, for which there are no real answers.[6]

COLD WAR LEGACY

Since the end of the Cold War the problem of the spread of nuclear weapons has become more complicated, not less. The legacy of the Cold War has played an important role. After the fall of the Berlin Wall and the collapse of the Soviet empire, the first challenge was to dismantle what Soviet premier Mikhail Gorbachev referred to as the "infrastructure of fear" that had dominated global security relations during the Cold War, and Washington and Moscow declared the arms race over with the signing of the

START Treaty in August 1991. Stopping it was one thing; reversing direction was quite another.

It is hard to find anyone who can offer a convincing argument as to why the United States and Russia both still need thousands of operational nuclear weapons in their stockpiles sixteen years after the end of the Cold War. Today, according to former Secretary of Defense Robert S. McNamara, the United States has deployed approximately 4,500 strategic offensive nuclear warheads and the Russians roughly 3,800. (The strategic forces of the UK, France and China are considerably smaller, with 200–400 nuclear weapons in each state's arsenal; the newer nuclear states of India and Pakistan have fewer than 100 weapons each.) Of the 8,000 active or operational U.S. warheads—each with the destructive power twenty times that of the Hiroshima bomb—2,000 are on hair-trigger alert, ready to be launched on fifteen minutes' notice. Moreover, the United States remains prepared to initiate the use of these weapons by the decision of one person, the president—against either a nuclear or nonnuclear enemy whenever the president believes that it is deemed in the national interest.

One of the most pressing concerns of security experts and policymakers in the early 1990s was to secure the weapons of the former USSR while that empire imploded. In 1991, the breakup of the Soviet Union left nuclear weapons in the former Soviet states of Ukraine, Belarus and Kazakhstan. These newly independent states, each of which was "born nuclear," were ultimately convinced to give up their inherited weapons, and all of those nuclear weapons were repatriated to Russia, but not without much anxiety. That the new states would simply give up these powerful bargaining chips was no foregone conclusion. The Nunn-Lugar program, with considerable U.S. funding to secure these weapons, aided in achieving a successful transfer. The sheer numbers of nuclear weapons even combined with this relatively modest dispersal illustrated the problem of command, control and security in an environment of deteriorating military infrastructure. Whether a cash-strapped military complex might look to liquidate its assets or the compromising of security measures allowed theft, the threat to the international community was acute.

The problem seemed even more worrisome with those weapons dispersed farther afield. During the Cold War, both sides deployed tens of thousands of nuclear weapons and nuclear-capable delivery vehicles, well beyond their own borders, in the name of forward defense and pre-positioning. The list of locations beyond the continental United States to which American nuclear weapons, both tactical and strategic, were dispersed is surprisingly long: Alaska, Canada, Greenland, Guam, Hawaii, Japan, Johnston Island, Kwajalein, Midway, Morocco, the Philippines, Puerto Rico, South Korea, Spain, Taiwan, Belgium, France, Greece, Italy, the Netherlands, Turkey, the United Kingdom and West Germany. In Europe alone, thousands of American nuclear weapons had been deployed since September 1954 in a constantly rotating inventory of obsolescence and replacement, peaking at approximately 7,300 in 1971.

The number of American nuclear weapons deployed overseas has been reduced markedly since the dissolution of the Soviet Union. In 1991, President George H. W. Bush ordered the withdrawal of all ground- and sea-based tactical nuclear weapons from their overseas bases. But the United States remains the only nation to continue basing land-based nuclear weapons beyond its own borders (other countries continue to deploy sea- and air-based weapons). The number of American nuclear weapons still based in Europe remains at about 480.

NUCLEAR DETERRENCE FOR
THE POST–COLD WAR ERA

The breakup of the Soviet Union augured a new reality in which the prospect of a Soviet invasion into Western Europe, launched with little or no warning, was no longer a realistic threat. Gorbachev shared the sentiment, describing it as a revolution in strategic thinking; no longer should the deterrent to war be the threat of war. "Our next goal," he said, "is to make full use of this breakthrough to make disarmament an irreversible process."

By the time Bill Clinton assumed the presidency, the euphoria of the end of the Cold War was giving way to more sober analysis. It had become increasingly apparent that the problems associated with nuclear weapons had not actually faded away—they had simply been transformed. Rather than opening an era of global peace and security, the end of the Cold War paved the way for instability and the resurfacing of regional issues that had long been suppressed. Sarajevo, Kosovo and Rwanda became household words.

Nevertheless, the Clinton administration pressed ahead with its efforts to align nuclear policy with new circumstances. In late 1993 it announced that the U.S. government had adopted a new understanding of deterrence. A wide-ranging and thorough "bottom-up review," conducted by the Pentagon during 1993, identified a number of key threats to U.S. national security. Foremost among them was the increased threat of proliferation of nuclear weapons and other weapons of mass destruction. The new deterrence, therefore, would be aimed at deterring not only the threat to use nuclear weapons but also the acquisition of atomic technology and materials. By employing significant military and economic disincentives, the administration hoped to neutralize some of the chief threats to stability such as North Korea, Iraq and Libya.

But the central thrust of U.S. nuclear policy remained the potential of a resurgent Russia. In keeping with its redefinition of deterrence, the Clinton administration announced in September 1994 that it was adopting a new nuclear doctrine. The doctrine of mutual assured destruction, or MAD, was to be replaced with a policy of mutual assured safety, aimed primarily at the Russian heartland. This served a dual purpose: first, to provide leadership for continuing reductions in nuclear weapons, and second, and more critically, to provide a hedge against a reversal of the reform process in Russia. Although it remained unlikely that Russia's weak economy could rebuild a conventional force of the magnitude that it had maintained during the Cold War, U.S. defense planners speculated that nuclear weapons might offer an attractive, cheaper option to a new generation of Russian leaders.

In November 1997, Clinton issued a presidential decision directive describing in general terms the purposes of U.S. nuclear weapons while providing broad guidance for developing operational plans. It was the first such presidential directive on the actual employment of nuclear weapons since the Carter administration. It was notable in that Washington finally abandoned the Cold War tenet that it must be prepared to fight a protracted nuclear war. The directive also noted that strategic nuclear weapons would play a smaller role in the U.S. security posture than at any other point during the second half of the twentieth century, but that they were still a vital part of U.S. efforts as a hedge against an uncertain future. But for those who believed that deterrence was a thing of the past, Clinton's directive served as a sharp reminder that not much had changed. In words still ringing from those at the height of the Cold War, the Clinton administration declared:

> Deterrence is predicated on ensuring that potential adversaries accept that any use of nuclear weapons against the United States or its allies would not succeed. . . . A wide range of nuclear retaliatory options are required to ensure that the United States is not left with an all-or-nothing response. . . . The United States will retain sufficient ambiguity of use that an adversary

could never be sure that the United States would not launch a counter-attack before the adversary's weapons arrive.[7]

At the same time, Aspin's successor, Secretary of Defense William Cohen, wondered aloud whether a smaller nuclear force made it a more attractive target and deliberately cultivated the ambiguity concept upon which deterrence rested. With transition to a coherent post–Cold War posture incomplete, the United States publicly considers Moscow an ally while Pentagon war game scenarios involving Moscow as the primary enemy continue. For its part, Russia maintains a nuclear force of considerable size, ostensibly to make up for the deterioration of its conventional capabilities.

NONPROLIFERATION

Nonproliferation efforts in recent years have enjoyed mixed results. On the one hand, nuclear stockpiles have been reduced markedly, with some of that fissile material being converted to peaceful purposes by blending down bomb-grade plutonium and uranium to lower-grade versions more suitable for nuclear power production. "One out of every ten light bulbs in the United States is powered by a former Soviet bomb," boasted Ambassador Linton Brooks, administrator of the U.S. National Nuclear Security Administration. On the other hand, the risk of nuclear weapons or fissile materials falling into the wrong hands seems greater than ever.

As of September 2005, there have been 220 cases of nuclear smuggling confirmed by the International Atomic Energy Agency since 1993. Eighteen of those cases involved highly enriched uranium. There are ongoing fears about Russian accountability for small, suitcase-sized bombs after former Russian national security adviser Alexander Lebed made a startling public claim in 1997 that up to one hundred of those bombs were unaccounted for. Originally envisaged for use by spies behind enemy lines for sabotage and demolition in the event of war, the weapons were designed to be highly portable and self-contained, possibly with short-cuts in their arming and detonation procedures. Put another way, they are a terrorist's dream. "More than a hundred weapons out of the supposed number of 250 are not under the control of the armed forces of Russia," Lebed said in a September 1997 interview on the American television program *60 Minutes*. "I don't know their location. I don't know whether they have been destroyed or whether they are stored or whether they've been sold or stolen, I don't know." Lebed's claims have been the subject of vigorous debate.

The issue is more than historical curiosity. On October 11, 2001, just one month after terrorists struck in New York and Washington, CIA Director George Tenet briefed President Bush that, according to a CIA source, Al Qaeda had stolen a small nuclear bomb from the Russian arsenal. That bomb, according to the source, was then in New York City. The intelligence proved false. Nonetheless, thefts of nuclear-usable material and attempts to steal nuclear weapons were no longer in the realm of the hypothetical but a proven, recurring fact of international life. According to Graham Allison, "Thousands of weapons and tens of thousands of potential weapons (softball-size lumps of highly enriched uranium and plutonium) remain today in unsecured storage facilities in Russia, vulnerable to theft by determined criminals who could then sell them to terrorists." In the years since the end of the Cold War, there have been numerous cases of theft of nuclear materials in which the thieves were captured, sometimes in Russia, on other occasions in the Czech Republic, Germany and elsewhere.[8]

There is also the problem of the spread of nuclear weapons to weak or failing states. Illustrating the immediacy of the problem was the case of the international trafficking of atomic technology and materials set up by Pakistani atomic scientist Dr. A. Q. Khan, a hero at home and a villain abroad. It amounted to a one-stop shopping network for nuclear weapons. By all accounts, Khan's operation was a highly sophisticated supply and production network spreading from Pakistan to Libya, North Korea, Iran, Malaysia and elsewhere. The network's customers for various nuclear technologies and equipment certainly included Libya, Iran and North Korea, though suspicion at times attached to Algeria, Saudi Arabia and Syria, too. Shutting it down had immediate, flow-on effects. Khan's network had played a crucial role in Libya's nuclear ambitions. Within months of the network being shut down in 2004, Libya had renounced its nuclear program, allowed international inspectors into the country, and given up much of the supporting technology.

It was a proliferation breakthrough of unusual drama. It was also sobering: the network was sophisticated, effective, and had operated undetected for several years. Though A. Q. Khan and his known cohorts are out of business, there is still the great unanswered question: Who else might have access to the nuclear technology he and his network proliferated? We simply don't know, according to London strategic studies think-tank chief John Chipman, as "Pakistan has never made public Khan's confession, the details of its investigation into the network, including who was arrested and who was simply detained 'for debriefing,' the charges and laws under which Khan's associates were detained, the grounds for their release, or the identities of those who were put under a form of continued 'house arrest.'" Pakistan has stopped providing information on the official grounds that the Khan case is closed. In addition, most of Khan's foreign accomplices remain free—only three have been convicted and imprisoned. The upshot is the real concern that the international framework of export controls still contains serious gaps that could well be exploited by a network similar to that of Khan.[9]

What do we know, then? We do know that the dismantling of the A. Q. Khan network had the appearance of a notable success of aggressive non-proliferation efforts and putatively led directly to tangible counterproliferation progress in compelling Libya to abandon its nuclear ambitions and its advanced weapons programs. At first glance, the Libyan case seemed a model of successful deterrence, but first appearances proved deceptive. Encouraged by the coincidence of timing with the invasion of Iraq and the heated domestic political environment, early news reports of Libya's decision to end its nuclear ambitions implied that deterrence had played a key role. Perhaps Colonel Qadafi had feared that Libya might face the same fate as Saddam Hussein's Iraq. The later exposure of Libya's reliance on Khan's network put events into a better perspective. While Qadafi might have been deterred to some extent, the shutdown of Khan's network was probably not the primary driving force behind Tripoli's decision. Libya had simply been caught red-handed, flaunting international rules against the trafficking of nuclear technology and materials. Confronted with undeniable evidence of its wrongdoing and deprived of its principal source for continuing the nuclear program, it probably saw more political advantage in confessing and renouncing nuclear weapons than in denying reality. Qadafi was proved right.

Another troubling complication in controlling proliferation is the blurred line between civilian atomic energy programs and weapons programs. Much effort in recent years has been directed toward establishing clear demarcation lines between them, but it always remains possible for a civilian atomic energy program to migrate to a nuclear weapons program. Civilian atomic energy programs build expertise, contribute technology and produce material. It is a characteristic recently exploited by two of the three countries President Bush notoriously identified as part of an "axis of evil." Iran has long insisted that its nuclear ambitions lie only in civilian atomic energy reactors; the international community, including the International Atomic Energy Agency, remains unpersuaded. Tehran's claim that is has a "peaceful" right to acquire all it needs to come within range of having a bomb served as a reminder of what the NPT was designed to avoid. Iran, for whatever reason, continues to reject international demands to suspend its uranium enrichment program.

By agreements concluded with the Clinton administration, North Korea was putatively allowed to maintain a strictly civilian atomic energy program. Clearly, North Korea was intent on using its energy reactors to enrich uranium, the key ingredient required for an atomic weapon. But problems with North Korea over nuclear proliferation were nothing new. The regime started building nuclear reactors in the 1960s and did not join the NPT until 1985, while the signing of a safeguards agreement that would permit the IAEA inspections of its nuclear program was postponed until 1992. When the overdue inspections suggested that the North Koreans were hiding nuclear material, the Democratic People's Republic of Korea became the first country to announce its withdrawal from the NPT, dramatically suspended one day before it became effective. Then came the period under the Agreed Framework in 1994, which for a number of reasons collapsed in 2002. The Agreed Framework, worked out by the Clinton administration, required the United States both to help North Korea to acquire modern, light-water reactors that would produce energy but not weapons and to move toward normal relations. Neither of these happened as Clinton's successor pushed for the so-called six-party talks on North Korea in which the two Koreas, China, Russia, Japan and the United States were jointly to reach a solution with Kim II Sung's Stalinist-style regime.

On October 9, 2006, North Korea, one of the poorest nations on this planet, exploded a plutonium bomb in a tunnel at a place called Punggye in the far north of the country, becoming the ninth country in history—and arguably the most unstable and dangerous—to proclaim that it had joined the club of nuclear weapons states. Why would North Korea want to acquire nuclear weapons—defense, offense, diplomatic bargaining chip? No one was quite sure. What to do about it was equally problematic. The normally sober *New York Times* editorialized that this was going to be a problem as North Korea "is too erratic, too brutal, and too willing to sell what it has built to have a nuclear bomb." The shortage of information on the generally reclusive North Korean nuclear program remains a serious issue for the international community, especially when this nation has repeatedly demonstrated antagonistic security policies. The possibility of some form of military conflict on the Korean peninsula in the years ahead remains high as it seems highly probable that North Korea would seriously contemplate using nuclear weapons in combat. The North Korean nuclear problem will not go away, despite Pyongyang's repeated counterproposal to rescind its nuclear program in exchange for energy and diplomatic concessions, particularly delisting from the U.S. Department of State's terrorism blacklist. At this juncture, it is hard to tell exactly what, if anything, it would take for North Korea to give up its nuclear ambitions.

Finally, there is the problem of the proliferation of weapons states in South Asia. Efforts to roll back the India-Pakistan nuclear arms race have been spectacularly unsuccessful. Admittedly, the problem had been handled very differently from the Libyan case. India joined the nuclear club with a successful test on May 18, 1974, having begun its program in response to the border clash with China in November 1962, and with China developing its own bomb two years later.[10] Since then, India maintained a dual-front approach to its defense planning, with Pakistan and China clearly in its sights. But it is the India-Pakistan front that has been the cause of intense global concern since things heated up considerably in mid-1998. The two countries have had a marked history of conflict during the relatively short life of the Pakistani nation. It is a rivalry fueled by many cultural and security issues. The injection of nuclear weapons into that volatile mix has naturally led to widespread concern. In May 1998, India tested five nuclear weapons. Before the month was out, Pakistan had hastily responded with six nuclear tests of its own. Each side engaged in saber-rattling rhetoric, and tension has built up on several occasions since, most notably in brinkmanship of dual mobilizations in 2002. The tests provoked widespread international condemnation aimed at both parties. That both countries were beyond the reach of the Nuclear Non-Proliferation Treaty and its watchdog, the International Atomic Energy Agency, would always make matters worse.

Whether nuclear weapons stabilize or destabilize the India-Pakistan rivalry remains a controversial question. Deterrence optimists argue that the risks of even a small-scale nuclear exchange on the subcontinent, where the urban environments would almost certainly lead to millions of deaths, should force each side back from the brink. Former Indian minister of external affairs Jaswant Singh fell in that camp, adding that those who were condemning India's nuclear policies loudest were engaging in what amounted to "nuclear apartheid." "If deterrence works in the West—as it so obviously appears to," he argued, "by what reasoning will it not work in India?"[11] The Pakistani leadership professed similar views: a nuclear conflict would surely have no victor. In South Asia, nuclear deterrence may, however, usher in an era of durable peace between Pakistan and India, providing the requisite incentives for resolving all outstanding issues, especially Jammu and Kashmir. This is the optimistic view. Deterrence pessimists argue, however, that such a view places far too much trust in the organizational integrity of the respective military establishments. Could either side actually control the escalation of a crisis, even if they wanted to? Many security experts think not.

The nuclear experience of recent years suggests that the underlying approach of creating rigorous international norms and inspection supervisory regimes remains the best and most effective way of controlling nuclear threats. Mohamed ElBaradei, director general of the International Atomic Energy Agency and winner of the 2005 Nobel Peace Prize, holds that, "We cannot respond to these threats by building more walls, developing bigger weapons or dispatching more troops. These threats require primarily multinational cooperation." The IAEA works with the atomic programs in more than one hundred countries. ElBaradei estimates that as many as forty-nine nations know how to make nuclear weapons and warns that global tension could well push some over the line. Still, the situation is not as bad as John F. Kennedy worried about in 1963 when he predicted that there could be well over fifteen or twenty nuclear powers by the end of the decade. Interestingly, his concern was not that developing nations would acquire the bomb, but rather that advanced industrial economies would do so, particularly West Germany and Japan. Several European nations, including neutral Sweden, which was then developing plans to build one hundred nuclear weapons to equip its armed forces, were already actively pursuing nuclear weapons programs.

On the other side of the ledger, the Bush administration's policies had been informed by a robust skepticism of the actual effectiveness of international controls and have often emphasized more aggressive counterproliferation efforts, turning its attention more and more to deterring the acquisition of atomic technology and materials, a policy initiated in the Clinton years. Bush revealed himself to be a deterrence pessimist of the first order. In justifying the invasion of Iraq, Bush declared: "I acted because I was not about to leave the security of the American people in the hands of a madman. I was not about to stand by and wait and trust in the sanity and restraint of Saddam Hussein."[12]

The invasion of Iraq in March 2003 was therefore presented mainly as an effort to destroy Iraqi weapons of mass destruction programs, for fear that Saddam could not be deterred and, implicitly, that he might try to turn the tables on the United States and its allies. "We don't want the smoking gun to be a mushroom cloud," then national security adviser Condoleezza Rice said in October 2002 in the lead-up to the war. As is well known, it turned out that Iraq had, in fact, no weapons of mass destruction, particularly of the nuclear kind. Less well known, paradoxically, is that the invasion reinvigorated the very argument that inspection regimes such as the one imposed on Iraq during the 1990s could indeed be effective instruments in slowing or stopping the spread of nuclear weapons. Unfortunately, for the people of Iraq—and the Coalition of the Willing—it was too late.

The clarity of the Cold War world has given way to the ambiguities and uncertainties of a world where global security is threatened by regime collapse, nuclear terrorism, new nuclear weapons states, regional conflict and preexisting nuclear arsenals. The dangers inherent in such a mix are in themselves greatly magnified by easier access to nuclear technology, inadequately protected stockpiles of plutonium and highly enriched uranium, the growing availability of missiles worldwide (thirty-one nations with ballistic missiles), black market nuclear supply networks, and a trend toward acquisition of latent nuclear weapons capabilities through the possession of the entire nuclear fuel cycle. The results are clear: of all the potential threats to the global community today (including global warming), nuclear weapons, the most deadly weapons ever invented—and really the only true weapons of mass destruction—probably pose the greatest risk to humankind today. The solution is imperative; the alternative, unbearable.

CHAPTER 7

ROADMAPS AND ROADBLOCKS: SECURING HUMANITY IN THE TWENTY-FIRST CENTURY

What does peace mean in a world in which the combined wealth of the world's 587 billionaires exceeds the combined gross domestic product of the world's 135 poorest countries? . . . What does peace mean to non-Muslims in Islamic countries or to women in Iran, Saudi Arabia and Afghanistan? What does it mean to the millions who are being uprooted from their lands by dams and development projects? What does peace mean to the poor who are being actively robbed of their resources and for whom everyday life is a grim battle for water, shelter, survival and, above all, some semblance of dignity? For them, peace is war.

—Arundhati Roy

The experience of World War Two provoked what Robert Lieber called a search for the "normative, legalistic and idealistic" bases of international order which, while intellectually impressive, did not match the realities of Cold War international relations.[1] Yet the idea of a moral or normative global order has not lost its appeal. The preceding chapters have mapped out many but not all of the security challenges or risks that confront human society at the start of the new millennium. We have examined the range of interconnected risk factors that make these security challenges dynamic and multifaceted. We have also examined impediments to the realization of policies designed to advance human security through international cooperation and global governance. The challenge of human security in the twenty-first century involves finding common agreement on the nature of global security risks and on the best strategies for ameliorating these at the global but also regional and local levels. Pessimists or realists maintain that such a level of maturity is not yet in evidence in the international system.

THE CHALLENGES OF HUMAN SECURITY

Nuclear proliferation renders traditional power-security calculations obsolete simply because the pivotal balancing principle of the Cold War era, deterrence, is gone. Nuclear weapons technologies have escaped the control of global superpowers, as was to be expected given long-established patterns of technological diffusion. At the same time, we have not reached a stage in human history where morality and pragmatism converge to deem war an unconscionable and counterproductive instrument of state policy. While alarm is registered at the spread of nuclear weapons, we have become sensitized to their existence, and military planners in nuclear-armed states calculate scenarios in which nuclear weapons might be tactically deployed for limited strategic gains.

To this must be added the risk of a "dirty bomb" being deployed in a major city. The possibility of a nonstate actor, a terrorist group, for example, gaining control of a nuclear bomb is cause for alarm—not necessarily because of the potential loss of human life, which would be relatively small compared with an intercontinental nuclear exchange, but because this kind of attack is harder to detect and there is no immediate target against which to retaliate. The existing international nuclear security architecture presupposes negotiations between sovereign states operating according to rational principles and led by people amenable to reason. Religious fundamentalists cherishing apocalyptic visions of Armageddon and the coming of a new messiah hold no such attachment to the system, to civilization or to human life.[2] One New York scenario based upon the terrorist detonation of a small 150-kiloton bomb at the foot of the Empire State Building calculated in excess of 800,000 immediate fatalities in a four-mile radius with an additional 900,000 injured. Clouds of radiation ensuing from the explosion would envelop and slowly poison and kill thousands more outside the immediate blast zone. So the scale of nuclear risks has mushroomed before our eyes.

The destructive potential of nuclear weapons presents a compelling case for the military use of nuclear technologies to remain at the top of the global security agenda. However, in this book we have examined many human security challenges and risks, from conflict and displacement to health and trafficking in drugs and humans. The human security agenda is lengthening as the world becomes more populous and complex. Population growth in the developing world combined with weak governance structures, poor medical facilities and the deleterious effects of severe income inequality gives rise to extensive development needs which, if not addressed, can lead to political chaos.

Ideas about globalization and the "end of the Cold War" interpretation of world history provide starting points for thinking about human security in the new millennium. The transcendence, though not the eclipse, of the nation-state brought into view the contradictions between ideologies of nationhood and the realities of difference—marked by ethnic and religious identity and by economic and political marginalization—that characterize the terrain of long-standing interstate rivalries and conflicts. In developing theoretical frameworks through which to interpret transformations in international affairs, multiple cross-cutting links between individuals across state boundaries also came into view, as did new and old vectors of transnational exchange.

The breakup of the Soviet Union has become the reference point for the discussion of security in the global era, coinciding as it did with new discourses of security from Buzan and the Copenhagen School. The trend toward sectioning off security issues into domains—military, environmental, economic, societal and political—has its advantages, but in this book we have sought to explain how human security concerns cut across these domains. There are dangers in presuming that security issues can be categorized when so much of what constitutes the landscape of security is invisible or unseen.

Writing from an environmentalist's perspective, Chris Bright identifies three types of processes that lead to surprise events. Habitat loss is a widely recognized threat to biodiversity and ultimately to the human food chain, although the secondary effects of such discontinuities might not be immediately noticed. Within ecosystems, therefore, there are multiple unseen events, invisible because they are ignored or undetectable, but which are causally related and which in combination produce a catastrophic event. *Discontinuity, unseen trend* and *synergism* are concepts that can be applied to generate a dynamic framework of security analysis.[3] In traditional international relations and state-centric readings of political affairs, humans are often the unseen agents and victims of change. Add to this the tendency to overlook gender and racial discrimination as factors in international affairs, which ensures than many human security deficits remain invisible until the consequences of neglect become a political problem for governments.

But is there a global or regional system of governance that can cope with this level of complexity? Robert Keohane and Joseph Nye argue that such a global architecture is emerging. Echoing the enthusiasm of radical thinkers like Falk, they argue that "complex interdependence" is increasing through new channels of communication and through social organization. Indeed, globalization is synonymous with pluralization in their interpretation of global change, and this plurality permits a greater flexibility and range of governance options with which to approach the challenge of human security—even if this also multiplies human security risks.[4]

Governance equations have changed dramatically as a consequence of globalization, but the proliferation of interested and organized actors has not simplified the policy choices to be made in pursuit of human security goals. The challenges posed by this array of policy considerations can be organized as follows:

1. *Problem definition*: For human security challenges to be acted upon, first there needs to be widespread agreement among those empowered or powerful enough to respond that there is, in fact, a problem to be addressed. Confronted by an array of present and future dangers, these actors have to agree upon a set of priorities for action and the methods by which these complex crises and risks will be approached. As discussed in chapter 2, problem definition is not straightforward.
2. *Network coordination*: The recruitment of nonstate actors into an evolving architecture of global governance is far from straightforward. It is a fact of life for INGOs and NGOs that funding for their

activities depends upon their ability to compete successfully for development dollars from donor countries, major multilateral donors and the general public. Fundraising is easier when there is extensive media coverage of a major and costly humanitarian crisis such as the December 26, 2004, Asian tsunami or famine in Ethiopia. Viewed cynically, disaster is big business, with the bulk of international development assistance flowing to those parts of the world in most immediate need, while the search for long-term sustainable development is deferred or ignored. Postconflict or postdisaster contexts can become saturated with governmental and nongovernmental aid organizations working at cross-purposes or duplicating relief efforts. The ideal that INGOs, governments and intergovernmental organizations can work cooperatively together to maximize efficiency is frequently confounded by the realities of the mistrustful world of international development.[5]

3. *Cooperation and compliance*: Coordination is also affected by the nature of global business competition. International regimes, from the protection of human rights to the control of nuclear technologies, rely not just upon voluntary cooperation of states but on cooperation of nonstate actors—in particular, transnational corporations. Pharmaceutical companies were forced by the pressure of public opinion to allow the manufacture of cheap generic equivalents of antiviral drugs used to treat HIV/AIDS sufferers. An architect of the UN's Global Compact, John Gerard Ruggie, argues that global businesses are becoming more socially and environmentally aware and are coming to the realization that the private sector has a role to play in the governance of global risk.[6] OECD leadership in forming guidelines for businesses operating in conflict zones and ethically challenging contexts suggests an increasing level of concern for the social impacts of international business activity. Monitoring of corporate compliance with international law is, however, in its infancy and, as discussed in this book, the financial incentives to avoid compliance can be lucrative.

4. *Corruption and transnational crime*: Recognition must also be given to the capacity of criminal groups to network globally and to inhibit relief work and longer-term humanitarian goals. The misallocation of development loans, be they with the World Bank or any national government, is one of the more insidious human security risks arising from inappropriate relations between government and business

in the developed and developing world. Ensuring that international aid is spent to benefit those most in need of assistance is problematic, given the weakness of monitoring regimes at the global and national levels. Corruption corrodes the institution of government and weakens the capacity of states to govern effectively. In extreme cases, where corruption is endemic and extensive, rights of individuals and communities are easily overridden by a powerful few. Without the support and compliance of global corporations and also the hundreds of thousands of transnational and subnational business enterprises, anticorruption regimes and international efforts to prevent human rights abuses are severely constrained. Corrupt officials, from customs officers at border checkpoints to ministers of state, are magnets for transnational criminals eager to circumvent state controls and international regimes. As the UN Oil-for-Food Programme demonstrates, the criminally inclined are adept at locating and exploiting human weaknesses in any chain of command. Tackling corruption, in spite of counterarguments from cultural relativists, is crucial to altering the dynamics of a great many human security risks.

5. *Priority setting*: Aid and development professionals work in a moral minefield. Confronted with often overwhelming human tragedies, relief workers and the organizations they work for must make immediate moral judgments about who must and who should be aided first. If aiding refugees on the brink of starvation is an organizational priority and there is no easy way to distinguish between a refugee and a nonuniformed combatant, then surely the moral imperative to prevent starvation takes precedence over the moral imperative to punish possible war criminals.[7] This is a localized example of how globally established priorities must confront realities on the ground for which pragmatic compromises are necessary—not sometimes, but often. Such microlevel concerns throw into relief the practical complexities of larger statements about freedoms, democracy and justice for all.

THE SOVEREIGNTY QUESTION

States' borders are unlikely to dissolve under the onslaught of economic globalization. While legal barriers to capital, goods and ideas are rapidly breaking down at the arrival of the borderless world of transnational production, investment and information should not obscure the enduring significance of geographical borders, states and governments in the international system.[8] Despite the rise of transnational corporations and the growth of international intergovernmental institutions, nation-states remain the primary actors in international relations. Indeed, scores of new states have joined the international community since the Berlin Wall came down. If nation-statehood was an anachronism, no one told the East Timorese or the republics that emerged from the ashes of the former Yugoslavia. In West Papua and the Gaza Strip, people are fighting to achieve political independence. But this does not mean that state sovereignty cannot or should not be reconceived.

Skeptics view international organizations as weak and bureaucratic and international laws as ineffective, often citing the failure of the United Nations to intervene to prevent genocide in Rwanda.[9] Humanitarian interventions to end human rights violations in Tibet, Chechnya, Burma or Sudan are unlikely to gain Security Council approval. China and Russia, both permanent members of the Security Council, oppose humanitarian intervention because both countries are sensitive about their respective positions in Tibet and Chechnya and wish to inhibit the evolution of an interventionist norm at the UN. Then again, according to Marc Weller, UN interventions in the Balkans, Southeast Asia and Africa during the 1990s have been more successful than not, and hence it is unreasonable to highlight extreme cases such as the Rwandan genocide while ignoring routine achievement.[10]

In this book we have reviewed interventions, humanitarian and otherwise, in Somalia, Afghanistan and Iraq, painting a picture of intervention as a high-risk venture. UN missions in Cambodia (1992) and East Timor (1999) occurred with the permission of the Cambodian and Indonesian governments and entailed no loss of life for occupying forces. Yet a body of expert opinion is emerging that unauthorized intervention on humanitarian grounds is desirable in certain circumstances. India's intervention in East Pakistan (Bangladesh), sparked by a mass exodus of Bangladeshi refugees across the border into India, prevented an even greater humanitarian disaster and brought about the birth of a new nation-state. Vietnam's invasion of Cambodia in 1979, though illegal under international law, brought an end to a four-year reign of terror by the Khmer Rouge during which as many as 1.7 million Cambodians were killed or allowed to die. Unauthorized air strikes against Serbian military targets by the United States in 1999, writes J. L Holzgrefe, arguably prevented a genocide of ethnic Albanians at the hands of the Serbian state and opened the possibility of Kosovo's peaceful secession from Serbia.[11]

The implication of Holzgrefe's reasoning is that humanitarian considerations can justify overriding the fundamental principle of state sovereignty where massive loss of civilian life is imminent. Further evidence of this shifting ground, submissions to the Commission on Intervention and State Sovereignty assert the continuing evolution of the concept of sovereignty to a point where there is recognition that sovereignty bears with it the responsibility for "states to protect persons and property and to discharge the functions of government adequately within their territories."[12] Sovereignty is clearly on the table for further discussion. Irrespective of how sovereignty was understood at the Treaty of Westphalia or at Versailles, and

---

HUMANITARIAN INTERVENTION AND INTERNATIONAL LAW

The legal argument for intervention to end genocide runs thus (in summary):

- There are no legal impediments to humanitarian intervention. Indeed, the UN Charter presents clear legal grounds to intervene where violations of Charter rights are a threat to peace. The charter restricts but does not ban intervention and indeed indirectly acknowledges the possibility of unauthorized humanitarian intervention.
- Articles 2/4 and 2/7 protect against invasion and colonization, not intervention to end political violence. Temporary intervention is thus consistent with international law and Chapter VII of the UN Charter. Obstacles to humanitarian interventions are political, not legal. The Security Council acts in ways that stymie enforcement. But, as said, there are grounds for action by UN member states without UNSC approval.
- Humanitarian interventions without UN approval, such as the 1999 NATO intervention in Kosovo, have succeeded in preventing major loss of civilian life, but repeated illegal actions can undermine international law and international institutions in the long run.

Source: J. L. Holzgrefe, "The Humanitarian Intervention Debate," 2003.

despite positivist objections, a dramatic reinterpretation of international law is underway. Robert Keohane argues for states in which the international community has intervened to have part of their sovereignty set aside and supervised at the regional level by an institution obliged and permitted to engage in further interventions to prevent or resolve political chaos. This was the UN solution to Kosovo in 1999, and Keohane suggests that this might be also be a long-term strategy to repair and rehabilitate Afghanistan, where the structures and the legitimacy of the state have been destroyed by decades of intrasocietal war.[13] This recommendation need not seem far-fetched, but much hinges upon the supportive international order. Buzan thinks such flexible approaches to sovereignty are possible in a system that encourages self-opening as a condition of "insider" status or where "sovereignty is operational within a collective relationship of insiders (international society)."[14]

The dynamics of globalization are forcing states to rethink sovereignty across a range of issues. The 1982 United Nations Law of the Sea Convention (UNCLOS) reaffirms the centrality of territorially bounded states. By extending the mapping of state boundaries into the world's oceans, UNCLOS establishes principles upon which maritime states can agree upon mutual seabed boundaries. In an era where the commercialization of the ocean floor intensifies resource competition and elevates the risk of international conflict, UNCLOS provides a framework for negotiation and resolution of disputed seabed claims.[15] The agreed delineation of maritime sovereignties is a linchpin of future global and regional order but also essential for apportioning responsibility for managing ocean resources and ocean traffic, from protecting fisheries to apprehending polluters or accepting responsibility for the welfare of refugees adrift on the high seas.

Overlapping seabed boundaries, exclusive economic zones and protected areas emerged along Australia's maritime boundaries with Papua New Guinea, Indonesia and, following independence in 1999, East Timor.[16] The Torres Strait Treaty (1978) established three coinciding boundaries: a seabed boundary that marks the Australia-PNG maritime border, an Australian fisheries protection line and a transborder protected zone. Australian fisheries' jurisdiction extends north of the seabed boundary, encompassing fifteen islands adjacent to the PNG coast and mutually recognized as Australian sovereign territory. Freedom of movement is permitted through the protected zone for inhabitants of a small number of designated villages on both sides of the border in recognition of historical cultural ties between communities on the PNG south coast and the Torres

Strait islands.[17] Similar concessions are accorded to fishermen from Indonesia, for whom islands within Australia's maritime boundary were once traditional fishing grounds.

The resultant patchwork of zones, boundaries and special transborder protected areas aptly illustrates the paradox of territoriality in an allegedly borderless world and the possibility that alternative and complementary sovereignties might be possible within a single territorial space. The fact that sovereign nations are prepared to admit flexibility in the application of international principles covering maritime territorial rights and jurisdiction is compelling evidence of the malleability of sovereignty. Such compromises are possible where common economic and political interests are perceived to be at stake. The Westphalian model of territorially bounded nation-states and the realist ideal of the state as a politically homogeneous space do not fit with the new realities of globalization, but then again, reports of the death of the nation-state appear to be exaggerated.

THE GOVERNANCE QUESTION

The UN system has many flaws, many of which stem from the attempt to superimpose a model of global decision making and intervention upon an interstate system that remains highly resistant to centralization on a global scale. The politics of nuclear nonproliferation highlight the many barriers to international cooperation. Despite the severity of human security risks detailed in the preceding chapters, there are many reasons for optimism. Multilevel and cross-sectoral approaches to governing risk are yielding positive results in arresting the rate of HIV/AIDS infection and in limiting the supply of narcotics.

These successes indicate that international efforts to address corruption and promote respect for human rights are making an impact. Yet campaigns to build human rights protections into international trading rules meet objections on two fronts. First, developing countries are sensitive to any attempts by developed nations, the United States especially, to attach rights or obligations with regard to wages and conditions to bilateral and multilateral trade treaties because, they argue, this is merely done to undermine their economic competitiveness by driving up the cost of labor. Powerful states are wary of the consequences of ratifying legal instruments that subordinate their citizens to an international court. As of 2008, the United States had yet to ratify the Rome Statute. Less explicable in terms of great power imperatives, U.S. failure to ratify CEDAW reflects how domestic political issues, in this case the legalization of abortion, can undermine the U.S. rhetorical commitment to international justice and human rights for all.

SUPERPOLARITY

Twenty years ago, international historian Paul Kennedy wrote a seminal account of how great powers emerge and then decline—the historian's corollary to Gilpin's cyclical theory of hegemonic stability. Kennedy's *The Rise and Fall of the Great Powers* (1989) set out the economic and political reasons that states become dominant powers only to gradually lose their preeminence. Kennedy's argument was simple: preeminent states reach a point where the costs of maintaining their global position outweigh the gains. "Imperial overreach" resulted in a gradual erosion of power for imperial states Spain, the Netherlands and Britain, while less-powerful states benefited from the opportunity to develop their power base without the burden of regional or global leadership.

The international system is thus one of fluctuating fortunes. Wrote Kennedy, "The relative strengths of the leading nations in world affairs never remain constant, principally because of the uneven rate of growth among different societies." Wealth and power are synonymous in his analysis.

> If, however, too large a proportion of the state's resources is diverted from wealth creation and allocated instead to military purposes, then that is likely to lead to a weakening of national power over the longer term. In the same way, if a state overextends itself strategically—by, say, the conquest of extensive territories or the waging of costly wars—it runs the risk that the potential benefits of expansion may be outweighed by the great exposure of it all.[18]

Kennedy's prophetic work carries weight even if the United States remains the world's foremost military power and largest economy. Kennedy assumed—like many writers on international affairs, historians and sociologists or futurists—that economic change led change in the international ordering of states. Kennedy paradoxically aligns with radical sociologists like Immanuel Wallerstein who also envisage U.S. long-term decline. According to this scenario, the United States will become only one world power among many and, as a consequence, will have to learn how to cooperate with other militarily powerful states if hegemonic war is to be avoided. The question, then, is what happens to the prevailing international order once its principal sponsor is no longer able to influence its underpinning values.

THE MISSING LINK

At the regional level there are signs from Europe that supranational political structures can function effectively. More structured and rule-based international cooperation is possible. The European Union is a rarefied example of how common approaches to security can be built and adhered to by sovereign states. While the European Union serves as an example of how state sovereignty can be ceded on some issues to a central supranational authority, this option is not currently available to most, if not all, other world regions. Yet promising regional cooperation dynamics are in evidence.

From a realist perspective, the rising density of transnational interconnections could increase the frequency and potency of disputes between states, which might trigger armed conflict. The expanding infrastructure of international business operates like a vast conduit for the signaling of risk, but common transport and communications networks, from roads, railways and bridges to airline routes, give governments reason to monitor political and economic developments in neighboring countries. It is no coincidence that Thailand's improving relations with Myanmar on the one hand and with Laos and Cambodia, border skirmishes aside, on the other has much to do with the development of a Mainland Southeast Asian land bridge between China and the Indian Ocean.[19] Malaysia and Thailand have reached accommodation over the joint exploitation of transborder natural gas reserves beneath their common continental shelf in the Gulf of Thailand. Separatists threaten the jointly owned gas pipeline spanning the border and with it the delivery of natural gas to Malaysian industry customers, giving both countries added incentive for security cooperation.[20] Integrated transport and communications networks are no guarantee of international peace, but in the context of contemporary regional and global enmeshment, common infrastructure, both existing and planned, constitutes an important integrative dynamic.[21]

It is worth remembering that Southeast Asia in the 1950s and 1960s was, to borrow the words of Milton Osborne, a "region in revolt." ASEAN brought together majority Buddhist, Christian and Islamic states whose governments were beset by internal Communist-led uprisings. Common security interests brought the ASEAN-5 to the negotiating table, where they agreed that economic development was the only long-term solution to the social challenges of poverty and food security. If anything, the centripetal forces working against regional cooperation were as intense, if not more so, at the formation of ASEAN as they are today.

The more modest inauguration of the ASEAN Free Trade Area in 1992 was a response to global shifts in regional cooperation in Europe and North America. The idea of an Asian Union and the proposed AFTA-CER (Australia and New Zealand) linkages make sense as risk-reducing responses.

Regionalization also allows multinational corporations to rationalize production at a regional level. There is a growing realization on the part of East Asian governments that financial cooperation is necessary to prevent the risk of economic catastrophe again descending to halt regional economic growth.[22] In this respect, regional sensitivity to financial risk further engenders cooperation, while resentment toward the West fuels a distinctive and, in some quarters, defiant assertion of East Asian identity.

SIX PRINCIPLES OF HUMAN SECURITY

In conceiving human security, therefore, we are confronted by a dazzling complexity of existential concerns from which we struggle to tease out meaningful theoretical abstractions. We can schematize and map out global patterns and trends, historical trajectories, correlations of risk and more. We can compose arguments that suggest advances in the cause of rights, peace and good governance, but although such arguments help illuminate a particular course of events, they are not predictive. In the marketplace of ideas, prediction sells, but prediction is a perilous enterprise. It is through the lens of history that we see how astonishingly simple are the prescriptions for a "better world" but also come to appreciate why such a secure new world remains elusive. In the face of these discomfiting realities, how can human security be defined?

1. *Human security is a new and useful organizing principle in a disordered world.* Accepting that concern for the protection of peoples from existential dangers and notions of moral authorities prior to and above the state constitute the central pillars of human security, we can argue that the elements of human security have been around for centuries. But the qualification of the term *security* marks a new synthesis in international affairs, capturing the salient truth that

states might not be the most effective providers of security goods. Instead of seeing a world mediated by states and states*men*, we comprehend a world composed of multiple agents pursuing complementary and competing agendas. Human security offers a "global" framework through which to impose some order on this disorderliness.

2. *Human security is an approach, not a prescription.* Policymakers and professionals in the field require serviceable frameworks to guide practice. This does not diminish the importance of debates about the nature of security or the means by which a common global future can be secured. This is because behind any global regime lies a host of competing interests seeking to shift the rules in their favor. Were a singular human security to achieve the mantle of uncontested global good, a rush to subvert its logic and rhetorical value for political ends would surely follow. The "securitization" of everything could perversely result in the denial of the very freedoms that human security advocates hold dear.

3. *Human security can be advanced under conditions of international stability and cooperation.* An international global order of some form is necessary if the development aims of the human security agenda are to be achieved. Global perspectives need to be matched with global strategies to reduce the risk of poverty, war, disease, famine and political oppression. Such strategies as that proposed by Annan (see chapter 1), however, depend upon international cooperation, which in turn hinges upon recognition of common interests and purposes. Again, strategies for ameliorating security risks have to be negotiated through the reefs and shoals of political, cultural and economic differences.

4. *International stability and cooperation are in themselves no guarantee that humans will enjoy greater security.* Asian industrialization went hand in hand with repressive government, ranging from authoritarian democracies to outright dictatorships. Without broad acceptance that the principal object of all security policy must be the individual and collective well-being of people, there can be no moral pressure for states and transnational actors to modify their behaviors. It is evident that there are governments and transnational entities whose size and influence render them impervious to moral pressure and for which human rights, peace and justice are at best secondary considerations. Even if the world were composed of sta-

ble, prosperous states, we cannot discount the possibility that one or more might collapse into anarchy through a sudden upsurge in political extremism.

5. *Human security is placed at greatest risk by sudden and drastic regime shifts.* In other words, revolutionary and hegemonic transformations have catastrophic human consequences. Totalizing political ideologies justify radical and violent change in pursuit of a fantastical future. Underpinning value systems are stripped away, leaving people unsure of their status and identity and vulnerable to either persecution or recruitment by their persecutors. Socialist transformations in the Islamic world, Afghanistan in the late 1970s being a prime example, gave impetus to Islamic extremists claiming the mantle of defenders of the faith. Without legitimating Islamism, it is not hard to see how both socialist and neoliberal challenges to Islamic tradition generated violent backlashes against secular modernity.

6. *Human security priorities, to be meaningful, must be stated with due recognition of the immense obstacles to their realization.* There is a tendency among proponents of human security to stress the moral imperatives for action. There can be little argument with the claim that peace, economic justice and human rights are desirable and mutually reinforcing ends. But in a self-help system where nascent and fragile structures for international cooperation are still in the early stages of their formation, impatience undermines the credibility of those attempting to wade through the practical challenges of effecting positive change through negotiation and compromise.

IMAGINING THE FUTURE

This book is structured around a debate between idealist and realist positions on the nature of security without seeking to negate either position. If national security must today be cast in multidimensional and regional or global terms, then effective forms of international cooperation have to be found to address the risks of an increasingly interdependent world. Alliance diplomacy is a confrontational option that reinforces international divisions and perpetuates policy dependence upon neorealist notions of power balances. There is a strengthening of transnational efforts outside the structures of the nation-state to build a normative global order from the ground up through international grassroots activism.

Governments and major corporations bear the heaviest responsibility to meet the challenges of human security in the twenty-first century. From achieving MDGs to preserving the global commons or limiting the proliferation of nuclear weapons, without cooperation between governments, businesses and people, our capacity to govern global risks is greatly diminished. Human security challenges, we hold, can be properly addressed only through a global or holistic appreciation of their complex nature and a realistic appreciation of the limitations of existing structures of global and regional governance. This should be the focus of the future debate.

NOTES

INTRODUCTION

1. National Commission on Terrorist Attacks Upon the United States, *The 9/11 Commission Report*, 1042, www.9-11commission.gov/report/911Report.pdf (accessed October 19, 2007).

2. UNDP, *Human Development Report, 1994* (New York: Oxford University Press, 1994).

3. Boutros Boutros-Ghali, *An Agenda for Peace: Preventive Diplomacy, Peace-Making and Peace-Building*, Report of the Secretary-General, United Nations, A/47/277-S/24111, June 17, 1992, www.un.org/docs/SG/agpeace.html (accessed January 21, 2008).

4. UN Commission on Human Security, *Human Security Now* (New York: United Nations, 2003), 2.

5. Hideaki Shinoda, "The Concept of Human Security: Historical and Theoretical Implications," in *Conflict and Human Security: A Search for New Approaches of Peace Building*, ed. Hideaki Shinoda and How-Won Jeong (Hiroshima: IPSHU, no. 19, 2004), 9. A Nobel Prize winner, Sen gave expression to his ideas in Amartya Sen, *Development as Freedom* (Oxford: Oxford University Press, 1999).

6. Barry Buzan, Ole Weaver, and Jaap de Wilde, *Security: A New Framework of Analysis* (London: Lynne Rienner, 1998); Barry Buzan, *People, States and Fear: The National Security Question in International Relations* (London: Wheatsheaf, 1983).

CHAPTER 1: GLOBALIZING NATIONAL SECURITY

1. Stéphane Courtois, "The Crimes of Communism," in *The Black Book of Communism: Crimes, Terror, Repression*, ed. Stéphane Courtois et al., trans. Mark

Kramer and Jonathan Murphy (Cambridge, MA: Harvard University Press, 2004), 146, 190.

2. Jean-Louis Margolin and Pierre Rigoulot, "Communism in Asia: Between Reeducation and Massacre," in Courtois et al., *The Black Book of Communism*, 495.

3. Francis Fukuyama, *The End of History and the Last Man* (London: Hamish Hamilton, 1992), xiii. Also see Norman A. Graebner, Richard Dean Burns, and Joseph M. Siracusa, *Reagan, Bush, Gorbachev: Revisiting the End of the Cold War* (Westport, CT: Praeger Security International, 2008), 137–46.

4. Stephan Haggard and Robert R. Kaufman, *The Political Economy of Democratic Transitions* (Princeton, NJ: Princeton University Press, 1995), 3–21.

5. Joseph Fewsmith, *China since Tiananmen: The Politics of Transition* (Cambridge: Cambridge University Press, 2001), 50–55, 81–83. For a vivid recounting of the events surrounding Tiananmen, see Nicholas D. Kristof and Sheryl WuDunn, *China Wakes: The Struggle for the Soul of a Rising Power* (New York: Vintage Books, 1995), 76–91.

6. Commission for Africa, *Our Common Interest: An Argument* (London: Penguin, 2005), 17.

7. This section of chapter 1 reproduces passages from P. Battersby, "A World Turned Upside Down: Risk, Refugees and Global Security in the 21st Century," in *Asylum Seekers: International Perspectives on Interdiction and Deterrence*, ed. Alperhan Babacan and Linda Briskman (Newcastle: Cambridge Scholars Publishing, 2008), 10–27.

8. Angus Maddison, *The World Economy*, vol. 2, *Historical Statistics* (Paris: OECD, 2003), 259, 261.

9. Milton Leitenberg, *Deaths in Wars and Conflicts in the 20th Century* (Occasional Paper no. 29, Peace Studies Program, Cornell University, 2006), www.cissm .umd.edu/papers/files/deathswarsconflictsjune52006.pdf (accessed June 21, 2007).

10. Martin Meredith, *The State of Africa* (New York: Free Press, 2005), 278–283.

11. Mary Kaldor, *New and Old Wars: Organized Violence in a Global Era* (Cambridge: Polity Press, 1999); V. P. Gagnon, *The Myth of Ethnic War: Serbia and Croatia in the 1990s* (Ithaca, NY: Cornell University Press, 2004).

12. President George W. Bush, "Address to the UN General Assembly: A More Hopeful World Beyond Terror and Extremism," www.whitehouse.gov/news/ releases/2006/09/20060919-4.html (accessed June 30, 2008).

13. Robert O. Keohane, *After Hegemony: Cooperation and Discord in the World Political Economy*, 2nd ed. (Princeton, NJ: Princeton University Press, 2005), 207.

14. United Nations Office on Drugs and Crime, *World Drug Report 2007* (Vienna: United Nations, 2007), 9.

15. President of the United States, *National Drug Control Strategy* (Washington: Office of National Drug Control Policy, 2004), 51.

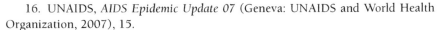

16. UNAIDS, *AIDS Epidemic Update 07* (Geneva: UNAIDS and World Health Organization, 2007), 15.

17. Nicholas Stern, *The Stern Review: The Economics of Climate Change*, prepublication ed. (London: HM Treasury, 2006), 56–57, www.hm-treasury.gov.uk/independent_reviews/stern_review_economics_climate_change/stern_review_re port.cfm (accessed March 20, 2008).

18. United Nations, *United Nations Millennium Development Goals Report, 2007*, www.un.org/millenniumgoals/pdf/mdg2007.pdf (accessed March 31, 2008).

19. Sen, *Development as Freedom*, 15, 87–110.

20. R. Paris, "Human Security: Paradigm Shift or Hot Air?" in *New Global Dangers: Changing Dimensions of International Security*, ed. M. E. Brown, O. R. Cote, Jr., S. M. Lynn-Jones, and S. E. Miller (Cambridge, MA: MIT Press, 2004), 254–55.

21. Human Security Centre, *Human Security Report, 2005* (Vancouver: University of British Columbia, 2006), 18–20.

22. Uppsala Conflict Data Program, "Definitions," http://www.pcr.uu.se/research/UCDP/data_and_publications/definitions_al l .htm (accessed September 18, 2007). Cited in Human Security Centre, *Human Security Report, 2005*, 18–20.

23. *Australia's Regional Security*, Ministerial Statement by the Senator the Hon. Gareth Evans QC, Minister for Foreign Affairs and Trade, December 1989 (Canberra: Commonwealth of Australia).

24. Foreign Affairs Minister Lloyd Axworthy, *Canada World View*, Canadian Ministry of Foreign Affairs and International Trade Official Publication, www .international.gc.ca/canada-magazine/special/se1t3-en.asp (accessed January 20, 2008).

25. Jim Whitman, *The Limits of Global Governance* (London: Routledge, 2005), 118.

26. Kofi Annan, *We the Peoples: The Role of the United Nations in the 21st Century* (New York: United Nations, 2000), 14, www.un.org/millennium/sg/report/ (accessed March 23, 2005).

27. Commission for Africa, *Our Common Interest*, 24.

28. Britta Sadoun, *Political Space for Non-Governmental Organizations in the United Nations World Summit Processes* (Civil Society and Social Movements Programme Paper No. 29, United Nations Research Institute for Social Development, 2007), 2–3; Manuel Mejido Costoya, *Toward a Typology of Civil Society Actors: The Case of the Movement to Change International Trade Rules and Barriers* (Civil Society and Social Movements Programme Paper No. 30, United Nations Research Institute for Social Development, 2007), 13–22.

29. Costoya, *Toward a Typology of Civil Society Actors*, 10–12.

30. Commission on Global Governance, *Human Security Now*, 32.

31. M. Lindenberg and C. Bryant, *Going Global: Transforming Relief and Development NGOs* (Bloomfield, CA: Kumarian Press, 2001), 3; Peter Willetts, "Transnational Actors and International Organizations in World Politics," in *The*

Globalization of World Politics: An Introduction to International Relations, ed. John Bayliss and Steve Smith (Oxford: Oxford University Press, 2005), 427.

32. Lindenberg and Bryant, *Going Global*, 3.

33. Peter Dicken, *Global Shift: Reshaping the Global Economic Map in the 21st Century*, 4th ed. (London: Sage, 2003), 381–82.

34. Nina Graeger and Alexandra Novosseloff, "The Role of the OSCE and the EU," in *The United Nations and Regional Security: Europe and Beyond*, ed. Michael Pugh and Waheguru Pal Singh Sidhu (Boulder, CO: Lynne Rienner, 2003), 81–83.

CHAPTER 2: THE ALCHEMY OF PEACE

1. This idea is discussed at length in Alexander Wendt, *Social Theory of International Politics* (Cambridge: Cambridge University Press, 1999).

2. Henry Kissinger, *Diplomacy* (New York: Touchstone, 1994), 19.

3. Geoffrey Robertson, *Crimes against Humanity: The Struggle for Global Justice*, 2nd ed. (London: Penguin, 2002), xxxii.

4. Kenneth Waltz, *Theory of International Politics* (Boston: McGraw-Hill, 1979), 112.

5. Carl Von Clausewitz, "Key Concepts," in L. Freedman (ed.), *War* (Oxford: Oxford University Press, 1994), 207.

6. John Keegan, *A History of Warfare* (London: Hutchinson, 1993), 58.

7. Geoffrey Blainey, *The Causes of War*, 3rd ed. (Melbourne: Sun Books, 1988).

8. Robert Jervis, *Perception and Misperception in International Politics* (Princeton, NJ: Princeton University Press, 1976), 62–67.

9. David J. Kilcullen, "New Paradigms for 21st Century Conflict," *Foreign Policy Agenda* 12, no. 5 (May 2007): 39–45, usinfo.state.gov/journals/itps/0507/ijpe/kilcullen.htm (accessed October 29, 2008); and Robert G. Berschinski, *AFRICOM's Dilemma: The "Global War on Terrorism," "Capacity Building," Humanitarianism, and the Future of U.S. Security Policy in Africa* (Strategic Studies Institute, November 2007), www.StrategicStudiesInstitute.army.mil (accessed June 10, 2008).

10. Barry Buzan, *People, States and Fear* (London: Wheatsheaf, 1983), 1.

11. Wendt, *Social Theory of International Politics*, 25.

12. Thomas Hobbes, *Leviathan* (London: Penguin, 1981), 188.

13. Hans Reiss, ed. and trans., *Kant: Political Writings*, 2nd ed. (Cambridge: Cambridge University Press, 1991), 93–106.

14. Mohammed Nuruzzaman, "Paradigms in Conflict: The Contested Claims of Human Security, Critical Theory and Feminism," *Cooperation and Conflict* 41 (2006): 300.

15. Michael Sheehan, *International Security: An Analytical Survey* (Boulder, CO: Lynne Rienner, 2005), 43–44.

16. Ted Gurr et al., *State Failure Task Force Report: Phase III Findings* (McLean,

VA: Science Applications International Corporation, 2000); Barbara Harff and Ted Robert Gurr, *Ethnic Conflict in World Politics*, 2nd ed. (Boulder, CO: Westview Press, 2004), 95–116.

17. Waltz, *Theory of International Politics*, 103.

18. Gagnon, *The Myth of Ethnic Wars*, 2–3.

19. Gagnon, *The Myth of Ethnic Wars*, 9.

20. Waltz, *Theory of International Politics*, 64.

21. Kaldor, *New and Old Wars*, 152.

22. Keegan, *A History of Warfare*, 21; Blainey, *The Causes of War*, 288.

23. Norman Angell, *The Great Illusion* (New York: Cosimo Classics, 2007), 341.

24. Karl Marx and Friedrich Engels, *The Communist Manifesto* (Harmondsworth: Penguin, 1981), 102.

25. V. I. Lenin, "Socialism and War," in Freeman (ed.), *War* (Oxford: Oxford University Press, 1994), 97.

26. W. W. Rostow, *The Stages of Economic Growth: A Non-Communist Manifesto* (Cambridge: Cambridge University Press, 1960), 4–16, www.mtholyoke.edu/acad/intrel/ipe/rostow.htm (accessed January 20, 2008).

27. Samuel P. Huntington, *Political Order in Changing Societies* (New Haven, CT: Yale University Press, 1968), 49–50.

28. For example, Immanuel Wallerstein, *The Decline of American Power: The U.S. in a Chaotic World* (New York: The New Press, 2003), 254–55.

29. Robert Gilpin, *The Political Economy of International Relations* (Hyderabad: Orient Longman, 2003), 93–97.

30. Paul Berman, *Power and the Idealists* (New York: W. W. Norton, 2005), 151–91.

31. Marx and Engels, *The Communist Manifesto*, 104.

32. Michael Hardt and Antonio Negri, *Empire* (Cambridge, MA: Harvard University Press, 2000).

33. Berman, *Power and the Idealists*, 181.

34. Council on Foreign Relations, "Hamas," *Backgrounder* (June 8, 2007), www.cfr.org/publication/8968 (accessed March 15, 2008); Are Knudsen, "Crescent and Sword: The Hamas Enigma," *Third World Quarterly* 26 (November 2005): 1384.

35. Claudia F. Fuentes and Francisco Rojas Aravena, *Promoting Human Security: Ethical, Normative and Educational Frameworks in Latin America and the Caribbean* (Paris: UNESCO, 2005), 152.

36. Mark Findlay, *The Globalization of Crime* (Cambridge: Cambridge University Press, 1999), 174–79.

37. Findlay, *The Globalization of Crime*, 68, 175.

38. In particular, the essay by Jim George, "Understanding International Relations after the Cold War: Probing beyond the Realist Legacy," in *Challenging*

Boundaries: Global Flows, Territorial Identities, ed. Michael J. Shapiro and Hayward R. Alker (Minneapolis: University of Minnesota Press, 1996), 42–45.

39. Susan McKay, "Women, Human Security, and Peace-building: A Feminist Analysis," in *Conflict and Human Security: A Search for New Approaches to Peace-Building*, ed. H. Shinoda and H. Jeong (Hiroshima: Institute for Peace Science, Hiroshima University, 2004), 158–63.

40. McKay, "Women, Human Security and Peace-building," 155–57.

41. Saskia E. Wieringa, "Measuring Women's Empowerment: Developing a Global Tool," in *Engendering Human Security: Feminist Perspectives*, ed. Thanh-Dam Truong, Saskia Wieringa, and Amrita Chhachhi (London: Zed Books, 2006), 214–15.

42. Cynthia Enloe, *Bananas, Beaches and Bases: Making Feminist Sense of International Politics* (Berkeley: University of California Press, 1990), 12–13.

43. Enloe, *Bananas, Beaches and Bases*, 11–18.

44. Jan Pettman, "Border Crossings/Shifting Identities: Minorities, Gender, and the State in International Perpsective," in *Challenging Boundaries: Global Flows, Territorial Identities*, ed. Michael J. Shapiro and Hayward R. Alker (Minneapolis: University of Minnesota Press, 1996), 265–66.

45. L. H. M. Ling, "Global Presumptions: A Critique of Sorensen's World-Order Change," *Cooperation and Conflict: Journal of the Nordic International Studies Association* 4, no. 4 (2006): 383.

46. Juanita Elias, *Fashioning Inequality: The Multinational Company and Gendered Employment in a Globalizing World* (Aldershot: Ashgate, 2004), 72.

47. Virginia Vargas, "Globalisation, Social Movements and Feminism: Coming Together at the World Social Forum," in *Engendering Human Security: Feminist Perspectives*, ed. Thanh-Dam Truong, Saskia Wieringa, and Amrita Chhachhi (London: Zed Books, 2006), 196–97.

48. Samuel P. Huntington, *The Clash of Civilizations and the Remaking of World Order* (New York: Simon & Schuster, 1997), 21.

49. Huntington, *The Clash of Civilizations*, 21.

50. Huntington, *The Clash of Civilizations*, 135.

51. Robert O. Keohane, *After Hegemony: Cooperation and Discord in the World Political Economy*, 2nd ed. (Princeton, NJ: Princeton University Press, 2005), 244.

52. Keohane, *After Hegemony*, 7.

53. Kenichi Ohmae, *The End of the Nation State: The Rise of Regional Economies* (London: HarperCollins, 1996), 15.

54. Stephanie Lawson, *Culture and Context in World Politics* (London: Palgrave, 2006), 171.

55. David Held, "From Executive to Cosmopolitan Multilateralism," in *Taming Globalization: Frontiers of Governance*, ed. D. Held and Mathias Koenig-Archibugi (Cambridge: Polity, 2003), 168.

56. Ulrich Beck, *World Risk Society* (Cambridge: Polity, 1999), 72–90; An-

thony Giddens, *Runaway World: How Globalization Is Reshaping Our Lives* (Cambridge: Polity, 1999), 27–33.

57. Ulrich Beck, *Power in the Global Age* (Cambridge: Polity, 2005).

58. Keohane, *After Hegemony*, 245.

59. Lucian W. Pye, *Asian Power and Politics: The Cultural Dimensions of Authority* (Cambridge, MA: Harvard University Press, 1985), 78–79.

CHAPTER 3: "BLACK HAWK DOWN"

1. Patrick Buchanan, "America First, and Second, and Third," *National Interest* 19 (Spring 1990): 77–82; William F. Gavin, "At the Roots of Pat Buchanan's Rhetoric," *WPNW* (Mar. 4–10, 1996): 24; and Owen Harries, "Pat's World," *The National Interest* 43 (Spring 1996): 108–111.

Portions of this chapter are adapted from *The United States and Post–Cold War Interventions* (Claremont, CA: Regina Books, 1998), with the permission of the publisher, Richard Dean Burns.

2. John Mueller, "The Common Sense," *National Interest* 47 (Spring 1997): 81–88; Barry Posen and Andrew Ross, "Contemporary Visions for U.S. Grand Strategy," *International Security* 21 (Winter 1996/97): 5–53. For the polls and Republicans' opposition to the UN and U.S. world concerns, see Jessica Mathews, "The U.N.—Are the Republicans Wrong Again?" *WPNW* (Mar. 11–17, 1996): 28.

3. Charles Krauthammer, "The Unipolar Movement," *Foreign Affairs* 70 (Winter 1990/91): 23–33.

4. Jesse Helms, "Fixing the U.N.," *Foreign Affairs* 75 (Sept./Oct. 1996): 2–7. For reactions to Helms: *Foreign Affairs* 75 (Nov./Dec. 1996): 172–79.

5. Joseph S. Nye, Jr., "What New World Order?" *Foreign Affairs* 71 (Spring 1992): 83–96; Joseph S. Nye, "The Case for Deep Support," *Foreign Affairs* 74 (July 1995): 90–102.

6. Lawrence Freedman, "Introduction," in *Military Intervention in European Conflicts*, ed. L. Freedman (London: Blackwell, 1994), 1–13.

7. Ted Robert Gurr, "Peoples against States: Ethnopolitical Conflict and the Changing World System," *International Studies Quarterly* 38 (Sept. 1994): 347–377.

8. Robert D. Blackwell, "A Taxonomy for Defining US National Security Interests in the 1990s and Beyond," in *Europe in Global Change*, ed. Werner Weidenfeld and Josef Janning (Gutersloh, Germany: Bertelsmann Foundation, 1993), 108; Boutros Boutros-Ghali, "Empowering the United Nations," *Foreign Affairs* 71 (Winter 1992/93): 89–102.

9. Josef Joffe, "The New Europe, Yesterday's Ghosts," *Foreign Affairs* 72 (Winter 1992/93): 33.

10. Kurt Andersen, "The Watchword Is Wariness: Weinberger Outlines Six Criteria for Sending Troops into Combat," *Time* 129 (Dec. 10, 1984): 1. For Shultz,

see Fareed Zakaria, "A Framework for Intervention in the Post Cold War World," in *U.S. Intervention Policy for the Post Cold War World*, ed. Arnold Kanter et al. (New York: Norton, 1994): 185–86. For a discussion of democracy and peace, see Henry Farber and Joanne Gowa, "Politics and Peace," *International Security* 20 (Fall 1995): 123–46 and *Correspondence* 20 (Winter 1996/97): 177–87; Edward Mansfield and Jack Snyder, "Democratization and the Danger of War," *International Security* 20 (Summer l995): 5–38 and *Correspondence* 20 (Spring 1996): 176–207.

11. Steven Kull and I. M. Destler, *An Emerging Consensus: A Study of American Public Attitudes on America's Role in the World* (College Park, MD: Center for International and Security Studies, University of Maryland, July 10, 1996).

12. I. M. Lewis, *A Modern History of Somalia: Nation and State in the Horn of Africa* (Boulder, CO: Westview, 1988).

13. Terrence Lyons and Ahmed Y. Samatar, *Somalia: State Collapse, Multilateral Intervention and Strategies for Political Reconstruction* (Washington, DC: Brookings Institution, 1995); Jonathan Stevenson, *Losing Mogadishu* (Annapolis, MD: Naval Institute Press, 1995), 7–11. On U.S. aid, see Jeffrey A. Lefebvre, *Arms for the Horn: U.S. Policy in Ethiopia and Somalia, 1953–91* (Pittsburgh: University of Pittsburgh Press, 1993); Donald Rothschild and John Ravenhill, "Subordinating African Issues to Global Logic," in *Eagle Resurgent? The Reagan Era in American Foreign Policy*, ed. Kenneth A. Oye, Robert J. Lieber, and Donald Rothschild (Boston: Little, Brown, 1987): 408–09; James G. Hershberg et al., "New East-Bloc Evidence on the Horn of Africa, 1977–1978," *Cold War International History Project Bulletin* 8/9 (Winter 1996–97): 18–102.

14. Mohamed Sahnoun, *The Somalia Challenge: The Missed Opportunities* (Washington, DC: Institute for Peace Press, 1994), 3–11; Jane Perlez, "Somalia Abandoned to Its Own Civil War," *New York Times*, Jan. 6, 1991, E-2.

15. Sahnoun, *The Somalia Challenge*, 25–37; Jonathan Stevenson, "Hope Restored in Somalia?" *Foreign Policy* 91 (Summer 1993): 138–54; Jane Perlez, "Profile: Mohammed Sahnoun; A Diplomat Matches Wits with Chaos in Somalia," *New York Times*, Sept. 26, 1992, E-4; Jane Perlez, "Aid's Departure Another Blow to UN in Somalia," *New York Times*, Oct. 31, 1992, A-2; Alex De Waal and Rakiya Omaar, "Doing Harm by Doing Good?" *Current History* 92 (May 1993): 198–202; Alex De Waal and Rakiya Omaar, "Somalia's Uninvited Saviors," *Washington Post*, Dec. 13, 1992, C1, 4. Another account of the UN problems in Somalia is Jeffrey Clark, "Debacle in Somalia," in *Enforcing Restraint*, ed. Lori Damrosh (New York: Council on Foreign Relations, 1993): 218–25.

16. Clifford Orwin, "Distant Compassion (Somalia)," *The National Interest* 43 (Spring 1996): 42–49; Peter Applebaum, "Scared by Faces of Need, Americans Say, 'How Could We Not Do This?'" *New York Times*, Dec. 13, 1992, A-16; Steven Hansh et al., *Excess Morality and the Impact of Health Intervention in the Somalian Humanitarian Emergency* (Washington, DC: Refugee Policy Group, 1994).

17. Robert B. Oakley and John L. Hirsh, *Somalia and Operation Restore Hope*

(Washington, DC: Institute of Peace, 1995), 35–46; Don Oberdorfer, "The Road to Somalia," *Washington Post National Weekly*, Dec. 14–20, 1992, 6–7; Colin Powell, *My American Journey* (New York: Random House, 1995), 524.

18. Keith Richberg, "Aid Workers Watching Country Favor Toughness toward Warlords," *Washington Post*, Nov. 27, 1992, A-1, 36; Henry Kissinger, "Somalia: Reservations," *Washington* Post, Dec. 13, 1992, C-7; Alex De Waal and Rakiya Omaar, "Doing Harm by Doing Good?" *Current History* 92 (May 1993): 198–202; Bruce W. Nelan, "Taking on the Thugs," *Time* 140 (Dec. 14, 1992): 26–35; Elaine Sciolino, "Getting in Is the Easy Part of the Mission," *New York Times*, Dec. 6, 1992, E-1, 3; Smith Hempstone, "Think Three Times before You Embrace the Somalia Tarbaby," *U.S. News and World Report* 113 (Dec. 14, 1992), 30; *New York Times*, "But Who'll Disarm the Thugs?" Dec 13, 1992.

19. Boutros-Ghali letter in UN Blue Book Series, Vol. VIII, *The United Nations and Somalia*, 1992–1996 (New York: UN Department of Public Information, 1996): Document 36 (Dec. 8, 1992): 216–217; Powell quotation in Sidney Blumenthal, "Why Are We in Somalia?" *New Yorker* 69 (Oct. 25, 1993): 48–71; John R. Bolton, "Wrong Turn in Somalia," *Foreign Affairs* 73 (Jan./Feb. 1994): 56–67; Walter Clark and Jeffrey Herbst, "Somalia and the Future of Humanitarian Intervention," *Foreign Affairs* 75 (Mar./Apr. 1996): 70–85; U.S. State Department, "Intervention in Somalia," *Foreign Policy Bulletin* 3 (Jan./Apr. 1993): 18–29.

20. Oakley and Hirsh, *Somalia and Operation Restore Hope*, 47–76; Lyons and Samatar, *Somalia: State Collapse*, 31–43; Diana Jean Schemo, "The World Moves on Somalia: The Warlords Move Faster," *New York Times*, Feb. 21, 1993, E-6.

21. Jane Perlez, "Rebels Take Control," *New York Times*, June 6, 1991, E-3; Lyons and Samatar, *Somalia: State Collapse*, 44–52.

22. Oakley and Hirsh, *Somalia and Operation Restore Hope*, 47–76; a more critical account is Stevenson, *Losing Mogadishu*, 54–70. UN Blue Book, *Somalia*, Document 49, 244–257, has the Boutros-Ghali report of March 3; Document 51, 261–263, is on establishing UNOSOM II.

23. Lyons and Samatar, *Somalia: State Collapse*, 53–57; Oakley and Hirsh, *Somalia and Operation Restore Hope*, 93–97; UN Blue Book, *Somalia*, Document 61, 279–295, is Boutros-Ghali's report of August 16 on UNOSOM forces and problems.

24. Thomas W. Lippman and Barton Gellman, "How Somalia Started Biting the Hand That Fed It," *Washington Post National Weekly*, Oct. 18–24, 1993, 14–15; U.S. State Department, "Walk, Don't Run to the Nearest Exit," *Foreign Policy Bulletin* 4 (Nov./Dec. 1993): 19–27; Powell, *My American Journey*, 588–604; UN Blue Book, *Somalia*, Document 75, 323–336, is Boutros-Ghali's report of Nov. 12, 1993.

25. Oakley and Hirsh, *Somalia and Operation Restore Hope*, 124–160; UN Blue Book, *Somalia*, Document 91, 426–429, is Boutros-Ghali's report on UNOSOM II of Aug. 14, 1994; Barton Gellman, "Pursuing Aideed into the Shifting Sands of U.S. Purpose," *Washington Post National Weekly*, Oct. 11–17, 1993, 7; Barton Gellman,

"A Deadly Round of Mixed Signals over Somalia," *Washington Post National Weekly*, Nov. 8–14, 1993, 31; Keith Richburg, "The Warlord's War," *Washington Post National Weekly*, Oct. 11–17, 1993, 6.

26. UN Blue Book, *Somalia*, Document 116 is the final report of Boutros-Ghali on Sept. 19, 1995, before the UN left Somalia and only kept political offices in Kenya available for negotiations. For an account favorable to Aideed, see Alex Shoumatoff, "The 'Warlord' Speaks," *Nation* 258 (Apr. 4, 1994): 442–50.

27. Associated Press, "Militia Says It Captured Somalia's Airport," *New York Times*, July 7, 1996, A-3; Donald G. McNeil, Jr., "Somalia Clan Leader Who Opposed U.S. Is Dead," *New York Times*, Aug. 3, 1996, A-1, 4; Donald G. McNeil, Jr., "Aideed's Son Sworn In," *New York Times*, Aug. 5, 1996; James McKinley, Jr., "How a U.S. Marine Became Leader of Somalia," *New York Times*, Aug. 12, 1996, A-3; James McKinley, Jr., "Islamic Movement's Niche," *New York Times*, Aug. 23, 1996, A-1, 6; James McKinley, Jr., "As Talks Stall, Somalia Strife Kills 300 over 5 Days," *New York Times*, Dec. 19, 1996, A-6; Stephen Buckley, "A Port in a Storm Amid Anarchy in Somalia," *Washington Post National Weekly*, Mar. 11–17, 1996, 18.

CHAPTER 4: A GLOBAL WEB OF RISK

1. Sections of this chapter also appear in Battersby, "A World Turned Upside Down."

2. Hearing before the Committee on Foreign Affairs, House of Representatives, One Hundred Tenth Congress, First Session, April 19, 2007, Serial No. 110–53, foreignaffairs.house.gov/110/34716.pdf (accessed January 20, 2008); Darren Brunk, "Dissecting Darfur: Anatomy of a Genocide Debate," *International Relations* 22 (2008): 27, 41.

3. Alex De Waal, "Darfur and the Failure of the Responsibility to Protect," *International Affairs* 83 (2007): 1040–42. See also Paul D. Williams and Alex J. Bellamy, "The Responsibility to Protect and the Crisis in Darfur," *Security Dialogue* 36 (2005): 27–47.

4. M. W. Daly, *Darfur's Sorrow: A History of Destruction and Genocide* (Cambridge: Cambridge University Press, 2007), 28–34.

5. Daly, *Darfur's Sorrow*, 178; Meredith, *State of Africa*, 344–347.

6. Meredith, *State of Africa*, 347.

7. Douglas Hamilton Johnson, *The Root Causes of Sudan's Civil Wars* (Oxford: James Currey, 2004), 41–42.

8. Daly, *Darfur's Sorrow*, 205.

9. Kithure Kindiki, *Intervention to Protect Civilians in Darfur: Legal Dilemmas and Policy Imperatives* (ISS Monograph Series, no. 131, May 2007), 3.

10. United Nations Environment Programme, *Sudan: Post-Conflict Environmental Assessment (Synthesis Report)*, www.humanitarianreform.org/humanitarian

reform/Portals/1/cluster%20approach%2 0p age/clusters%20pages/Environment/ UNEP_Sudan_synthesis_E.pdf (accessed March 24, 2008), 7–10.

11. Kindiki, *Intervention to Protect Civilians in Darfur*, 3.

12. Daly, *Darfur's Sorrow*, 273.

13. Jessica Stern, *Terror in the Name of God: Why Religious Militants Kill* (New York: Ecco, 2003), 45–46; Bassam Tibi, "The Totalitarianism of Jihadist Islamism and Its Challenge to Europe and to Islam," *Totalitarian Movements and Political Religions* 8 (March 2007): 35–54.

14. *9/11 Report*, 59–62; Meredith, *State of Africa*, 590–93; Coll, *Ghost Wars*, 162–64.

15. Christopher Thompson, "The Scramble for Africa's Oil," *New Statesman*, June 14, 2007, www.newstatesman.com (accessed December 5, 2007).

16. Daly, *Darfur's Sorrow*, 272.

17. International Crisis Group, *Darfur's New Security Reality*, Africa Report no. 134, November 26, 2007, 1; Steve Bloomfield, "The Thin Blue Line," *Melbourne Age*, June 17, 2008, 9.

18. Navnita Chadha Behera, *Demystifying Kashmir* (Washington: Brookings Institution Press, 2006), 4, 14–16.

19. A tragic miscalculation detailed in Steve Coll, *Ghost Wars*.

20. A. Rasanayagam, *Afghanistan: A Modern History* (London: I. B. Tauris, 2005), 184–88.

21. "US Casualties in Iraq," www.globalsecurity.org/military/ops/iraq_casualties.htm, (accessed October 29, 2008).

22. Iraq Body Count (IBC), "Documented Civilian Deaths from Violence," www.iraqbodycount.org/database (accessed December 13, 2007).

23. Gilbert Burnham, Riyadh Lafta, Shannon Doocy, and Les Roberts, "Mortality after the 2003 Invasion of Iraq: A Cross-sectional Cluster Sample Survey," *The Lancet* 368 (October 12, 2006): 1421–28.

24. Peter W. Galbraith, *The End of Iraq: How American Incompetence Created a War without End* (London: Pocket Books, 2007), 70–82.

25. Fromkin, *Peace to End all Peace* (London: Penguin, 1989), 449–54.

26. Dilip Hiro, *Iraq: A Report from the Inside* (London: Granta, 2003), 71–94.

27. Hiro, *Iraq from the Inside*, 71–94; Ian Bickerton and Michael Pearson, *43 Days: The Gulf War* (Sydney: ABC Books, 1991).

28. Jeffrey A. Meyer and Mark G. Califano, *Good Intentions Corrupted: The Oil-for-Food Scandal and the Threat to the UN* (New York: Public Affairs Reports, 2006), 74–75, 120–30.

29. K. M. Pollack and D. L. Bryman, "Iraqi Refugees: Carriers of Conflict," *Atlantic*, November 2006, www.brookings.edu/views/articles/byman/2061101.htm (accessed February 7, 2007).

30. J. G. Ruggie, "Taking Embedded Liberalism Global: The Corporate Con-

nection," in *Taming Globalization: Frontiers of Governance*, ed. D. Held and Mathias Koenig-Archibugi (Cambridge: Polity, 2003), 102–103.

31. Henk Driessen, "The 'New Immigration' and the Transformation of the European-African Frontier," in *Border Identities: Nation and State and International Frontiers*, ed. Thomas M. Wilson and Hastings Donnan (Cambridge: Cambridge University Press, 1998), 100–102.

32. Tim Costello, "Seeing the Whole: Population in a Global Context," in *Australia's Population Challenge: The 2002 Australian Population Summit*, ed. Steve Vizard, Hugh J. Martin, and Tim Watts (Melbourne: Penguin, 2003), 197–98.

33. Michael Barnett and Martha Finnemore, *Rules for the World: International Organizations in Global Politics* (Ithaca, NY: Cornell University Press, 2004), 96–97.

34. United Nations Population Fund, *State of the World Population 2006, A Passage to Hope: Women and International Migration*, www.unfpa.org/swp/2006/english (accessed September 12, 2007); Commission on Human Security, *Human Security Now*, 41.

35. Moises Naim, *Illicit: How Smugglers, Traffickers and Copycats Are Hijacking the Global Economy* (New York: Doubleday, 2005), 88; P. Shifman, "Trafficking and Women's Human Rights in a Globalised World," *Gender and Development* 11, no. 1 (May 2003), 126–27.

36. Naim, *Illicit*, 12–24; United Nations Office on Drugs and Crime (UNDOC), *World Drug Report, 2007* (Vienna: United Nations, 2007).

37. Naim, *Illicit*, chapters 4 and 5, 65–85, 86–108; UNDOC, *World Drug Report, 2007*, 170–73.

38. International Crisis Group, "Executive Summary," *Latin American Drugs 1: Losing the Fight* (Latin America Report no. 25, March 14, 2008).

39. Ronald D. Renard, *The Burmese Connection: Illegal Drugs and the Making of the Golden Triangle* (Boulder, CO: Lynne Rienner, 1996), 22.

40. John Braithwaite and Peter Drahos, *Global Business Regulation* (Cambridge: Cambridge University Press, 2000), 360–63.

41. Martin Smith, *Burma: Insurgency and the Politics of Ethnicity*, 2nd ed. (London: Zed Books, 1993), 76–95.

42. Alan Dupont, *East Asia Imperiled: Transnational Challenges to Security* (Cambridge: Cambridge University Press, 2001), 198–99.

43. Smith, *Burma*, 27–38.

44. Indochina Information Centre, *Indochina Review* (Bangkok: Manager Group, 1994), 114–15.

45. *Bangkok Post*, March 3, 1995, February 1, 1997.

46. William R. Keylor, *The Twentieth Century World: An International History*, 2nd ed. (New York: Oxford University Press, 1992), 22; Richard W. Van Alstyne and Joseph M. Siracusa, "Loans and Debt Resolution," in *Encyclopedia of American*

Foreign Policy, vol. 2, *E–N*, 2nd ed., ed. Alexander DeConde, Richard Dean Burns, and Frederik Longevall (New York: Charles Scribner's Sons, 2002), 366.

47. Theodore Roosevelt, quoted in Richard W. Van Alstyne and Joseph M. Siracusa, "Loans and Debt Resolution," in *Encyclopedia of American Foreign Policy*, vol. 2, *E–N*, 2nd ed., ed. Alexander DeConde, Richard Dean Burns, and Frederik Longevall (New York: Charles Scribner's Sons, 2002), 367.

48. John Ward, *Latin America: Development and Conflict since 1945*, 2nd ed. (London: Routledge, 2004), 60–61.

49. J. Humberto Lopez and Guillermo Perry, *Inequality in Latin America: Determinants and Consequences* (Policy Research Working Paper no. 4504, World Bank, February 2008), 4.

50. Ward, *Latin America*, 74–75.

51. Marshall C. Eakin, *The History of Latin America: Collision of Cultures* (New York: Palgrave Macmillan, 2007), 354–55; Ward, *Latin America*, 72–77.

52. Marc Chernick, "Economic Resources and Internal Armed Conflicts: Lessons from the Colombian Case," in *Rethinking the Economics of War: The Intersection of Need, Creed and Greed*, ed. Cynthia Arnson and I. William Zartman (Baltimore: Johns Hopkins University Press, 2005), 190–92.

53. Eakin, *The History of Latin America*, 355; Ward, *Latin America*, 73; International Crisis Group, *Latin American Drugs 1*, 6–9; International Crisis Group, *Colombia: Moving Forward with the ELN* (Latin American Briefing no. 16, Bogota/Brussels: October 11, 2007) 2–5; Stephanie Hanson, "Colombia's Right-Wing Paramilitaries and Splinter Groups," *Backgrounder* (January 11, 2008), www.cfr.org/publication/15239 (accessed March 31, 2008).

54. Michael Kenney, "The Architecture of Drug Trafficking: Network Forms of Organisation in the Colombian Cocaine Trade," *Global Crime* 8 (August 2007): 233–59.

55. Hanson, "Colombia's Right-Wing Paramilitaries and Splinter Groups."

56. UNAIDS, *AIDS Epidemic Update 07* (Geneva: UNAIDS and World Health Organization, 2007), 24.

57. Commission on Human Security, *Human Security Now*, 99–101.

58. Alan Whiteside, *HIV/AIDS: A Very Short Introduction* (Oxford: Oxford University Press, 2008), 124–26.

59. Kenrad E. Nelson, "The Demographic Impact of the HIV Epidemic in Thailand," *AIDS* 12 (1998): 813–14.

60. UNAIDS, *AIDS Epidemic Update 07*, 11, 24.

61. Nedra Weerakoon, "International Female Labour Migration: Implications of the HIV/AIDS Epidemic in the Asian Region," in *No Place for Borders: The HIV/AIDS Epidemic and Development in Asia and the Pacific*, ed. Geoffrey Linge and Doug Porter (Sydney: Allen & Unwin, 1997).

62. Statistical data from Tony Barnett and Alan Whiteside (2006), cited in Collette Schultz-Herzenberg, *A Lethal Cocktail: Exploring the Impact of Corruption on HIV/AIDS Prevention and Treatment Efforts in South Africa* (Pretoria: Institute for

Security Studies, 2007), 14. South African responses to HIV/AIDS are discussed at length in Tony Barnett and Alan Whiteside, *AIDS in the Twenty-First Century: Disease and Globalization* (Basingstoke: Palgrave Macmillan, 2002).

63. Schultz-Herzenberg, *A Lethal Cocktail*, 20.

64. Kerry Cullinan, "Health Officials Promote Untested uBejane," *Health-e*, March 22, 2006, www.health-e.org.za/news/article.php?uid=20031380 (accessed June 15, 2008); Anso Thom, "It's All Over for Rath," *Health-e*, June 13, 2008, www.health-e.org.za/news/article.php?uid=20031993&PHPSESSID=e229128d 9445673ab928a3b417ba4bfc (accessed June 22, 2008). Schultz-Herzenberg, *A Lethal Cocktail*, 61–63.

65. Joseph Tumushabe, *The Politics of HIV/AIDS in Uganda* (Geneva: The United Nations Research Institute for Social Development, Paper no. 28, 2006), 10–12.

66. Jonathan Cohen and Tony Tate, "The Less They Know the Better: Abstinence-Only HIV/AIDS Programs in Uganda," *Human Rights Watch* 17 (March 2005), 5.

67. Cohen and Tate, "The Less They Know," 58.

68. Karyn Kaplan and Rebecca Schleifer, "Deadly Denial: Barriers to HIV/AIDS Treatment for People Who Use Drugs in Thailand," *Human Rights Watch* 19 (November 2007), 1, 26. For Russian data, see Genine Babakian, "Positively Abandoned: Stigma and Discrimination against HIV Positive Mothers and Their Children in Russia," *Human Rights Watch* 17 (June 2005).

69. Nada Mustafa Ali, "Hidden in the Mealie Meal: Gender-Based Abuses and Women's HIV Treatment in Zambia," *Human Rights Watch* 19 (December 2001).

70. Tumushabe, *The Politics of HIV/AIDS in Uganda*, 11.

71. Johann Graf Lambsdorf, "Corruption Perceptions Index 2004," in *Transparency International, Global Corruption Report, 2005* (London: Pluto Press, 2005), 236.

72. Schultz-Herzenberg, *A Lethal Cocktail*, 32–52.

73. Susan Rose-Ackerman, *Corruption and Government: Causes, Consequences and Reform* (Cambridge: Cambridge University Press, 1999), 166–67.

74. Peter Eigen, "Introduction," in *Transparency International Global Corruption Report, 2005* (London: Pluto Press, 2005), 1.

75. World Bank, *World Development Report 2000/2001: Attacking Poverty* (Oxford: Oxford University Press, 2001), 15.

76. Amartya Sen, *Development as Freedom* (Oxford: Oxford University Press, 1999), 44.

77. Sen, *Development as Freedom*, 44.

78. Commission for Africa, *Our Common Interest*, 17.

79. UN Office of the High Representative for the Least Developed Countries, Landlocked Developing Countries and Small Island Developing Countries, www.un.org/special-rep/ohrlls/ldc/list.htm (accessed April 15, 2008).

80. Gurr et al., *State Failure Taskforce Report*, 12; UNCTAD, *The Least Developed Countries Report 2004* (Geneva: United Nations, 2004), 162.

CHAPTER 5: HUMAN RIGHTS
AND HUMAN SECURITY

1. Michael Freeman, *Human Rights: An Interdisciplinary Approach* (Cambridge: Polity, 2002), 62.

2. International Covenant on Civil and Political Rights, Office of the High Commissioner for Human Rights, www.unhchr.ch/html/menu3/b/a_ccpr.htm (accessed January 24, 2008); Freeman, *Human Rights*, 18–26; Geoffrey Robertson, *Crimes against Humanity: The Struggle for Global Justice*, 2nd ed. (London: Penguin, 2002), 4, 35.

3. Simon Leys, ed. and trans., *The Analects of Confucius* (New York: Norton, 1997), 58–59.

4. R. Goodin, "Globalising Justice," in *Taming Globalization: New Frontiers of Governance*, ed. D. Held and M. Koenig-Archibugi (Cambridge: Polity Press, 2003), 72.

5. Sumner B. Twiss, "A Constructive Framework for Discussing Confucianism and Human Rights," in *Confucianism and Human Rights*, ed. W. Theodore De Barry and Tu Weiming (New York: Columbia University Press, 1998), 30.

6. Andrew Clapham, *Human Rights: A Very Short Introduction* (Oxford: Oxford University Press, 2007), 42–51.

7. Henry Dunant, *A Memory of Solferino* (Geneva: International Committee of the Red Cross, 1986); "Henry Dunant, The Nobel Peace Prize 1901," nobelprize.org/nobel_prizes/peace/laureates/1901/dunant-bio.html (accessed June 28, 2008).

8. The Avalon Project at Yale Law School, Laws of War: Pacific Settlement of International Disputes (Hague 1), July 29, 1899, www.yale.edu/lawweb/avalon/lawofwar/hague01.htm (accessed April 28, 2008).

9. Jackson Nyamuya Maogoto, *War Crimes and Realpolitik: International Justice from World War 1 to the 21st Century* (Boulder, CO: Lynne Rienner, 2004), 24–27.

10. Inazo Nitobe, *Bushido: the Soul of Japan* (Alcester, UK: Read Books, 2007), 100–105.

11. Yuki Tanaka, *Hidden Horrors: Japanese War Crimes in World War II* (Boulder, CO: Westview Press, 1996), 206–211; Chalmers Johnson, "The Looting of Asia," *London Review of Books*, November 20, 2003, www.lrb.co.uk/v25/n22/john04_.html (accessed April 28, 2008).

12. Maogoto, *War Crimes and Realpolitik*, 102–04.

13. Michael Byers, "The Laws of War, US Style," *London Review of Books*, February 20, 2003, www.lrb.co.uk/v25/n04byer01_.html (accessed May 16, 2008).

14. Condoleezza Rice (keynote address, Annual Meeting of the World Eco-

nomic Forum, Davos, Switzerland, January 23, 2008), www.state.gov/secretary/rm/2008/01/99624.htm (accessed January 31, 2008).

15. Renee de Nevers, "The Geneva Conventions and New Wars," *Political Science Quarterly* 121 (2006), 369–71.

16. Kenneth Roth, "Drawing the Line: War Rules and Law Enforcement Rules in the Fight against Terrorism," *World Report 2004: Human Rights and Armed Conflict* (New York: Human Rights Watch, 2004), 178.

17. Thomas E. Skidmore and Peter H. Smith, *Modern Latin America*, 6th ed. (Oxford: Oxford University Press, 2005), 133–37.

18. Marshall C. Eakin, *The History of Latin America: Collision of Cultures* (New York: Palgrave, 2007), 270.

19. Chen Guidi and Wu Chuntao, *Will the Boat Sink the Water? The Struggle of Peasants in 21st-Century China* (Sydney: HarperCollins, 2007), 1–16.

20. Chen and Wu, *Will the Boat Sink the Water?*, 16–28.

21. Sen, *Development as Freedom*, 260.

22. Mahatir Mohamad, *A New Deal for Asia* (Kuala Lumpur: Pelanduk, 1999), 71.

23. Fareed Zakaria, "Culture Is Destiny: A Conversation with Lee Kuan Yew," *Foreign Affairs*, March/April 1994, www.fareedzakaria.com/articles/other/culture.html (accessed May 5, 2008).

24. Zakaria, "Culture Is Destiny."

25. Wejen Chang, "Confucian Theory of Norms and Human Rights," in *Confucianism and Human Rights*, ed. W. Theodore De Barry and Tu Weiming (New York: Columbia University Press, 1998), 116–125.

26. Sen, *Development as Freedom*, 15.

27. Stephanie Lawson, "Cultural Relativism and Democracy: Political Myths about 'Asia' and the 'West,'" in *Pathways to Asia: The Politics of Engagement*, ed. Richard Robison (Sydney: Allen & Unwin, 1996), 115.

28. Twiss, "A Constructive Framework for Discussing Confucianism and Human Rights," 30.

29. Greg Sheridan, *Asian Values, Western Dreams: Understanding the New Asia* (Sydney: Allen & Unwin, 1999), 294.

30. Organization of the Islamic Conference, *Cairo Declaration on Human Rights in Islam*, August 5, 1990, www1.umn.edu/humanrts/instree/cairodeclaration.html (accessed April 28, 2008).

31. Freeman, *Human Rights*, 112–13.

32. Sharifah Zuriah Aljeffri, "Islam and the Status of Women" (address to the Hawke Centre, University of South Australia, May 1, 2003), www.unisa.edu.au/hawkecentre/events/2003events/islam_transcript.asp (accessed April 28, 2008).

33. Gita Sen, "Reproductive Rights and Gender Justice in the Neo-conservative Shadow," in *Engendering Human Security: Feminist Perspectives*, ed. Thanh-Dam

Truong, Saskia Wieringa, and Amrita Chhachhi (London: Zed Books, 2006), 43–45.

34. Sunila Abeyasekera, "Gendering Transitional Justice: Experiences of Women in Sri Lanka and Timor Leste in Seeking Affirmation of Rights," in *Engendering Human Security: Feminist Perspectives*, ed. Thanh-Dam Truong, Saskia Wieringa, and Amrita Chhachhi (London: Zed Books, 2006), 7–10.

35. LaShawn R. Jefferson, "In War as in Peace," in *World Report 2004* (New York: Human Rights Watch, 2004), 328–29.

36. Eva Brems, "Protecting the Human Rights of Women," in *International Human Rights in the 21st Century: Protecting the Rights of Groups*, ed. Gene M. Lyons and James Mayall (Lanham, MD: Rowman & Littlefield, 2003), 103.

37. Joseph Amon, "Preventing the Further Spread of HIV/AIDS: The Essential Role of Human Rights," Human Rights Watch, www.humanrightswatch.org (accessed March 27, 2007).

38. Patricia Feeny and Tom Kenny, "Conflict Management and the OECD *Guidelines for Multinational Enterprises*," in *Profiting from Peace: Managing the Resource Dimensions of Civil War*, ed. Karen Ballentine and Heiko Nitschke (Boulder, CO: Lynne Rienner, 2005), 347–60.

39. Paul Battersby and Preecha Uitragool, "Managing Risk through Community Empowerment: Village-centred Knowledge Networks in Lower Isaan, Thailand," *Proceedings of the Conference on Community Development in a 'Global Risk Society': Selected Papers*, April 20–22, 2006 (Melbourne: Centre for Citizenship and Human Rights, Deakin University).

40. Rosli Omar, "Sungai Selangor Dam: Orang Asli and the Environment," in *People Before Profits: The Rights of Malaysia Communities in Development*, ed. Kua Kia Soong (Kuala Lumpur: Vinlin Press, 2001), 87–88.

41. BBC News, "Giant China Dam Seeks Funds," Business News, April 12, 2002, news.bbc.co.uk/2/hi/business/1868237.stm (accessed May 18, 2008); "Millions More Face Relocation from the Three Gorges Reservoir Area, Wang Honjiang," China View, October 11, 2007, news.xinhuanet.com/english/2007–10/11/content_6864252.htm (accessed May 18, 2008).

42. BBC News, "Three Gorges Activist Beaten Up," June 13, 2006, news.bbc.co.uk/2/hi/asia-pacific/5074922.stm (accessed May 18, 2008); Jill McGivering, "Three Gorges Dam's Social Impact," BBC News, May 20, 2006, news.bbc.co.uk/2/hi/asia-pacific/5000198.stm (accessed May 18, 2008); Calum MacLeod and Lijia MacLeod, "China's Dambusters Protest Controversial Resettlement Project," *The Independent*, July 19, 2001, www.independent.co.uk/news/world/asia/chinas-dam-busters-protest-controversial-resettlement-project-678191.html (accessed May 18, 2008).

43. Elliot Sperling, *The Tibet-China Conflict: History and Polemics* (Washington: East-West Center, 2004), 5–7.

44. Sperling, *The Tibet-China Conflict*, 16.

45. Brad Adams and Ian Gorvin (eds.), "'It Was Like Suddenly My Son No Longer Existed': Enforced Disappearances in Thailand's Southern Border Provinces," *Human Rights Watch* 19 (March 2007), 16–18.

46. United Nations, *Declaration on the Rights of Indigenous Peoples*, 61/295, October 2, 2007, daccessdds.un.org/doc/UNDOC/GEN/N06/512/07/PDF/N0651207.pdf?OpenElement (accessed February 24, 2008).

47. Rodolfo Stavenhagen, "Report of the Special Rapporteur on the Situation of Human Rights and Fundamental Freedoms of Indigenous People" (UN General Assembly, A/60/358, September 16, 2005), 15, daccessdds.un.org/doc/UNDOC/GEN/N05/513/14/PDF/N0551314.pdf?OpenElement (accessed April 28, 2008).

48. Human Rights Watch, "The Price of Oil," www.hrw.org/reports/1999/nigeria/Nigew991-01.htm (accessed December 18, 2007); Human Rights Watch, "Update on Human Rights Violations in the Niger Delta," hrw.org/backgrounder/africa/nigeriabkg1214.htm (accessed December 18, 2007).

49. Tim Clark, *Canadian Mining Companies in Latin America: Community Rights and Corporate Responsibility* (Centre for Research on Latin America and the Caribbean (CERLAC) and MiningWatch, Colloquia Papers Series, 2003), 10, http://www.yorku.ca/cerlac/documents/Mining-report.pdf (accessed May 25, 2008). See also Aneli Tolvanen, *The Legacy of Greenstone Resources in Nicaragua* (Canada: MiningWatch, 2003), www.miningwatch.ca/updir/Nicaragua_studies.pdf (accessed June 30,2008).

50. *Rome Statute of the International Court* (The Hague: ICC Public Information and Documentation Service, 2002), 7.

51. Yasmin Naqvi, "Amnesty for War Crimes: Defining the Limits of International Recognition," *International Review of the Red Cross* 851 (2003), www.icrc.org/Web/eng/siteeng0.nsf/htmlall/5SSDUX/$File/irrc_851_Naqvi.pdf (accessed June 27, 2008).

CHAPTER 6: AVERTING NUCLEAR ARMAGEDDON

1. Portions of this chapter have been adapted from my recent study, *Nuclear Weapons: A Very Short Introduction* (Oxford: Oxford University Press, 2008).

2. Quoted in David G. Coleman and Joseph M. Siracusa, *Real-World Nuclear Deterrence: The Making of International Strategy* (Westport, CT: Praeger Security International, 2006), 108.

3. Pierre Gallois, "NATO's New Teeth," *Foreign Affairs* 39 (October 1960): 73.

4. Susanna Schrafstetter and Stephen Twigge, *Avoiding Armageddon: Europe, the United States, and the Struggle for Nuclear Nonproliferation, 1945–1970* (Westport, CT: Praeger, 2004), 2.

5. George Perkovich, *India's Nuclear Bomb: The Impact on Global Proliferation* (Berkeley: University of California Press, 1999), 3.

6. See George Perkovich et al., *Universal Compliance: A Strategy for Nuclear Security* (Washington, DC: Carnegie Endowment for International Peace, 2005).

7. Quoted in Coleman and Siracusa, *Real-World Nuclear Deterrence*, 116.

8. Graham Allison, *Nuclear Terrorism: The Ultimate Preventable Catastrophe* (New York: Times Books, 2004), 1.

9. *Nuclear Blackmarkets: Pakistan, A.Q. Khan and the Rise of Proliferation Networks: A Net Assessment* (London: IISS, 2007).

10. Allen Whiting, *The Chinese Calculus of Deterrence: India and Indochina* (Ann Arbor: University of Michigan Press, 1975); Neville Maxwell, *India's China War* (Garden City, NY: Anchor Books, 1972). For new insights into why China's leaders and military thinkers see the United States as their country's major potential nuclear threat, see Larry M. Wortzel, *China's Nuclear Forces: Operations, Training, Command, Control, and Campaign Planning* (Washington, DC: U.S. Army War College, 2007).

11. Jaswant Singh, "Against Nuclear Apartheid," *Foreign Affairs* 77 (September/October 1998): 5.

12. Quoted in Coleman and Siracusa, *Real-World Nuclear Deterrence,* 120.

CHAPTER 7: ROADMAPS AND ROADBLOCKS

1. Robert J. Lieber, *No Common Power: Understanding International Relations* (Glenview, IL: Scott, Foresman and Company, 1988), 10–11.

2. Andrew O'Neil, "Terrorist Use of Weapons of Mass Destruction: How Serious Is the Threat?' *Australian Journal of International Affairs* 57, no. 1 (2003): 99–110.

3. Chris Bright, "Anticipating Environmental 'Surprise,'" in *State of the World 2000*, ed. L. R. Brown et al. (London: Earthscan, 2000), 22.

4. Robert Keohane and Joseph Nye Jr., "Globalization: What's New? What's Not? (And So What?)," *Foreign Policy* 4 (Spring 2000): 104–19.

5. A. Cooley and James Ron, "The NGO Scramble: Organizational Insecurity and the Political Economy of Transnational Action," in *New Global Dangers: Changing Dimensions of International Security*, ed. M. E. Brown, O. R. Cote, Jr., S. M. Lynn-Jones, and S. E. Miller (Cambridge, MA: MIT Press, 2004), 488–89.

6. John Gerard Ruggie, "Taking Embedded Liberalism Global: The Corporate Connection," in *Taming Globalization: Frontiers of Governance*, ed. David Held and Mathias Koenig-Archibugi (Cambridge: Polity, 2003), 106–14.

7. Cooley and Ron, "The NGO Scramble," 500.

8. As explored in J. E. Thompson, "State Sovereignty in International Relations: Bridging the Gap between Theory and Empirical Research," *International Studies Quarterly* 39 (1995), 213–33.

9. Dore Gold, *Tower of Babel: How the United Nations Has Fuelled Global Chaos* (New York: Crown Forum, 2004), 6, 13, 22.

10. Marc Weller, "Human Rights in Weak, Divided and Threatened States," in *International Human Rights in the 21st Century: Protecting the Rights of Groups*, ed. Gene M. Lyons and James Mayall (Lanham, MD: Rowman & Littlefield, 2003), 150–57.

11. J. L. Holzgrefe, "The Humanitarian Intervention Debate," in *Humanitarian Intervention: Ethical, Legal and Political Dilemmas*, ed. J. L. Holzgrefe and Robert Keohane (Cambridge: Cambridge University Press, 2003), 36–43.

12. International Commission on Intervention and State Sovereignty, *The Responsibility to Protect: Research, Bibliography, Background* (Canada: International Development Research Centre, 2001), www.idrc.ca/openebooks/963-1/#page_7 (accessed January 20, 2008).

13. Robert Keohane, "Political Authority after Intervention," in *Humanitarian Intervention: Ethical, Legal and Political Dilemmas*, ed. J. L. Holzgrefe and Robert Keohane (Cambridge: Cambridge University Press, 2003), 276–77.

14. Buzan, Waever and de Wilde, *Security*, 153.

15. M. T. Klare, *Resource Wars: The New Landscape of Global Conflict* (New York: Owl Books, 2002), 109–37.

16. V. L. Forbes, "Geopolitical Change: Direction and Continuing Issues," in *Southeast Asia Transformed: A Geography of Change*, ed. Chia Lin Sien (Singapore: Institute of Southeast Asian Studies, 2003), 47–94.

17. "Treaty between Australia and the Independent State of Papua New Guinea Concerning Sovereignty and Maritime Boundaries in the Area between the Two Countries, Including the Area Known as Torres Strait, and Related Matters," December 18, 1978, *Australian Treaty Series* 4 (1985).

18. Paul Kennedy, *The Rise and Fall of the Great Powers: Economic Change and Military Conflict from 1500 to 2000* (London: Unwin Hyman, 1989), xvi.

19. P. Battersby, "Border Politics and the Broader Politics of Thailand's International Relations in the 1990s: From Communism to Capitalism," *Pacific Affairs* 71 (Winter 1998–1999): 473–88.

20. *Bangkok Post*, January 13, 2001.

21. M. Richardson, "Australia-Southeast Asia Relations and the East Asia Summit," *Australian Journal of International Affairs* 59 (September 2005): 364.

22. Hans Dieter and Richard Higgott, *Exploring Alternative Theories of Economic Regionalism: From Trade to Finance in Asian Co-operation* (working paper no. 89/02, University of Warwick Centre for the Study of Globalisation and Regionalisation, January 2002), 27–33.

BIBLIOGRAPHICAL ESSAY

GLOBALIZATION

The concept of globalization has gathered a rich bibliography in a relatively short space of time and become embedded in the social science lexicon. A good general and brief study of the idea of globalization is Manfred Steger's *Globalization: A Very Short Introduction* (2003). For a comprehensive and multilayered introduction from an international politics perspective, see John Bayliss and Steve Smith (eds.), *The Globalization of World Politics* (2005). Bayliss and Smith bring together authored chapters on history, political theory, conflict and security, international institutions, environmental politics and human rights. The processes of what we recognize as globalization span several centuries. For very different historical perspectives, see David Held, Anthony McGrew, David Goldblatt and Jonathan

Perraton, *Global Transformations: Politics, Economics and Culture* (2000) and A. G. Hopkins (ed.), *Globalization in World History* (2002).

Globalization has received extensive treatment by sociologists and economists. In the field of sociology, Ulrich Beck's *What Is Globalization?* (1999) and Anthony Giddens, *Runaway World: How Globalization Is Reshaping Our Lives* (1999), clarify globalization's reflexive nature. A detailed examination and mapping of global economic relations is given in Peter Dicken, *Global Shift: Reshaping the Global Economic Map in the 21st Century* (2003), which seeks to balance the macroeconomic with the political in contemporary patterns of global exchange. Representative of the business studies genre, Kenichi Ohmae's *The End of the Nation State: The Rise of Regional Economies* (1996) examines globalization as if politics did not matter. For further introductory reading see Mark Rupert and M. Scott Solomon, *Globalization and International Political Economy* (2006).

Critical views questioning our conception of globalization are provided by Richard Falk, *Predatory Globalization: A Critique* (1999), John Gray, *False Dawn: The Delusions of Global Capitalism* (2002), Paul Hirst and Grahame Thompson, *Globalization in Question* (1999) and Michael Veseth, *Globaloney: Unravelling the Myths of Globalization* (2006).

WORLD HISTORY AND POLITICS

World histories play a significant part in defining the contemporary global agenda. Possibly the most provocative historical study of globalization is Francis Fukuyama's *The End of History and the Last Man* (1992), which still generates frequent, and usually disparaging, references. In many ways as controversial as Fukuyama's book is Samuel Huntington's *The Clash of Civilizations and the Remaking of World Order* (1997), which remains a widely cited and much criticized study of the relationship between culture and historical change. The finest exemplar of a genre of international historical writing that strives to capture the breadth of human experience is Eric Hobsbawm, whose *Age of Extremes* (1996) sets a benchmark for modern generalist world histories. William R. Keylor's *The Twentieth Century World: An International History* (1992) attends to major political events, bringing together important historical strands that bear upon our contemporary interest in human security. Henry Kissinger's landmark *Diplomacy* (1994) gives an Atlantic view of global history and a sympathetic reading of the role of American power in international affairs. John Keegan's *A History of Warfare* (1993) remains an important study of the nature of armed conflict. Geoffrey Blainey's seminal study, *The Causes of War* (1988), bridges international history and international relations to examine wars and their causes across the nineteenth and twentieth centuries. Jessica Stern's *Terror in the Name of God: Why Religious Militants Kill* (2003) helps to clarify causal factors in the rise of global terror networks.

Paul Kennedy's *The Rise and Fall of the Great Powers* (1989) sets out the declinist interpretation of American history echoed in Immanuel Wallerstein's *The Decline of American Power: The U.S. in a Chaotic World* (2003). U.S. foreign relations are expertly covered in Alexander DeConde, Richard Dean Burns and Frederik Longevall (eds.), *Encyclopedia of American Foreign Policy*, 2nd edition, Volume 2, *E–N* (2002). See also Norman A. Graebner, Richard Dean Burns, and Joseph M. Siracusa, *Reagan, Bush, Gorbachev: Revisiting the End of the Cold War* (2008). Journal articles reflecting upon world order in the 1990s and which can be considered important historical documents in their own right are Joseph S. Nye, Jr., "What New World Order?" in *Foreign Affairs* 71 (Spring 1992) and Barry Posen and Andrew Ross, "Contemporary Visions for U.S. Grand Strategy," in *International Security* 21 (Winter 1996/97).

More statistical or quantitative studies of world economic and social history are presented in Angus Maddison's *The World Economy: Volume 2, Historical Statistics* (2003), while Patrick Manning's *Migration in World History* (2005) is a very accessible introduction to global population movements. Mention should also be given to useful collections of country-specific information: the annual *SBS World Guide* and the *CIA World Factbook*, www.cia.gov/library/publications/the-world-factbook.

REGIONAL AND NATIONAL HISTORIES

AFRICA

Martin Meredith's *The State of Africa: A History of Fifty Years of Independence* (2005) explains the continent's tortured historical development and prepares the ground for more specialized studies of individual countries such as M. W. Daly's highly regarded book *Darfur's Sorrow: A History of Destruction and Genocide* (2007). For other studies of Sudan and neighboring countries, see Douglas Hamilton Johnson, *The Root Causes of Sudan's Civil Wars* (2004), and I. M. Lewis, *A Modern History of Somalia: Nation and State in the Horn of Africa* (1988). For journal articles examining the issues of humanitarian intervention in Somalia and Sudan, see Alex De

Waal and Rakiya Omaar, "Doing Harm by Doing Good?" in *Current History* 92 (May 1993): 198–202, and Alex De Waal, "Darfur and the Failure of the Responsibility to Protect," *International Affairs* 83 (2007): 1039–1054.

THE MIDDLE EAST

The connections between early-twentieth-century history and modern Middle Eastern affairs are the subject of David Fromkin's *A Peace to End All Peace: Creating the Modern Middle East* (1989), which, as its subtitle announces, examines how post-1918 peace settlements altered the terrain of regional politics and sowed the seeds of current regional tensions. Fred Halliday in *The Middle East in International Relations: Power, Politics and Ideology* (2005) presents a contemporary analysis of regional affairs and explains the Middle East's enduring global geostrategic and geoeconomic significance.

For contemporary histories addressing important questions in late-twentieth-century international affairs, see Steve Coll's *Ghost Wars: The Secret History of the CIA, Afghanistan and Bin Laden, from the Soviet Invasion to September 10, 2001* (2005), a thorough and also riveting account of CIA activities in the Middle East and South and Central Asia. Dilip Hiro's *Iraq: A Report from the Inside* (2003) sets the scene in Iraq before the 2003 invasion, while Peter W. Galbraith, *The End of Iraq* (2007), backgrounds and critiques U.S. strategy in the Middle East.

ASIA

Cambridge offers excellent historical series covering all world regions, South Asia, Southeast Asia, Africa and the Middle East being the most relevant here. China and India dominate the physical, cultural and political geography of Asia. For general histories of each, see Rafe de Crespigny's *China This Century* (1992) and Hermann Kulke and Dietmar Rothermund, *History of India* (1986). The study of Chinese culture would be meaningless without reading the teachings of Confucius or Sun Tzu. See Simon Leys (trans.), *The Analects of Confucius* (1997), and John Minford (trans.), *The Art of War: Sun-tzu* (2003). Lucian W. Pye's *Asian Power and Politics: The Cultural Dimensions of Authority* (1985) offers insights into the enduring cultural importance of Asian tradition. China's modernization is explored from an intensely personal and compelling point of view in Nicholas D. Kristof and Sheryl WuDunn's *China Wakes: The Struggle for the Soul of a Rising Power* (1995). Greg Sheridan's *Asian Values, Western Dreams: Understanding the New Asia* (1999) is an insightful Australian perspective on the region in the 1990s. Navnita Chadha Behera's *Demystifying Kashmir* (2006), as the title suggests, deconstructs the stereotypes of Kashmiri politics in the context of India and Pakistan's continuing territorial rivalry. Angelo Rasanayagam's *Afghanistan: A Modern History* (2005) presents a timely study of Afghanistan's emergence as a modern state. Frank Tipton's *The Rise of Asia: Economics, Society and Politics in Contemporary Asia* (1998) examines Asian economic development during the past century. David Chandler's *The Tragedy of Cambodian History* (1991) is still the most comprehensive study of the Khmer Rouge era, while Martin Smith's *Burma: Insurgency and the Politics of Ethnicity* (1993) remains a significant study of that country's political turmoil.

Mention should also be given to refugee accounts of historical and current events. Personal testimonies give insights into the lived experience of human tragedies. Two different examples of this genre that were used in this book are Alex Klaits and Gulchin Gulmamadova-Klaits, *Love and War in Afghanistan* (2005) and Theary C. Seng, *Daughter of the Killing Fields: Asrei's Story* (2005).

LATIN AMERICA

Generalist English-language studies of Latin America are in short supply. Stephan Haggard and Robert R. Kaufman in *The Political Economy of Democratic Transitions* (1995) examine the relationship between economic crises and regime changes in Asia and Latin America. Marshall C. Eakin's *The History of Latin America* (2007) fills an important gap in the historical literature. Covering a shorter timespan, John Ward, *Latin America: Development and Conflict since 1945* (2004) and Thomas E. Skidmore and Peter H. Smith, *Modern Latin America* (2005) examine Latin America's post–World War Two economic and political fortunes.

GLOBAL GOVERNANCE

John Braithwaite and Peter Drahos in *Global Business Regulation* (2000) present an important empirical study of the evolution and complexity of global governance regimes. Ulrich Beck, *Power in the Global Age* (2005) revisits the counterhegemonic thrust of his *World Risk Society* (1999). David Held and Mathias Koenig-Archibugi (eds.), *Taming Globalization:*

Frontiers of Governance (2003) presents an eclectic collection of articles that assess the governability of globalization. Paul Kennedy, *The Parliament of Man: The United Nations and the Quest for World Government* (2006) is a historical account of the UN's evolution. Jim Whitman in *The Limits of Global Governance* (2005) offers a realistic assessment of the capacity of global institutions and regimes to address global challenges. Anthony Payne, *The Global Politics of Unequal Development* (2005) usefully describes the many institutions that constitute the architecture of global governance. Michael Pugh and Waheguru Pal Singh Sidhu (eds.) in *The United Nations and Regional Security: Europe and Beyond* (2003) present a collection of essays exploring the complementarities between global and regional governance. Ha-Joon Chang, *Bad Samaritans: Rich Nations, Poor Policies and Threats to the Developing World* (2007) and Joseph Stiglitz, *Globalization and Its Discontents* (1999) present insider critiques of global financial institutions.

INTERNATIONAL RELATIONS THEORY

International relations theory developed appreciably after publication and extensive critiquing of Norman Angell's *The Great Illusion* (2007/1912). Hans J. Morgenthau's *Politics among Nations* (1945) encapsulates the realist view of international relations. Kenneth Waltz's *Man, State and War* (1984) and *Theories of International Politics* (1979) established the credentials of neorealism. Waltz's theoretical formulation was advanced by the likes of Robert Gilpin in *The Political Economy of International Relations* (2003), Robert Keohane's works *Neorealism and Its Critics* (1986) and *After Hegemony: Cooperation and Discord in the World Political Economy* (2005/1984) and Robert J. Lieber, *No Common Power: Understanding International Relations* (1988). Robert Jervis's *Perception and Misperception in International Politics* (1976) remains a classic study of the role of subjectivity in world affairs. Michael J. Shapiro and Hayward R. Alker (eds.), *Challenging Boundaries: Global Flows, Territorial Identities* (1996) is a collection of critical studies in international relations theory. Alexander Wendt's *Social Theory of International Politics* (1999) is a thorough investigation of the corpus of international relations theory from a constructivist perspective. A useful exploration of different theoretical conceptions of human security is provided by Mohammed Nurruzaman, "Paradigms of Conflict: The Contested Claims of Human Security, Critical Theory and Feminism," in *Cooperation and Conflict: Journal of the Nordic International Studies Association* 41

(2006). One of the best introductory surveys of the state of play in international relations theory is Martin Griffiths's *Fifty Key Thinkers in International Relations* (1999). (Note that feminist contributions to the field are addressed separately below.)

In their different ways, the following have been influential in forming international relations theory: Thomas Hobbes, *Leviathan* (1981/1651); Hans Reiss (ed. and trans.), *Kant: Political Writings* (1991); and Karl Marx and Friedrich Engels, *The Communist Manifesto* (1981).

SECURITY AND CONFLICT

The following display the broad spectrum of work in the area of security and conflict studies. Barry Buzan's *People, States and Fear* (1983) is a seminal analysis of the nature and dynamics of national and international security, followed up by Buzan, Ole Waever and Jaap de Wilde's *Security: A New Framework for Analysis* (1998). Exemplary of a new trend in thinking about business and war is Cynthia Arnson and I. William Zartman (eds.), *Rethinking the Economics of War: The Intersection of Need, Creed and Greed* (2005) and Karen Ballentine and Heiko Nitschke (eds.), *Profiting from Peace: Managing the Resource Dimensions of Civil War* (2005). Other influential studies are Michael E. Brown et al. (eds.), *New Global Dangers: Changing Dimensions of International Security* (2004); Jared Diamond, *Collapse: How Societies Fail or Choose to Survive* (2005); Valere Gagnon, *The Myth of Ethnic War: Serbia and Croatia in the 1990s* (2004); Barbara Harff and Ted Gurr, *Ethnic Conflict in World Politics* (2004); Mary Kaldor, *New and Old Wars: Organized Violence in a Global Era* (1999); Michael T. Klare, *Resource Wars: The New Landscape of Global Conflict* (2002); Stephanie Lawson, *Culture and Context in World Politics* (2006); Michael Sheehan, *International Security: An Analytical Survey* (2005); Hideaki Shinoda and How-Won Jeong (eds.), *Conflict and Human Security: A Search for New Approaches to Peace-Building* (2004); Ted Robert Gurr, "Peoples against States: Ethnopolitical Conflict and the Changing World System," *International Studies Quarterly* 38 (Sept. 1994) and Edward Mansfield and Jack Snyder, "Democratization and the Danger of War," *International Security* 20 (Summer 1995).

NUCLEAR WEAPONS

This subject is a subset of security studies, perhaps, but one worthy of a separate category and heading. See Graham Allison, *Nuclear Terrorism: The*

Ultimate Preventable Catastrophe (2004); George Perkovich, *India's Nuclear Bomb: The Impact on Global Proliferation* (1999); George Perkovich et al., *Universal Compliance: A Strategy for Nuclear Security* (2005); Susanna Schrafstetter and Stephen Twigge, *Avoiding Armageddon: Europe, the United States, and the Struggle for Nuclear Nonproliferation, 1945–1970* (2004); Allen Whiting, *The Chinese Calculus of Deterrence: India and Indochina* (1975); and Larry M. Wortzel, *China's Nuclear Forces: Operations, Training, Command, Control, and Campaign Planning* (2007).

HUMAN RIGHTS AND INTERNATIONAL LAW

Human rights: Amartya Sen, *Development as Freedom* (1999). An accessible introductory study is Andrew Clapham, *Human Rights: A Very Short Introduction* (2007). Geoffrey Robertson strides majestically through the evolution of human rights law and the International Criminal Court in *Crimes against Humanity* (2002). Michael Freeman surveys the human rights debate in *Human Rights: An Interdisciplinary Approach* (2002). Minority and gender rights are discussed in Gene M. Lyons and James Mayall (eds.), *International Human Rights in the 21st Century: Protecting the Rights of Groups* (2003). For a different cultural perspective, see W. Theodore De Barry and Tu Weiming (ed.), *Confucianism and Human Rights* (1998). The law of war is assessed in Jackson Nyamuya Maogoto, *War Crimes and Realpolitik: International Justice from World War 1 to the 21st Century* (2004). Legal questions surrounding the use of terror tactics and legitimate responses are debated in James P. Sterba (ed.), *Terrorism and International Justice* (2003). War crimes and crimes against humanity are detailed extensively in Yuki Tanaka, *Hidden Horrors: Japanese War Crimes in World War II* (1996) and Stéphane Courtois et al. (eds.), *The Black Book of Communism: Crimes, Terror, Repression* (2004).

GENDER RELATIONS

The study of gender in international relations was pioneered by J. Ann Tickner in *Gender in International Relations: Feminist Perspectives on Achieving International Security* (1992) and *Gendering World Politics: Issues and Approaches in the Post-Cold War Era* (2001); Cynthia Enloe, *Bananas, Beaches and Bases: Making Feminist Sense of International Politics* (1990); and Jan Jindy Pettman, *Worlding Women: A Feminist International Politics* (1994). Notable recent contributions to feminist studies of global security include Thanh-Dam Truong, Saskia Wieringa and Amrita Chhachhi (eds.), *Engendering Human Security: Feminist Perspectives* (2006). L. H. M. Ling, "Global Presumptions: A Critique of Sorensen's World-Order Change," *Cooperation and Conflict: Journal of the Nordic International Studies Association* 4 (2006) succinctly captures the feminist critique of grand world-order narratives.

DEVELOPMENT STUDIES

Paul Harrison's *Inside the Third World* (1993) explains the persistence of poverty in developing countries. Jeffrey Sachs, *The End of Poverty: How We Can Make It Happen in Our Lifetime* (2005) is something of a self-congratulatory survey of policy success and failure in tackling poverty around the world. Sunil Bastian and Robert Luckham (eds.) in *Can Democracy be Designed? The Politics of Institutional Choice in Conflict-Torn Societies* (2003) ask and find some possible answers to the question of how democratic ideas can be transplanted in societies outside the Western world. Health is a major determinant of development, and HIV/AIDS dominates the literature on public health in the developing world. Important studies of HIV and development include Tony Barnett and Alan Whiteside, *AIDS in the Twenty-First Century: Disease and Globalization* (2002); Alan Whiteside, *HIV/AIDS: A Very Short Introduction* (2008); Geoffrey Linge and Doug Porter (eds.), *No Place for Borders: The HIV/AIDS Epidemic and Development in Asia and the Pacific* (1997). For studies of the development of transnational civil society organizations, see M. Lindenberg and C. Bryant, *Going Global: Transforming Relief and Development NGOs* (2001) and papers for the United Nations Research Institute for Social Development by Britta Sadoun, *Political Space for Non-Governmental Organizations in the United Nations World Summit Processes* (2007) and Manuel Mejido Costoya, *Toward a Typology of Civil Society Actors: The Case of the Movement to Change International Trade Rules and Barriers* (2007).

CORRUPTION AND TRANSNATIONAL CRIME

Susan Rose-Ackerman, *Corruption and Government: Causes, Consequences and Reform* (1999); Cynthia Arnson and I. William Zartman (eds.), *Rethinking the Economics of War: The Intersection of Need, Creed and Greed* (2005); Moises Naim, *Illicit: How Smugglers, Traffickers, and Copycats Are Hijacking the Global Economy* (2005); Alan Dupont, *East Asia Imperilled*

(2001); Ronald Renard, *The Burmese Connection* (1996); UN Office of Drug Control and Crime Prevention's annual *Drug Report*; Jeffrey A. Meyer and Mark G. Califano, *Good Intentions Corrupted: The Oil-for-Food Scandal and the Threat to the U.N.* (2006); and Simon Tay and Maria Seda (eds.), *The Enemy Within: Combating Corruption in Asia* (2003). The South African Institute for Strategic Studies publishes voluminously on topics spanning the entire human security spectrum. See, for example, Collette Schultz-Herzenberg, *A Lethal Cocktail: Exploring the Impact of Corruption on HIV/AIDS Prevention and Treatment Efforts in South Africa* (2007).

OFFICIAL REPORTS AND POLICY STATEMENTS

There is a wealth of intergovernmental reports and policy statements addressing global and human security issues: Kofi Annan, *"We the Peoples"* (2000) and *In Larger Freedom* (2005) and Boutros Boutros-Ghali, *An Agenda for Peace: Preventive Diplomacy, Peacemaking and Peace-Keeping* (1992). Apart from the UNDP's *World Development Report* (1994), the Agency's annual *Human Development Report* contains up-to-date information on country performance against human quality-of-life indicators.

Setting out the UN's human security agenda is the Commission on Human Security's *Human Security Now* (2003). UNESCO regional reports on human security offer extensive and informative regional and national overviews. See, for Latin America, Claudia F. Fuentes and Francisco Rojas Aravena, *Promoting Human Security: Ethical, Normative and Educational Frameworks in Latin America and the Caribbean* (2005). UNCTAD reports on international economic and development trends in its *World Investment Report* and *Least Developed Country Report* series. UNAIDS provides annual HIV/AIDS updates, while the World Health Organization's annual *World Health Report* addresses wider global health issues and statistics. The UN Office for Drug Control and Crime Prevention publishes an annual *World Drug Report*, which remains the most comprehensive source of statistical information on narcotics production and trafficking.

The UN High Commissioner for Refugees publishes annual refugee statistical reports, as does the UN Population Fund. Key websites: UNAIDS: www.unaids.org/en; UNCTAD: www.unctad.org; Commission on Human Security: www.humansecurity-chs.org; UNODC: www.unodc.org; UNFPA: www.unfpa.org; UNHCR: www.unhcr.org; Organization for Security and Co-operation in Europe: www.osce.org.

INTERNATIONAL NONGOVERNMENTAL AGENCIES

The Human Security Centre's *Human Security Report* (2005 and 2006) provides analytical discussion of human security data, including the incidence of conflict. Human Rights Watch monitors human rights violations across a wide range of issue areas. See, for example, Human Rights Watch, *Deadly Denial: Barriers to HIV/AIDS Treatment for People Who Use Drugs in Thailand* (2007). For Russian data, see Human Rights Watch, *Positively Abandoned: Stigma and Discrimination against HIV Positive Mothers and Their Children in Russia* (2005). Also see Human Rights Watch, *Hidden in the Mealie Meal: Gender-Based Abuses and Women's HIV Treatment in Zambia* (2001). Corruption, corporate involvement in human rights abuses and transnational crime are emerging as pivotal human security concerns. See, for example, Anita Ramasastry and Robert C. Thompson, *Commerce, Crime and Conflict: Legal Remedies for Private Sector Liability for Grave Breaches of International Law, A Survey of Sixteen Countries* (2006). In South Africa, the Institute for Security Studies offers an extensive database of publications addressing humanitarian issues. See, for example, Festus B. Aboagye (ed.), *Complex Emergencies in the 21st Century: Challenges of New Africa's Strategic Peace and Security Policy Issues* (2007) and Cheryl Hendricks (ed.), *From State Security to Human Security in Southern Africa: Policy Research and Capacity Building Challenges* (2006). Websites: Canadian Consortium on Human Security: www.humansecurity.info; Fafo Institute for Applied International Studies: www.fafo.no/ais/projectoverview.htm; Global Policy Forum: www.globalpolicy.org; Human Rights Watch: www.hrw.org; Institute for Security Studies: www.iss.co.za; International Crisis Group: www.crisisgroup.org/home/index.cfm.

INDEX

ABOUT THE AUTHORS

Paul Battersby is associate professor of international relations in the School of Global Studies, Social Science and Planning at the Royal Melbourne Institute of Technology University (RMIT), Melbourne, Australia, where he specializes in global governance, transnational crime and human security, Asian business cultures, development studies, curriculum internationalization and Australia-Asia relations. Born in the United Kingdom, he received his doctorate from James Cook University in 1996 and taught at universities and colleges in Australia and Thailand before joining RMIT in 2000. Since then he has developed and led the International Studies and Global Studies program areas, developed academic links and exchanges with universities in Thailand and Chile and published on subjects ranging from international project-based learning to the history of Australia-Asia relations. His first book, *To the Islands: White Australians and the Malay Archipelago since 1788*, was published in 2007. He has also published numerous book chapters and contributed articles to *Pacific Affairs* and the *Australian Journal of International Affairs*.

Joseph M. Siracusa is professor in global studies in the School of Global Studies, Social Science and Planning at the Royal Melbourne Institute of Technology, where he is also a fellow in the Human Security Program. A native of Chicago and long-time resident of Australia, he studied at the University of Denver and the University of Vienna and received his PhD from the University of Colorado, Boulder. He is internationally known for his writings on nuclear weapons, diplomatic history and presidential politics. Professor Siracusa is also a frequent political affairs commentator in the Australian media, including ABC Radio National. He has worked at Merrill Lynch in Boston and at the University of Queensland, and for three years he served as senior visiting fellow in the Key Centre for Ethics, Law, Justice and Governance, Griffith University. Among his numerous books are *A History of United States Foreign Policy*; *Depression to Cold War: A History of America from Herbert Hoover to Ronald Reagan* (with David G. Coleman); *Presidential Profiles: The Kennedy Years*; *Real-World Nuclear Deterrence: The Making of International Strategy* (with David G. Coleman); *Nuclear Weapons: A Very Short Introduction*; and *Reagan, Bush, Gorbachev: Revisiting the End of the Cold War* (with Norman A. Graebner and Richard Dean Burns).